The Psychology of the Foreign Exchange Market

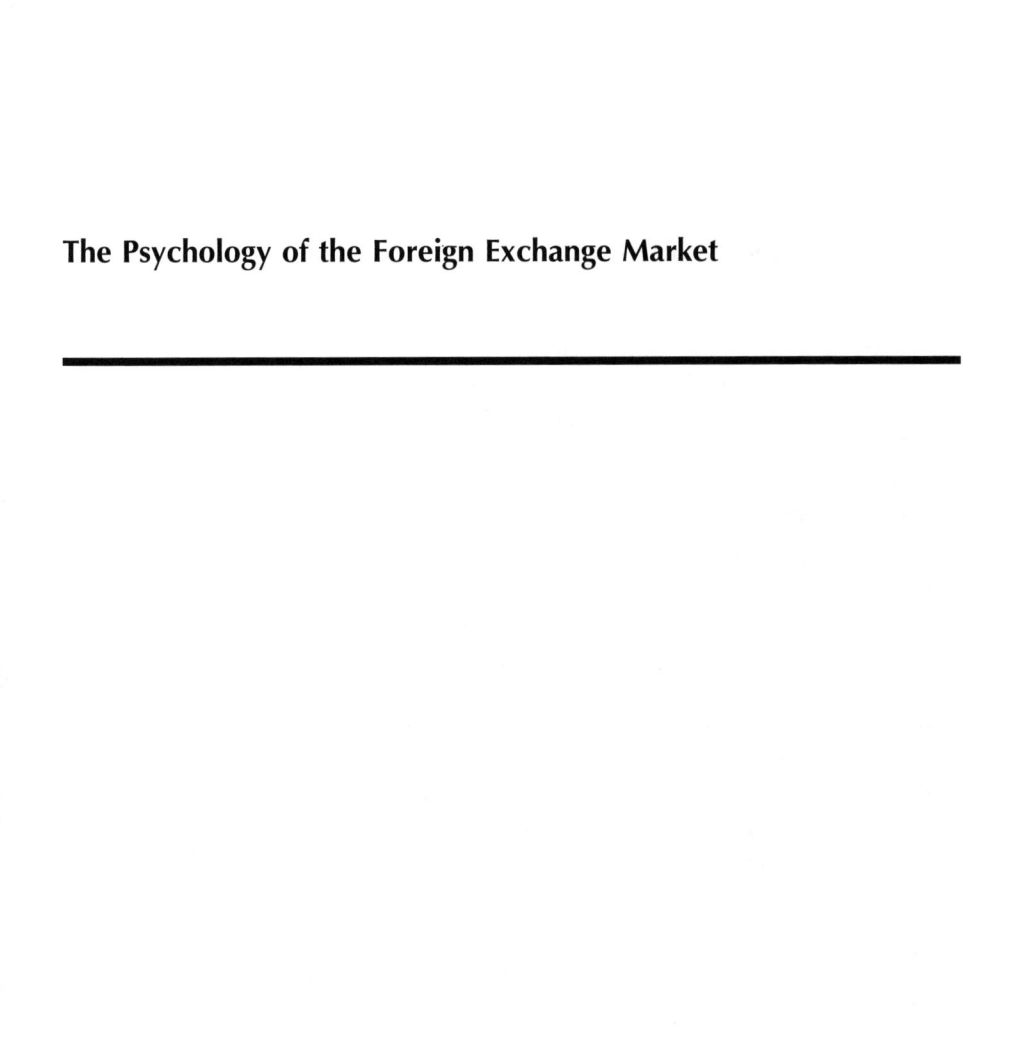

WILEY TRADING SERIES

Single Stock Futures: A Trader's Guide
Patrick L. Young and Charles Sidey

Uncertainty and Expectation: Strategies for the Trading of Risk
Gerald Ashley

Bear Market Investing Strategies
Harry D. Schultz

The Psychology of Finance, revised edition
Lars Tvede

The Elliott Wave Principle: Key to Market Behavior
Robert R. Prechter

International Commodity Trading
Ephraim Clark, Jean-Baptiste Lesourd and René Thiéblemont

Dynamic Technical Analysis
Philippe Cahen

Encyclopedia of Chart Patterns
Thomas N. Bulkowski

Integrated Technical Analysis
Ian Copsey

Financial Markets Tick by Tick: Insights in Financial Markets Microstructure
Pierre Lequeux

Technical Market Indicators: Analysis and Performance
Richard J. Bauer and Julie R. Dahlquist

Trading to Win: The Psychology of Mastering the Markets
Ari Kiev

Pricing Convertible Bonds
Kevin Connolly

At the Crest of the Tidal Wave: A Forecast for the Great Bear Market
Robert R. Prechter

THE PSYCHOLOGY OF THE FOREIGN EXCHANGE MARKET

Thomas Oberlechner

John Wiley & Sons, Ltd

Copyright © 2004 John Wiley & Sons Ltd, The Atrium, Southern Gate, Chichester,
West Sussex PO19 8SQ, England
Telephone (+44) 1243 779777

Email (for orders and customer service enquiries): cs-books@wiley.co.uk
Visit our Home Page on www.wileyeurope.com or www.wiley.com

All Rights Reserved. No part of this publication may be reproduced, stored in a retrieval system, or transmitted in any form or by any means, electronic, mechanical, photocopying, recording, scanning or otherwise, except under the terms of the Copyright, Designs and Patents Act 1988 or under the terms of a licence issued by the Copyright Licensing Agency Ltd, 90 Tottenham Court Road, London W1T 4LP, UK, without the permission in writing of the Publisher. Requests to the Publisher should be addressed to the Permissions Department, John Wiley & Sons Ltd, The Atrium, Southern Gate, Chichester, West Sussex PO19 8SQ, England, or emailed to permreq@wiley.co.uk, or faxed to (+44) 1243 770620.

Designations used by companies to distinguish their products are often claimed as trademarks. All brand names and product names used in this book are trade names, service marks, trademarks or registered trademarks of their respective owners. The Publisher is not associated with any product or vendor mentioned in this book.

This publication is designed to provide accurate and authoritative information in regard to the subject matter covered. It is sold on the understanding that the Publisher is not engaged in rendering professional services. If professional advice or other expert assistance is required, the services of a competent professional should be sought.

Other Wiley Editorial Offices

John Wiley & Sons, Inc., 111 River Street, Hoboken, NJ 07030, USA

Jossey-Bass, 989 Market Street, San Francisco, CA 94103-1741, USA

Wiley-VCH Verlag GmbH, Boschstr. 12, D-69469 Weinheim, Germany

John Wiley & Sons Australia Ltd, 33 Park Road, Milton, Queensland 4064, Australia

John Wiley & Sons (Asia) Pte Ltd, 2 Clementi Loop #02-01, Jin Xing Distripark, Singapore 129809

John Wiley & Sons Canada Ltd, 22 Worcester Road, Etobicoke, Ontario, Canada M9W 1L1

Wiley also publishes its books in a variety of electronic formats. Some content that appears in print may not be available in electronic books.

British Library Cataloguing in Publication Data

A catalogue record for this book is available from the British Library

ISBN 0-470-84406-X

Project management by Originator, Gt Yarmouth, Norfolk (typeset in 10.4/13pt Times)
Printed and bound in Great Britain by TJ International Ltd, Padstow, Cornwall
This book is printed on acid-free paper responsibly manufactured from sustainable forestry in which at least two trees are planted for each one used for paper production.

Contents

Preface ix

Acknowledgments xi

Introduction xv

1 From Rational Decision-Makers to a Psychology of the Foreign Exchange Market 1
    Traditional vs. behavioral finance: A paradigmatic shift in approaching financial markets 3
    Economic defense of the efficient market view 7
    Traders' views of rationality in the foreign exchange market 10
    Toward a market psychology 14
    Abbreviated references 18

2 Psychology of Trading Decisions 21
    Trading decisions: The view of traders 21
    Excursion: Understanding decision-making in financial markets 27
    From objective prices to psychological theories of decision-making 27
    Normative–economic and descriptive–psychological approaches 30
    Social herding dynamics 34
    Herding and psychological conformity 34
    Herding dynamics in the foreign exchange market 36
    Affects 41
    Status quo tendency 44
    Overconfidence 47
    Trading intuition: Bridging affects and cognitions 51

	Cognitions	55
	Heuristics	57
	Representativeness	58
	Availability	63
	Anchoring and adjustment	64
	Hindsight bias	66
	Abbreviated references	67
3	Risk-Taking in Trading Decisions	71
	Asymmetric risk-taking	72
	Framing and mental accounting	77
	Managing trading risk: Institutional and personal strategies	83
	Abbreviated references	87
4	Expectations in the Foreign Exchange Market	89
	Expectations: A market time machine	92
	Fundamental and technical/chartist analysis	94
	Psychological attitudes and market expectations	108
	Social dynamics, meta-expectations, and the financial news media	117
	Abbreviated references	123
5	News and Rumors	125
	Characteristics of important information	127
	From news sources to information loops	131
	Information sources of foreign exchange traders	131
	Information sources of financial journalists	135
	Implications for collective market information-processing	137
	Reporting trends and interdependency	139
	Market rumors	143
	Abreviated references	148
6	Personality Psychology of Traders	149
	The role of personality in trading	150
	What makes successful traders?	153
	Disciplined cooperation	154
	Tackling decisions	156
	Market meaning-making	157
	Emotional stability	157
	Information-processing	159

	Interested integrity	159
	Autonomous organization	159
	Information handling	160
	Market applications	163
	Abbreviated references	164
7	Surfing the Market on Metaphors	167
	Main market metaphors	168
	The foreign exchange market as a bazaar	171
	The foreign exchange market as a machine	172
	The foreign exchange market as a living being	173
	The foreign exchange market as gambling	175
	The foreign exchange market as sports	176
	The foreign exchange market as war	177
	The foreign exchange market as an ocean	178
	Metaphors shape market perspectives	180
	Market metaphors are about the psychological "other"	180
	Market metaphors are about market predictability	183
	Explicit and implicit metaphors of the foreign exchange market	185
	Market metaphors in action	188
	What we can learn from market metaphors	192
	Abbreviated references	193
8	The Foreign Exchange Market—A Psychological Construct	195
	The market as a construct and illusion	198
	Market constructs change	200
	Abbreviated references	204
9	The Basics	207
	Function and scope of the market	207
	Instruments	211
	Trading	212
	Dealing room structure	213
	Market players	216
	Commercial and investment banks	216
	Central banks	217
	Brokers	218
	Investment companies, pension funds, and hedge funds	219
	Corporations and multinational companies	220
	Individuals	221
	Global financial news agencies	222
	Abbreviated references	222

Appendix: The European and the North American Survey 225
    Abbreviated references 227

References 229

Index 249

Preface

If you are interested in how *psychology* influences the foreign exchange market, this is the book for you. This book sheds light on spectacular market phenomena as well as on subliminal psychological processes in trading decisions. New insights are gathered from psychological theory, survey research studies with leading foreign exchange participants, and finally one-on-one interviews with trading experts. Combining these insights, the book offers an innovative psychological understanding of the daily decisions that determine exchange rates.

The following statements from foreign exchange experts provide a first glimpse at the variety of topics explored.

1. *Personality characteristics* involved in successful trading—the trading manager of a leading bank declares:

    "I think you could be a *good* trader based on trading and experience, but you can't be *excellent*. There is something that is inherent in the very best traders that other people just don't have."

2. *Asymmetric risk-taking* after gains and after losses may lead traders to take excessive risk to make up for previous losses. As one trader explains the case of Nick Leeson, whose trading losses brought down an entire bank:

    "He was just emotionally attached to his position; he just couldn't ever believe that he was going to be wrong."

3. *Meta-expectations* (i.e., market participants' expectations about the expectations of other market participants):

    "That is what I call market psychology: understanding what people are thinking, why they are thinking it, or what stage of the game they are at."

4. *Trading intuition*: Explaining a recent trading decision, one experienced trader remarks:

 "People asked me, 'Why did you do that?' I said, 'I don't know.' And that's the truth, I don't know. For instance, I walked in last Monday, and I was just wandering around. And then I just got this light shining on me, and I said '[the pound] sterling is going a lot lower today!' There is no economics; there is no chart; there is no anything, except for 'Well, I think.' And I sold quite a lot of it, and it collapsed, and I made a hell of a lot of money. And I could not explain why I had done it."

5. *Market rumors*:

 "Rumors are in the markets all the time and markets move!"

6. *Market metaphors* translate the abstraction of the market into psychological reality. In the words of one trader:

 "I think it is a battlefield—like boxing every day. I compete and struggle with the markets. They are very tough, always, and they test me. I need to always be ready to fight."

 As another trader explains, these metaphors have important consequences for trading decisions:

 "If you don't like a certain counterparty, for example, you end up like you try to fight against him, with sometimes taking silly positions which under normal circumstances you would not. And this normally causes a lot of losses!"

Centuries ago, seafarers who engaged in historic journeys of discovery struggled with images of demons on the borders of their maps, indicating the dangers of the unknown. Likewise today, the new field of market psychology is another vast ocean whose many riches have only begun to be discovered. The book promises to take the reader on this exhilarating voyage, explaining the psychological dynamics that shape today's foreign exchange market.

Thomas Oberlechner
Cambridge, Massachusetts and Vienna

Acknowledgments

My being a psychologist not only explains my research focus on the actual participants in the market, it also makes me acutely aware of the numerous relationships, research and otherwise, this research has rewarded me. I am extremely thankful and indebted to everybody who has been involved in my research and who has contributed to this book, including many persons who are not explicitly named in the following. Not only has the process of researching and writing been a thoroughly inspiring and rewarding experience, it has also allowed me to work with, and learn from, truly exceptional individuals.

The book would not exist without the generosity of foreign exchange experts at many of the world's leading market institutions who shared with me their knowledge of the market. The institutions I had the privilege to work with in Europe and in the U.S. include ABN-AMRO, AIG International, AP-Dow Jones, Bank Austria, Bank of England, Bankers Trust, Bank of Montreal, Bank of New York, Bank of Tokyo Mitsubishi, Barclays, BAWAG, Bayerische Landesbank, Bear Stearns, Bloomberg, *Börsen-Zeitung*, Brown Brothers Harriman, CIBC World Markets, Citigroup, CNBC, CNN Business Report, Comerica Bank, Commerzbank, Creditanstalt Bankverein, Credit Suisse First Boston, Den Norske Bank, Deutsche Bank, Deutsche Börse, Dresdner Bank, *The Economist*, Erste Bank, European Business News, *Financial Times*, Financial Times Television, Finanz Markt Austria, FleetBoston Financial, Giro Credit, Goldman Sachs, Handelsblatt, HSBC, JP Morgan Chase, Keybank, Knight Ridder, Mellon Bank, Merrill Lynch, Morgan Stanley, National City Bank, Nat West, Natexis Banques Populaires, *Neue Zürcher Zeitung*, Nomura, Oesterreichische Nationalbank, ÖTOB, P.S.K., RBC Capital Markets, Reuters, RZB, SBC Warburg, SEB, Standard Americas Inc., State Street Corporation, Svenska Handelsbanken, Schweizerische Nationalbank, UBS Warburg, Union Bank of California, U.S. Bank, VWD,

Wall Street Journal, Wells Fargo Bank, and Westdeutsche Landesbank Girozentrale. Dozens, indeed *hundreds* of foreign exchange experts at these institutions volunteered to participate in extensive surveys on the psychological aspects of the foreign exchange market, to discuss the market in comprehensive research interviews, and to share their market experience informally in many private conversations. Because all research interviews and surveys were conducted under the premise of confidentiality, I want to thank each of these experts anonymously but with no less degree of thankfulness for their valuable insights into the dynamics of this exciting market. Their openness in supporting my research has been tremendous.

For their ready assistance with my studies and for establishing contact with market participants, I am grateful to Clifford Asness, James Borden, Lynne Browne, Marshall Carter, Christine Cumming, Thomas Healey, Ira Jackson, Richard Kopcke, Dino Kos, Peter Nielsen, and Werner Studener.

I am indebted to Brandon Adams, Karl Berger, Eduard Brandstätter, Erich Kirchler, Mark Kritzman, Guy-Charles Mahic, Charles McFerren, Anna Nordström, Carol Osler, Aurel Schubert, Martin Senn, John Shue, and Meir Statman, who graciously volunteered to read sections of the manuscript or even the entire manuscript. Their precious suggestions provided a much needed corrective of my own lack of knowledge, strengthening the argument of the book in substantial ways.

A large number of other distinguished academic colleagues provided me with valuable support and comments at various stages of the writing process. I would like to particularly thank Max Bazerman, John Carroll, Boris Groysberg, Richard Hackman, Nicole Kronberger, David Laibson, David Lazer, John van Maanen, Ashok Nimgade, Al Roth, Andrej Shleifer, Thomas Slunecko, and Richard Zeckhauser. While I can only hope that they all still remember the various ways they found to support me, I certainly do.

Harvard University, University of Vienna, and Webster University provided valuable institutional and academic support. At Harvard, Viktor Mayer-Schönberger gave me all the personal and professional support for my research imaginable and unimaginable. Adri Chaikin's and Katharine Olson's editing skills ensured that progressive versions of the manuscript became more and more readable. Minwoo Jang assisted with collecting data from North American market participants, while Grace Gui led my way through the maze of advanced statistics in retrieving results. Many thanks go to friendly and helpful staff at the Baker and Kennedy School libraries. At the University of Vienna, Giselher Guttmann and Peter Vitouch advised my dissertation on the topic of this book, while Reinhold Stipsits generously shared his publishing experience. At Webster University Vienna, Sherri

Speck, Eva Berger, Steve Chaid, Dessislava Dantcheva, Clemens Dudek, Arturo Cruz Esparza, Guy Kehila, Karl Kinsky, Thomas Krenn, Gernot Mittendorfer, Irena Radman, Ingrid Schörghuber, and Claudia Westermayr were part of the highly synergistic team that collected data from European market participants. Samia Bishun expertly edited the book as well as a number of scholarly articles on which parts of the book are based, turning into a market psychologist herself.

It has been a great pleasure to cooperate with the publication team at John Wiley & Sons. Peter Baker, Sam Hartley, Carole Millett, Patricia Morrison, Samantha Whittaker, Viv Wickham, and Rachael Wilkie have consistently provided me with the most competent, flexible, and motivating assistance; as has Bruce Shuttlewood of Originator.

Above all, I want to thank Gerlinde Berghofer. I cannot think of any aspect of this book she did not support with encouragement and her own expertise in writing and conducting research. My deepest gratitude also goes to Sam Hocking, now at Banc of America, who inspired my interest in the foreign exchange market and without whose friendship and research partnership this book would not exist.

Introduction

> *I think psychology is the biggest driver of foreign exchange rates, more than anything else in the market.*
>
> Foreign exchange trader

"The market is made up of people. So, invariably, psychology plays a role," one trader summarizes years of experience in the foreign exchange market. Based on the first-hand experience of this as well as of hundreds of other traders, this book explores the role of psychology in the market in which currencies are traded and priced. It shows how the "psyche" of the foreign exchange market is a driving force at all levels: from the individual trader, to collective market processes, to actual exchange rates.

The foreign exchange market is the largest financial market worldwide, easily ten times the size of other market giants such as the NYSE. The influence of this market is pervasive: Wherever you live, exchange rates affect the prices of goods you buy such as rice from Thailand, software from the U.S., cars from Japan, and beer from Germany. Every day, the rates at which currencies are bought and sold determine the success of national economic policies and, ultimately, such fundamental aspects of well-being as the level of unemployment.

Like the center of a spider web, the foreign exchange market connects to all other financial markets around the world. In the words of one trader, "There are aspects of all the other markets that influence behavior in the foreign exchange market." The market has almost as many interpretations as it has observers. Historically, the market for currencies was possibly the first financial market. Functionally, the foreign exchange market is where capital flows among countries and where exporters are paid. Normatively, the market has often been lauded as an efficient, smoothly functioning source of necessary liquidity and, just as frequently, slammed as a playground for irresponsible speculators. To many, the foreign exchange market is a mystery, and the exchange rates it produces are ultimately incomprehensible. Changes in exchange rates seem random or, at best, governed by complex mathematical principles understood by a select few.

This book demystifies these processes in the foreign exchange market by focusing on the actual decision-makers who comprise it. Drawing on the first-hand expertise of the very professionals whose decisions shape the market, the book demonstrates that each of the currency transactions on which exchange rates ultimately rest is driven by a thinking, feeling person, not by a detached computer or by randomly thrown dice. The people who decide and interact in the market do so in *human* ways, pursuing human goals and attempting to satisfy human needs. Thus, as the market consists of a network of people, we can only understand the market by considering the psychology involved in their buying and selling decisions. In the words of one trader, "If you understand what everyone else is doing, and why everyone else is doing it, it makes it very, very easy to understand what is going to happen. And to me, that's psychology!"

BACKGROUND

A large part of the presented findings are based on two comprehensive research studies conducted with market participants in Europe and North America. Details about these studies and participants are provided in the Appendix.

Hundreds of active traders completed surveys, and dozens participated in one-on-one interviews. In addition to surveying traders at the world's leading foreign exchange institutions, I also surveyed financial journalists working for internationally recognized news media. The views of these market participants, both traders and journalists, were often quite distinct from the academic theories of the foreign exchange market. Though this might surprise some academic economists, it might not surprise those who actively participate in the market. As one trader remarked matter-of-factly: "I found a lot of stuff you learn in economics classes not very useful."

In the 1996 survey with European market participants (called the "European survey" in this book),[1] I had the privilege of working with Samuel Hocking, now at Bank of America. Sam's background in journalism and the news media led me to explore the role of financial news in the foreign exchange market, including the information dynamics between trading participants and news

Introduction

media. More than 300 foreign exchange traders and 70 financial journalists participated. In the 2002 survey in North America (called the "North American survey" in this book),[2] I surveyed more than 400 foreign exchange professionals.

Complementing the two surveys, 70 foreign exchange experts from trading institutions and financial news media shared their perspectives in extensive research interviews. All interviews were recorded and transcribed verbatim after the interview. The transcriptions of the interviews resulted in nearly 1,000 pages of text.

Thus, a very comprehensive set of empirical data, both quantitative and qualitative, forms the basis for the insights presented in this book. These insights reflect the first-hand knowledge and real-life experience of market participants. Each chapter of this book is an acknowledgment of their market experience.

CHAPTER BY CHAPTER

The chapters of this book explore the psychology of the foreign exchange market from a variety of perspectives. Some perspectives are theoretical; others are practical. Some perspectives focus on individual decision makers, others on how these decision makers interact to form collective market processes, and yet other perspectives focus on the relationship of the players that have traditionally been defined as "market participants" to their broader environment, such as the financial news media. The variety of topics, stories, and research results discussed portray the foreign exchange market as a deeply psychological phenomenon.

Chapter 1, "From Rational Decision-Makers to a Psychology of the Foreign Exchange Market," compares the psychological and traditional economic approaches to understanding financial markets. The traditional economic approach postulates that all agents' decisions are rational, that market prices efficiently reflect all relevant information, and that market prices are always consistent with "fundamentals." The psychological approach stresses common departures from perfect rationality that may permit informational inefficiencies and may drive market prices away from fundamental values. The chapter also highlights how the young discipline of behavioral finance has made important strides toward integrating insights from cognitive psychology. However, a comprehensive understanding of the foreign exchange market must incorporate insights from a variety of psychological perspectives, including social and personality psychology.

Decision-making forms the center of a psychological understanding of the foreign exchange market. Chapter 2, "Psychology of Trading Decisions," discusses the social dynamics of herding, which permeates the market in subtle ways and becomes especially prominent during financial crashes. Because to traders *feelings* are the most important aspect of trading decisions, the chapter also explains affective phenomena, such as trading overconfidence and intuition next to so-called cognitive heuristics (i.e., psychological rules of thumb traders use to accelerate trading decisions).

Chapter 3, "Risk-Taking in Trading Decisions," explains the psychological dynamics leading to asymmetric risk-taking and shows that so-called framing phenomena may dramatically influence the risk-taking of market participants. This chapter also discusses participants' strategies to reduce biased risk-taking in their trading decisions.

Chapter 4, "Expectations in the Foreign Exchange Market," identifies expectations as the key psychological link between market participants and exchange rates. The chapter shows how forecasts based on technical analysis, in contrast to purely fundamental analyses based on economic theories, incorporate rudimentary market psychology. The chapter however further shows that a complete understanding of expectations must also consider subjective attitudes, social dynamics, and meta-expectations.

Chapter 5, "News and Rumors," shows that participants in the foreign exchange market do not occupy a separate world. This chapter examines the various sources of market participants' information and how important these sources are to participants. It discusses the role of the financial news media, as well as current trends in the reporting of financial news. The dynamics of market rumors is explained partly through the interdependence between traders and news providers.

Chapter 6, "Personality Psychology of Traders," explores the importance of individual personality characteristics to trading performance, showing that certain traits promote profits and other measures of trading success.

Chapter 7, "Surfing the Market on Metaphors," develops a novel understanding of the foreign exchange market based on the experience of market participants. This understanding questions the static concept of the market as a machine implicit in economic theories. Instead, the chapter shows that participants usually understand the market in terms of dynamic and organic metaphors, such as "the market war" or "the market as a living being." These metaphors have important implications for the behavior of participants and the dynamics of the market.

Chapter 8, "The Foreign Exchange Market—A Psychological Construct," synthesizes the earlier chapters to shed new light on the nature of the foreign exchange market. Departing from the observation that human beliefs function in part to reduce uncertainty, the chapter shows that theories of the foreign exchange market are illusions rather than objective facts. These theories do not address a permanent structure but rather a social and human construction in constant change. Market participants need to adjust to the changing construction of the market. Using the knowledge of the market's psychology described here, market participants may even shape the development of the market to their advantage.

For readers less acquainted with financial markets and the technical aspects of trading, Chapter 9, "The Basics," introduces the main players in the foreign exchange market and explains how they trade currencies.

The Appendix provides detailed information about the participants of the two comprehensive research studies I conducted in the European and in the North American foreign exchange market on which many of the findings presented in the book are based.

Embarking on the journey of this book, readers will encounter some of the theoretical and practical cornerstones on which the psychology of the foreign exchange market builds. Along the journey, the book aims to be understandable and engaging for the expert and the non-expert alike. For foreign exchange professionals and private investors, the book dwells on the firsthand experiences of actual market participants. For scholars in economics and psychology who are interested in the psychological aspects of financial markets, the book includes substantial new, rigorous evidence.

It is important to share two caveats. First, this book does not offer investment advice. While the insights presented here will doubtless be useful to traders, I do not spell out the connections from market understanding to trading strategies. Second, the book is not encyclopedic. Given the vast influence of psychology on individual behavior, the list of possible topics for this book is very long. Inevitably, some psychological, economic, and financial concepts will not be covered or will be dealt with only briefly. For further information, the references provide a good guide to relevant original research in both psychology and economics.

ABBREVIATED REFERENCES

See the reference chapter at the end of the book for full details.

1 Oberlechner, T. and Hocking, S. (1997)
2 Oberlechner, T. (2003)

1
From Rational Decision-Makers to a Psychology of the Foreign Exchange Market

> *What is the foreign exchange market? Is it a part of human rationality? I don't know. Ask Rene Descartes or somebody, not me!*
>
> Foreign exchange trader

From the outside, financial markets appear "dry, technical, and economic in nature—[all about] percentage declines, volume, margin calls, and paper losses. [However, their] inner mechanism is psychological. All markets, financial or otherwise, are arrangements where goods, money, and real and financial assets change hands. It is vital to remember that the hands are *human* and are attached to thinking, feeling hands and bodies," according to economist Shlomo Maital.[1] Or, as articulated by James Grant, of *Grant's Interest Rate Observer*, markets "are normally as objective as people watching the ninth inning of the seventh game of the World Series, with the teams at a tie."[i]

The contrast between the outcome-based outside appearance and the inner decision-making dynamics of such financial markets as the foreign exchange market is reflected in substantial differences between the traditional economic and the psychological views. "There aren't many human beings populating the world of economic models," economist Richard Thaler observes.[2] Focusing on aggregate pricing dynamics, traditional economic models of the market have

---
[i] Personal communication.

assumed that individuals are "fully rational" and make decisions optimally. In contrast, psychology has observed how they *fail* to be rational from an economic viewpoint when making decisions in the markets.[3-6]

In this book, I demonstrate that the notions that market participants are rational and the foreign exchange market is efficient have to be supplemented by a more complex understanding of *psychological* and *social* market processes. The traditional economic models of financial markets have provided innumerable valuable insights into optimal portfolio allocations and into how markets operate in an ideal world. While these models will always serve as important benchmarks against which to evaluate competing concepts, they are fundamentally and critically incomplete, as there are many important aspects of real-life financial market behavior that they simply cannot explain. Departures from market efficiency, such as the stock market valuing the entire 3Com Corporation less than one of its subsidiaries in 2000,[7] are not just exotic exceptions. Instead, these "exceptions" reflect departures from perfect rationality that are so pervasive as to be inherent to financial markets. Indeed, it is possible that psychology and—to put it in the words of finance—"imperfect rationality" influence the foreign exchange dynamics more than do perfect rationality and efficiency.

Placing the emphasis on psychology in understanding financial markets closely reflects the actual experience and observations of those who take part in financial markets. In the words of one trader, "Psychology does play a huge role in people making decisions and influencing [market] behavior." As the chapters of this book illustrate, market participants themselves readily acknowledge their inability to achieve full rationality in the economic sense. Accordingly, they frequently observe that their information-processing capabilities are limited and that in the second-to-second dynamics of the market, there is not enough time for a full analysis of relevant information. Such insights were the inspiration for economic models of "bounded" rationality developed some decades ago by economic Nobel laureate Herbert Simon.[8] In recent years, economists have built on this foundation, integrating many psychological insights into their models, and thus building a bridge between finance and psychology, which promises a more accurate and a more differentiated understanding of human actors in financial markets. Fortifying this bridge and fostering a new understanding of the markets, this book shows that, rather than being rational and efficient, the very nature of the foreign exchange market is *psychological*.

TRADITIONAL VS. BEHAVIORAL FINANCE: A PARADIGMATIC SHIFT IN APPROACHING FINANCIAL MARKETS

Contemporary financial markets, such as the foreign exchange market, can be approached from a variety of useful perspectives. To give some examples, history, sociology, political science, psychology, and economy all provide exciting angles for examining the complex meanings and inner workings of financial markets. While these disciplines often complement each other, they certainly are not always in agreement. Indeed, a closer examination of how economists have thought about financial markets and market participants reveals plainly that, even within the same discipline, approaches may contradict and even conflict entirely with each other. Thus, one of the core questions posed by economists today is the extent to which psychology may help in understanding and explaining the workings of financial markets, and in the building of more accurate market models.

Traditional economic models assume that all market participants are *fully rational*. This means that participants process information using the best known statistical techniques, that they fully understand the structure of the market, and that their decisions are optimally suited to achieving their personal goals. In the context of portfolio formation, for example, the assumption of perfect rationality has helped to define how portfolios should be allocated when investors care primarily about expected return and volatility.[9] Some readers will be familiar with the powerful concepts of "mean-variance optimization" and "efficient frontiers," both of which come from this literature.[ii] Rationality is especially important in the context of how market participants form expectations, where it implies that their forecasts should not consistently be biased in any direction, that forecasters should learn from their mistakes, and that forecasts should not be amenable to improvement using readily available information.

On the assumption that all investors are rational, financial theorists have been able to characterize how markets should price individual assets. They have found that only the price risk that is correlated with the overall market should be valued, while asset-specific price risk should not: Rational investors can eliminate asset-specific price risk through diversification, but they are stuck with the price risk that is correlated with the overall market no matter what they do. The analogy of an ocean ship illustrates this concept. The risk that the

---

[ii] Mean-variance optimization determines how investors should combine various financial assets for the highest return at a given level of risk (as measured by volatility). The group of all optimal portfolios is called the efficient frontier.

ship will reach its destination depends not only on the ocean conditions (i.e., the market risk), but also, among other factors, on the sobriety of the crew (i.e., the asset-specific risk). While freighters can control the risk related to the crews, the risk related to the ocean remains. These insights, in turn, have spawned an entire industry devoted to measuring "market risk," and such related concepts as "alpha," the excess of expected return over its theoretically appropriate value.

Another implication of universal rationality is that market prices should be "informationally efficient." This means that prices should always be at their fundamentally correct values, which, in turn, implies that public news generally brings quick, once-and-for-all price changes: rational agents will immediately drive prices to the value consistent with existing information. Economists often summarize an efficient market as one in which market prices appropriately reflect all available information at all times.[10] Because all relevant information is already factored into current prices, a perfectly efficient market provides no opportunities to earn excess (risk-adjusted) profits.

For decades, the concepts of rationality and market efficiency have provided the economic analysis of financial markets with a consistency never enjoyed by psychological approaches.[11] In contrast to the concept of universal rationality, psychological theories address human motivation, cognition, and behavior. For example, Sigmund Freud's notion of personality is certainly a far cry from the extremely rational decision-maker depicted in economic textbooks. Freud describes the fundamental part of personality as a "cauldron full of seething excitations"[12]; indeed, central to psychoanalysis are the notions of the unconscious and the primacy of the pleasure principle, which is irrational, over the reality principle, which is based on reason. In stark contrast, the behaviorism of B. F. Skinner conceives of the human mind as an impenetrable black box. Instead, behaviorism focuses first on behavior, which it perceives as governed by antecedents and consequences in the outside world or as learned by observing others.[13] Cognitive-behavioral approaches, a more recent offspring of behaviorism, focus on thinking and information-processing in how people feel and in what they do.[14-16] A third disparate branch of psychology, Carl Rogers' and Abraham Maslow's humanistic theory, emphasizes people's subjective experience, free will, and human self-determination.[17-19]

Some economists object that these theories are perhaps valuable in personal therapy, but have little significance in financial markets. As economists point out, financial market participants are motivated by high pay to process information rationally. Since departures from rationality hinder them from maximizing profits (or more generally maximizing well-being), individuals will either become rational or go bankrupt and leave the market.[20]

However, the traditional economic view is crumbling. Debate now rages about whether imperfect rationality, and the psychology research that documents it, may be critical to financial markets. The two central points of debate concern the very nature of financial markets: (1) Are market participants rational? (2) Are financial markets efficient?

Are market participants rational? In recent years economists have begun to look beyond optimal human behavior to focus on actual human behavior in financial markets. They now often turn to psychology and sometimes even do their own original research. The consistent conclusion from this new focus is that full rationality is not an accurate description of human decision-making. There are regular divergences from what economists define as rational even in such professional settings as financial markets, where the goals of participants are seen as clearly defined and the results of their decisions as easily measurable. Financial decision-makers, for example, typically take mental shortcuts inconsistent with full rationality. Additionally, they are influenced by such "irrelevant" information as the way things are presented as opposed to the information content of the presentation.[iii] Market participants' forecasts violate three critical dimensions of economic rationality: they are biased, they do not incorporate lessons from past mistakes, and they can be improved using readily available information.[21–24]

Are financial markets efficient? Evidence against the efficient markets hypothesis has also accumulated rapidly in recent years. Simple trading rules of when to buy and sell currencies were quite profitable in currency markets for many years and may still be;[25,26] an efficient market would not allow such rules to exist. For if indeed the market were *truly* efficient, then individual market participants could not systematically outsmart the market and there should be no possibility for trading rules or strategies that systematically perform better than other strategies, as there is by definition no piece of information that is not already factored into the market's rates.[27,28] Just as telling is the fact that "market risk" does not appear to matter for stock prices, while other factors apparently unrelated to risk—such as the ratio of a firm's stock market value to its accounting (or "book") value—do appear to matter.[29–33]

Also, the so-called momentum and reversal effects that have been observed in market prices contradict the assumption of efficient markets. If the markets were efficient, they would behave according to a random walk (i.e., there would not be any correlation between present, past, and future market prices).[34]

[iii] Examples of such mental shortcuts (also called "heuristics") and "framing effects" (in which the way a situation is presented or perceived, not its objective content, influences decisions) are discussed in Chapter 2, "Psychology of Trading Decisions".

However, empirical studies on the returns of various financial assets have shown that market prices autocorrelate positively in the short term (momentum), and negatively in the long term (reversal). For example, stocks with a successful recent performance have a tendency to perform highly over the following month,[35] while stocks that have performed either extremely well or extremely badly over longer horizons of some years reverse this pattern.[36] Finally, market prices have been shown to be affected by irrelevant news; this also contradicts efficient markets theory. For example, returns and volumes of stocks with similar ticker symbols correlate with each other significantly, due to the confusion of investors,[37] and newspaper reports about old information that was already publicly available affect stock prices.[38] In one striking case in point, a potential breakthrough on cancer research reported in a Sunday edition of the *New York Times* caused the company owning licensing rights to soar massively. On the following Monday morning, stocks of EntreMed opened at more than seven times their Friday closing price, and they sustained a considerable portion of these gains over the following weeks. However, the newspaper report provided no relevant new information whatsoever. The "news" had already been reported in a scientific journal and in various newspapers (including the *New York Times* itself) some months earlier.[39]

Such market "anomalies" (from the viewpoint of traditional economics) are found in real-life markets, as well as in experimental market settings.[3] Increasingly, the evidence against full rationality and the efficient markets hypothesis has encouraged some financial economists to challenge the traditional view of finance. The young discipline of "behavioral finance" has paved the way to a new paradigm of financial markets.[40] Why, behavioral finance researchers ask, should the people who form trading decisions in the ambiguous complexity of the daily markets always have perfectly rational solutions for problems that even trained economists have a hard time analyzing?[2] "Even in the Olympics," in the apt words of finance professor David Hirshleifer, "no one runs at the speed of light; some cognitive tasks are just too hard for any of us."[41] Thus, proponents of behavioral finance claim that a more realistic and complete understanding of investors' decisions and market dynamics comes from considering psychology.

Unlike traditional economics, the view of financial markets offered by behavioral finance builds on less-than-perfectly rational traders and investors, and explains investor behavior and market phenomena by *human decision-making characteristics*.[2,42–45] Thus, the representatives of behavioral finance have started to build market models that explain how psychological aspects of decision-making translate into deviations from market efficiency, for instance, how these processes may lead to the observed short-term momentum and long-term reversals in stock returns and the ability of market-to-book-value ratios to forecast returns.[46–48] Behavioral market models are based on such aspects as considering the representativeness bias (people often form likelihood judgments by simply viewing events as typical of some class and by ignoring their knowledge about base rate probabilities); conservatism (people update their expectations and models in the face of new evidence only slowly); biased self-attributions (people usually perceive the reasons for their successes as internal—i.e., as due to their own abilities—and the reasons for their failures as external—i.e., due to the environment); and overconfidence (people tend to overestimate their own knowledge and skills), particularly overconfidence about the accuracy of their private information.

ECONOMIC DEFENSE OF THE EFFICIENT MARKET VIEW

"Market efficiency survives the challenge," economist Eugene Fama vehemently declares,[49] and, indeed, mainstream economists defend the efficient market paradigm against behavioral finance in a variety of ways. Often they will attempt to provide explanations for apparent anomalies consistent with the theory. For instance, they argue that if a firm's ratio of market-to-book-value matters for its stock price, then that ratio must somehow be related to risk, even if it is not apparent just how.[50] Consistent with the efficient markets hypothesis itself, these explanations sometimes rely on an underlying assumption of full rationality.

To support the notion of efficient markets, economists also appeal to the famed economist Milton Friedman's "as if" defense (namely, that theories should be judged by the validity of their *predictions*, not by their assumptions).[20] These economists maintain that finance theory based on the notion of full rationality has, after all, still been very successful in predicting market outcomes and that markets are efficient to a first approximation. A successful baseball player helps to exemplify this line of thinking. Without actually knowing the underlying physical forces that determine a baseball's voyage, and with no inkling of the equations expressing these forces, celebrated hitters from Babe Ruth to Barry Bonds frequently connect with the ball.

However, the success of the baseball player in this metaphor—and likewise the success of economic theory—can be disputed. One could, for example, suggest that Ruth could have hit the ball more frequently had he known the physical forces and critical equations. Likewise, behavioral economist Richard Thaler points out that finance theory is not very useful at predicting market developments.[2] Moreover, the very nature of the "as if" defense is problematic when it is contrasted with the truthfulness requirement demanded of science by philosopher Michael Polanyi. Truthfulness rests on an actual link between theory and reality.[51] "Scientific knowing," Polanyi asserts, "consists in discerning Gestalten ['figures'] that are aspects of *reality*."[52, emphasis added] In other words, an accurate description of financial markets (i.e., one close to reality) is critical if we want to more fully understand them.[53]

An accurate description of financial markets must include the fact that some agents are *not* perfectly rational, as noted earlier. Still, traditional finance argues that markets can still be efficient, provided that the mistakes of the imperfectly rational agents are mutually independent. Individual irrationalities will then effectively cancel each other out at the level of the overall market. Suppose, for example, that the dollar–yen exchange rate is at its fundamentally correct value of ¥110/$, but one trader mistakenly thinks that the correct rate is ¥100/$ (maybe because this trader is Japanese and highly optimistic of the Japanese economy) and another trader mistakenly thinks it is ¥120/$ (maybe because this trader is from the U.S., and because this is the price where the trader bought the yen some time ago). The first trader will choose to sell dollars at ¥110/$ while the second trader will choose to buy dollars. In this way, the two traders' decisions will cancel each other out, leaving the yen stable at ¥110/$. Thus, despite the presence of imperfectly rational individual investors, the market overall could efficiently reflect the fundamentally correct price.

Unfortunately for this argument, there is ample empirical evidence that the decisions of people are psychologically influenced in *systematic* ways and not just randomly. In other words, in the above scenario psychological processes may lead to misvaluations of the dollar–yen exchange rate that show the same trend for the traders; although the fundamental value is ¥110/$, these processes make them both willing to trade (say, at ¥100/$ or at ¥120/$). For example, as we will see in Chapter 2, "Psychology of Trading Decisions," the so-called framing effects found by psychologists Daniel Kahneman and Amos Tversky describe methodical deviations from what economic rationality would suggest.[43,54,55] Framing influences decision-making by how the situation that requires a decision is described and subjectively perceived, as opposed to the objective information content of the situation. Framing effects have been found to have a crucial influence on the risk-taking of investors. Because these and other psychological factors in decision-making constitute a systematic departure from the traditional economic model of rational decision-makers, aggregation does not make them vanish but may even reinforce them.[56]

On the market level, the resulting inefficiencies may even be additionally intensified by self-reinforcing patterns among investors who imitate each other.[57] To give an example, people tend to find patterns with predictive power where there are none.[58,59] This tendency has contributed to an entire industry, known as "technical analysis," in which people believe that price patterns predict future price movements. As technical analysis is now widely disseminated in organized courses (e.g., by the New York Institute of Finance) and through textbooks, many of whose authors are familiar names within finance, any mistakes fostered by this discipline will be shared by many market participants. Finance researchers Jennifer Chu and Carol Osler, for example, find that even though the famous "head-and-shoulders pattern" has no predictive power, it nonetheless generates additional trading equivalent to 60% of a day's normal trading volume.[60] Moreover, technical analysis influences price levels in the market, as many technical strategies involve positive feedback trading, in which price rises generate purchases and price declines generate sales. As a result, technical analysis may contribute to sustained price changes beyond fundamentally correct values.[61] Such a possibility was apparently the concern of Federal Reserve chairman Alan Greenspan in 1996, when he famously asked if "irrational exuberance" might have let U.S. stock market prices soar excessively.[iv]

Still, there is a final line of defense that traditional finance uses in favor of efficient markets. This defense concedes that unsophisticated market participants may indeed exhibit shared psychological biases and thus distort the efficient market equilibrium. However, the distortions will not last because other market forces will neutralize them. Overall market efficiency, in this line of reasoning, is guaranteed by rational market participants, called "arbitrageurs," who hasten to exploit the profit opportunities created by imperfectly rational ones.[56] Because the arbitrageurs know the rational and correct prices, they can trade profitably with anybody behaving irrationally. When the market is overpriced due to "irrational exuberance," for example, the "smart money" will sell aggressively, thus bringing prices down to more sensible levels. Although the two traders in our example, and the majority of the other traders, are willing to trade dollar–yen at ¥120/$, some rational arbitrageurs suffice to bring the overpriced dollar down to its fundamentally correct value of ¥110/$.

The arbitrageurs have two important consequences. First, they ensure that the market reaches its "efficient" price level. Second, they profit handsomely at the expense of the irrationally exuberant individual investors. Thus, the irrational market participants either learn to trade rationally or they run out of funds and leave the market. Accordingly, it is argued, that through expertise

---

[iv] Speech at the American Enterprise Institute on December 5, 1996.

and learning effects, the market will in the long run always be dominated by rational players.

Once again, market reality fails to support this particular line of argument. "Very much does not support the strong versions of the experts-get-things-right and in-the-real-world-people-learn hypotheses," economist Matthew Rabin summarizes in his discussion of psychological findings relevant to economics.[62] People are often very resistant to learning from their past mistakes,[63] and the rich mental representations of such complex subject matters as financial markets held by experts may even introduce a paradoxical hazard of *increased* noise and scatter in their predictions, as compared with those of novices.[64] Moreover, as Harvard finance professor Andrej Shleifer argues, in real life possibilities for arbitrage are limited and they bring along risks.[42] For example, most "rational" assessments of the U.S. stock market in 1997 indicated that it was overvalued by fundamental measures. This led some arbitrageurs to sell short, in the expectation that they would buy stocks back cheaply soon thereafter, exactly according to theory. However, this strategy led to losses for two straight years. Indeed, because the market "mispricing" became worse for a while, rather than disappearing, those arbitrageurs paid dearly. The well-regarded Brandywine mutual fund, for example, went heavily into cash at the end of 1997 and then hemorrhaged funds when the market shot forward the next quarter. This happened even though earnings reports were disappointing, as the fund had forecast.

"Nothing is more suicidal than a rational investment policy in an irrational world," the eminent economist John Maynard Keynes is alleged to have declared, in reference to his 1936 book, *The General Theory of Employment, Interest, and Money*. In a trader's words, "[if] you find someone else is making [a price] just as bad as you, hopefully worse than you, then you make money, and you actually make more money when people are trading on a rational price." In short, arbitrage to bring prices into line with fundamentally appropriate values may be extremely limited. As the following section discusses in depth, these limitations also play a central role in traders' own observations of market rationality.

TRADERS' VIEWS OF RATIONALITY IN THE FOREIGN EXCHANGE MARKET

One may well ask what foreign exchange traders themselves think about rationality and market efficiency in response to all the academic ink that has been spilt over the question. In answer, while some traders observe that the foreign exchange market is "completely rational," this view does not refer to the traditional economic notion that the market at all times correctly reflects all economically relevant market information; instead, this observation expresses that exchange rate movements always *reflect the decisions of market participants* and that, even when these movements seem inexplicable at first sight, they *ultimately can be explained*. Thus one trader observes frankly, "I don't think there is any irrationality in the foreign exchange market, because it's driven by supply and demand—that defines the foreign exchange market. You may have an opinion that is totally one way, but your opinion is not the foreign exchange market; it could not matter less. If [the market] is going higher and you are short, *you* are wrong. Because it is all about supply and demand, and any opinion you have beyond that is really a second-order sort of thing!" The same understanding of market rationality can be found in the response given by another trader: "If you have the information, [the market] is very logical. For example, an economic figure comes out and the dollar should be bought, that would be logical. But just one big fund decides, 'I've made enough money, I'll switch out of the currency.' So the market drops rather than rises. To those who don't know that the fund sold out, it is very illogical, very irrational. But can you say that the market has behaved irrationally?"

In the accounts of traders, market rationality thus frequently emerges as a *subjective explanatory concept* that depends on the subjective point of view. "What is perhaps rational for me, is irrational to someone else, and vice versa. In the places where I say the market is irrational, for somebody else it is rational," one trader explains. This makes it evident that to these market practitioners, "rationality" lies in the eye of the beholder, and assessing a certain market development as rational or irrational is a matter of perspective. Accordingly, traders observe that recourse to so-called irrationality is often used as a reaction to events that contradict a previous expectation or the personal point of view. Irrationality is then defined by the question of whether or not the decision-maker can retrospectively explain a market process. "People call irrational what they don't understand," one trader declares unequivocally. Another trader concurs with this statement, remarking dryly that "irrational is always used by those who can't explain." Likewise, some traders comment that in the context of actual trading, the term irrational is often used to describe the reasons for trading losses. "If you are the wrong way around, you call it irrational, and if you are the right way around, it's rational," one trader notices. "I have never seen a trader that made a ton in trading gold [say] 'that was an irrational move but I got rich,'" another trader sagely remarks.

In seeming agreement with traditional economic theory, some traders observe that there may be individual irrationalities that become neutralized by opposing market forces on the collective market level. "There is some irrationality on a single level behavior. But that is washed out of course when you go over that because you have those buying and you have those selling, and at the end it is zero. So the market is not irrational but individual traders in their initial decision-making process may be," one trader asserts. Another trader agrees, commenting that "At some point, there are rational players in the markets that take a look at things at a more fundamental or value basis, and there are flows out there that provide the necessary adjustment." In additional support of traditional economic theory, traders also observe that the quality of information available to large market players allows them to benefit at the expense of those who are ill-informed. In the words of one trader, "There are ways to take advantage of some of that irrational behavior ... provided you have some information advantage."

However, traders stress that possibilities for arbitrage are limited in market reality and that trading at a price level that may seem rational to economists may turn out to be costly. In the ironic words of one trader, "if you have a degree in economics, I think you would lose a lot of money, because the market is completely the opposite!" The limits and dangers of arbitrage in the real-life market are addressed by another trader who vividly describes the dilemma of a rational market player during a phase of prolonged market "irrationality." "You say, well, there has to come red; I can put my chips on red. Now black comes once again. What are you doing to not lose money? You double up with red ... and as long as you can double up, you gain back what you have lost, *as long as you can double up*. But there are certain situations when you are stopped: you might run out of money or the casino might set a table limit. Then you are wiped out and you lose. And this is the same situation you might encounter in foreign exchange. You will reach a limit, your risk-taking capacity is full, so at times you are no longer influenced by what happens in the market in terms of information and macroeconomic data!"

Far from being homogeneous, the picture of rationality and irrationality on the market level portrayed by traders is differentiated and variable. Traders observe, for instance, that the market knows of more and less rational periods; in the words of a trader, at times, "the market is totally irrational; there is no rational reason behind any move. And then, for a certain period of time, the market reacts quite, as you would say, rational." Moreover, various aspects of the foreign exchange market such as different decision time horizons, trading locations, trading instruments, and roles of market participants are associated with different degrees of rationality. With regard to different time horizons, traders remark that, "Rationality, of course it exists to a certain extent, but in the daily market, it does not," and "short-term logic and rational do not apply to this market." To this, another trader adds that, "In terms of minutes, I would say 80% is emotional. [But] as you go forward through time, in which case the information can be processed and analyzed, it is more of a rational reaction, and much less of an emotion ... Long-term investors tend to be more influenced by analysis than by feelings." "Over time, the markets are largely rational in terms of major trends," yet another trader agrees. "But," he adds meaningfully, "most of the market participants do not or cannot have a time horizon that is consistent with that because of their own earning pressures, or accounting treatment on trading positions, or their own risk appetite!"

While most foreign exchange traders thus agree that the role played by rationality in the market overall is limited, they differ in their views on how the market has changed over time. On the one hand, some traders observe that the role of irrationality has increased. "When I started in the business ... the market was behaving in a more logical way than it is today," one trader notes, to which another trader adds his description of the market as, "mostly irrational, and more and more!" One important reason for this development is seen in the growing importance of international investment flows relative to trade flows: "With the liberalization of capital flows, you have more people and individuals that have access to money, that handle money, that are rich. And consequently they go cross-border, they go from one currency into another currency, and then they get a part of that pure speculation. The motivation behind [their trading] is purely speculative," one trader explains. On the other hand, other traders address market aspects that are seen as signs of enhanced rationality. For example, one trader notices that today, "a lot of noise is eliminated, and the market now tends to shift very quickly from price point to price point. So, [the traders] will all be stuck at a point for a reasonable amount of time, and then there will be some news or flow coming into the market, and it will move to the next price point and stop. Whereas previously, because price discovery was less efficient, what would happen when news or flows came into the market, it was like an elastic band: it would go down and come back up until it settled."

The list of examples for irrational market behavior given by foreign exchange traders is long. One important source for the observed deviations from the economic notion of rationality stems from the different needs and motivation of participants. In the frank words of one trader, "You have many participants in the foreign exchange market who take actions for radically divergent reasons." Addressing an equally important reason for irrationalities, another trader explains: "To the extent that the market is much faster [than before], it means that emotions play a bigger role, because people don't have enough time to do a rational analysis of the information. [However,] they have to act. So, you will see irrational moves, reactions, price actions very often in a market like the foreign exchange!" Adding to this statement, another trader remarks on exchange rate dynamics that, "75% is rumor-driven and 25% is really rational." Other relevant areas of market irrationalities are seen by traders in "the behavior of crowds and the madness of speculative movement," exaggerated exchange-rate movements when, "news is hitting the market at a very strategic moment ... and the market is taken by surprise," or institutional trading regulations that force individual traders to take trading suboptimal decisions: "Because the trader has a limit, he has to cut his position and has to get back into his limit. And although he may think that the market goes in this direction, if it has not moved in his direction and if he has a certain loss he has to cut his position. And that is, with respect to the market, irrational. You see this always in the evening; the market goes in one way and the traders had to cut their positions and the New Yorkers wait for the Europeans and know what positions they have, and they make the big money!"

Thus the interviews with traders provide a striking and significant window on the question of rationality in the foreign exchange market. The observations of traders suggest that for market practitioners, the line between rational and non-rational market behavior is quite variable, blurred, and of limited practical use. "I have a bit of a problem with saying what is rational and what is irrational," one trader admits, while another declares that, "The borderline between rationality and non-rationality is floating." Unlike traditional economic theory, traders stress the *subjective* aspects of what makes trading decisions rational or irrational. "I think there is no objective rationalism or irrationalism," in the words of one trader. "Irrational is not quite the word, I would rather say subjective. If you rather wear a black than a blue dress I do not think it is irrational!" These observations suggest a need to go beyond the abstract and theoretical notions of rationality and market efficiency, and to explore the subjective perspectives, preferences, and decisions of market participants. This inevitably leads to psychology; in the laconic words of one trader, "Psychology is not rationality!"

TOWARD A MARKET PSYCHOLOGY

To move beyond the notions of rationality and market efficiency, it is not enough to merely look at such market outcomes as share prices in the stock market or exchange rates in the foreign exchange market on a collective level. Instead, we need to explore the driving forces underlying trading decisions and build bridges between the experience and behavior of individuals and collective market results. Doing so not only contributes to the new paradigm of behavioral finance, but it also marks the advent of a new field within psychology: market psychology.

Why do we need a market psychology if there is behavioral finance?

(1) *Psychology offers an understanding of financial market processes which goes beyond cognitive aspects alone.* Of all fields of psychology, the subdiscipline of cognitive psychology has been most influential in behavioral finance, since it directly addresses such market-relevant topics as information-processing, decision-making, and problem-solving.[65,66] This dominant influence of cognitive psychology on behavioral finance can also be explained by the fact that behavioral finance has mostly been driven by economists. Similar to traditional economics, cognitive psychology is based on an implicit computer metaphor of the human mind. However, while cognitive psychology correctly emphasizes that people have only limited ability to process information,[v] additional vital insights into financial markets are offered by other psychological fields, such as social, personality, evolutionary, and developmental psychology.[68–72]

For example, economic approaches often overlook the fact that financial markets are social systems: a psychologically informed approach considers the group psychological dynamics that influence the link between market information and the behavior of market participants.[73] Social psychologists stress that such dynamics, like individuals' cognitive biases, are systematic and not random. As Chapter 2, "Psychology of Trading Decisions," and Chapter 5, "News and Rumors in the Foreign Exchange Market" will show, conformity and herding among investors may augment rather than reduce "irrationalities" on the collective market level, and feedback loops among decision makers result in strongly self-reinforcing patterns of perception and behavior.

Social psychology might also help to answer the question of whether the irrationalities of individual market participants neutralize each other on the collective level of the market. Social psychologists describe powerful phenomena in the problem-solving dynamics of groups, which influence the efficiency of their work and the results they produce. In so-called compensatory judgment tasks, the solution of the group integrates individual judgments to produce a result that reflects some theoretically correct value (e.g.,

---

[v] For a more detailed comparison of the neoclassical economic and psychological approaches to decision making, see Anderson and Goldsmith.[67]

estimating the number of coins in a jar). Supposedly, the group's decision quality should increase with the number of group members because the errors of individual group members cancel each other out. For example, asking a group of investors to remember where the Dow Jones index stood on January 1, 2000 is likely to produce a better result than asking a single investor; the more investors are asked, the better the result should be. However, in practice, groups in such tasks suffer from considerable *process loss* (i.e., the quality of the group's judgment is not as good as it should be in theory, and after the group has reached a certain size, adding additional group members may even *decrease* group performance rather than increase it). How can this happen? In the social dynamics of groups, there is always a large number of factors unrelated to the ability and knowledge of individual group members (such as their social status, their rank in the organization, their verbal dominance) which influence the groups' decision-making and lead to distorted group results.[74,75]

(2) *Psychology provides insights into the connection between the subjective experience of market participants and objective market processes.* Psychology may lead to an understanding of market process which reflects the subjective experience and inner processes of participants. For instance, the analysis of market metaphors provides a key to understanding the experience of financial markets, for these metaphors make the abstraction of the market tangible to decision-makers on an experientially meaningful level. Moreover, far from being trivial and without consequences, these metaphors influence the way participants act, decide, and form predictions about the market (see Chapter 7, "Surfing the Market on Metaphors"). Psychology also explores the role of subjective attitudes in the expectations of market participants, thus moving beyond the hypothetical groups of rational "arbitrageurs" and irrational "noise" traders, or of purely "fundamental" and purely "technical" forecasting groups (see Chapter 4, "Expectations in the Foreign Exchange Market").

(3) *Psychology offers insights into the differences between market participants.* So far, the models of behavioral finance have paid only scant attention to individual differences between market participants. Market psychology may help fill this gap; one important application may lie in the traits and personal styles of participants. For example, examining the role of *personality* in trading decisions helps to determine whether trading performance is simply a manifestation of chance and of survivorship, or if there are psychological characteristics that systematically allow some participants to outperform others (see Chapter 6, "Personality Psychology of Traders").

From the perspective of market psychology, the economic focus on the notion of rationality needs to be questioned for a far-reaching reason:

placing the emphasis on rationality may obstruct the view of what actually happens in financial markets and keep observers from adequately perceiving and understanding so-called irrationalities. This limiting consequence of the rationality paradigm is captured perfectly by an episode described in Norse mythology. Woden, the wisdom god, once demanded to know of the king of the trolls how to vanquish the chaos that threatened to intrude middle earth. In exchange for his answer, the king of the trolls claimed Woden's left eye, which the wisdom god gave him without hesitation: "The secret is, you must watch with both eyes!"[76, cited in 77]

How does the rationality paradigm blind market observers in one eye when, metaphorically speaking, they require both eyes? Taking rationality as the point of departure restricts our understanding of the actual dynamics of financial markets. Focusing on rationality usually implies the tacit assumption that rational market behavior is natural and that it, therefore, requires no explanation. This assumption greatly limits how we see the decisions and actions of human market participants: Psychology is considered important only when the decisions of participants or market behavior diverge from this assumed natural state.[78] Moreover, the focus on rationality often equates all market processes that do not conform to it (i.e., non-rationality) with anomaly, irrationality, and something negative.[79] When rationality is the paradigm, psychology is activated merely to supply secondary adjustments to economic theory and to explain phenomena construed as eccentric quirks in decision-making, evolutionary psychologists Leda Cosmides and John Tooby observe.[80]

Thus, to see with both eyes and to fully appreciate the role of psychology in the markets, a different perspective is needed. It is vitally important to recognize that the behavior of market participants which does not fulfill the economic criteria for rationality does not have to be "unreasoned." A case in point, Chapter 7, "Surfing the Market on Metaphors," shows that not one, but indeed different "rationalities" characterize how participants construe their decisions in the market. These rationalities are frame-dependent; in other words, they depend on participants' subjective understanding of what the market is about. Also, when market participants use psychological heuristics for their decision-making, they do not comply with the perfectly calculating Bayesian statisticians implied in rational models. Nevertheless, such heuristics represent systematic cognitive processes, and their use generally leads to fairly good predictions. Thus, economic rationality is not required for explanation and for prediction; many psychological theories do *not* depend on rationality assumptions and accurately explain human behavior. Likewise, the behavior of foreign exchange market participants who do not act rationally (in the traditional economic definition) can also be explained;[25] basing our approach to the analysis of financial markets on psychological dynamics does not make them unexplainable or subject to random predictions.[81] On the contrary, psychology promises to offer more adequate, more differentiated, and less judgmental vantage points for understanding financial markets *the way they are experienced and enacted by human participants.*

Such an understanding of the markets not only explains better how decisions in the markets are actually formed, but psychology may also pay off financially.[82] Thus, the following point, by one of the traders in the interviews, is key both to researchers and practitioners in the foreign exchange market. "The question is," he inquired rhetorically, "Can [you] adjust yourself, your thinking, in the same way as the market?"

ABBREVIATED REFERENCES

See the reference chapter at the end of the book for full details.

1 Maital, S. (1982)
2 Thaler, R. H. (1992)
3 Frey, B. S. (1990)
4 Katona, G. (1975)
5 Shapira, Z. (1986)
6 Van Raaij, W. F. (1986)
7 Lamont, O. A. and Thaler, R. H. (2003)
8 Simon, H. A. (1959)
9 Markowitz, H. (1952)
10 Fama, E. F. (1970)
11 Hogarth, R. and Reder, M. W. E. (1987)
12 Freud, S. (1933/1965)
13 Skinner, B. F. (1974)
14 Ellis, A. and Harper, R. A. (1961)
15 Beck, A. T. (1967)
16 Lazarus, A. A. (1971)
17 Rogers, C. (1951)
18 Rogers, C. (1961)
19 Maslow, A. H. (1962)
20 Friedman, M. (1953)
21 Froot, K. A. and Frankel, J. A. (1989)
22 Frankel, J. A. and Froot, K. A. (1987)
23 Ito, T. (1990)
24 Lovell, M. C. (1986)
25 Harvey, J. T. (1996)
26 Chang, P. H. K. and Osler, C. L. (1999)

27 Lucas, R. E. (1978)
28 Muth, J. F. (1961)
29 Banz, R. W. (1981)
30 Basu, S. (1983)
31 Chan, L. K. C. et al. (1991)
32 Hawawini, G. and Keim, D. B. (2000)
33 Rosenberg, B. et al. (1985)
34 Malkiel, B. (1990)
35 Jegadeesh, N. and Titman, S. (1993)
36 De Bondt, W. F. M. and Thaler, R. (1985)
37 Rashes, M. S. (2001)
38 Ho, T. S. Y. and Michaely, R. (1988)
39 Huberman, G. and Regev, T. (2001)
40 Dreman, D. (1995)
41 Hirshleifer, D. (2001)
42 Shleifer, A. (2000)
43 Kahneman, D. and Tversky, A. (1979)
44 Shefrin, H. (2000)
45 Thaler, R. H. (1991)
46 Barberis, N. et al. (1998)
47 Daniel, K. D. et al. (2001)
48 Daniel, K. et al. (1998)
49 Fama, E. F. (1998)
50 Fama, E. F. and French, K. R. (1992)
51 Polanyi, M. (1962)
52 Polanyi, M. (1964)
53 Lopes, L. L. (1995)
54 Kahneman, D. and Tversky, A. (1984)
55 Tversky, A. and Kahneman, D. (1981)
56 De Bondt, W. F. M. and Thaler, R. H. (1994)
57 Shiller, R. J. (1984)
58 Chapman, L. J. and Chapman, J. P. (1967)
59 Wagenaar, W. A. (1971)
60 Chu, J. and Osler, C. L. (2004)
61 Frankel, J. A. and Froot, K. A. (1990a)
62 Rabin, M. (1998)
63 Stael von Holstein, C. A. (1972)
64 Yates, F. J. et al. (1991)
65 Anderson, J. R. (1990)
66 Sternberg, R. J. (2002)
67 Anderson, M. A. and Goldsmith, A. H. (1994)
68 Aronson, E. (2004)
69 Myers, D. G. (2002b)
70 Hall, C. S. et al. (1998)
71 Barkow, J. H. et al. (1992)
72 Miller, P. H. (2001)
73 Scharfstein, D. S. and Stein, J. C. (1990)

74 Steiner, L. D. (1972)
75 Hackman, R. J. (2002)
76 Gardner, J. (1978)
77 Land, D. (1996)
78 Abelson, R. P. (1976)
79 Etzioni, A. (1988)
80 Cosmides, L. and Tooby, J. (1994)
81 Katona, G. (1972)
82 Ferguson, R. (1989)

2
Psychology of Trading Decisions

> *Sixteen thousand things a day go into making your decision. And you are really making so many decisions every time you trade.*
>
> Foreign exchange trader

TRADING DECISIONS: THE VIEW OF TRADERS

In the contemporary foreign exchange market, exchange rates are determined by the decisions taken by thousands of traders and investors. It is the dynamics of human decisions which form the very heart of the market, and if there is one single topic that most closely relates to *all* market aspects, it is decision-making. All market behavior—each single currency transaction, each movement of an exchange rate—is ultimately based on underlying decisions.

Whether they are conscious of it or not, market participants take decisions constantly and in a broad variety of appearances. Their decisions may come in the form of *choices* between alternatives (e.g., corporations hedging their foreign exchange risk or not taking any action), *evaluations* of one single alternative (e.g., currency strategists evaluating the prospective value of a currency), and *constructions* of limited resources into the most satisfactory alternative (e.g., proprietary traders attempting to transform limited information, money, and time into optimal investment decisions).[1]

Usually, observers of financial markets pay attention only to what happens once decisions are already made. Focusing on averaged *decision outcomes* that manifest themselves on the collective level, they analyze trading volume, percentage rates of exchange-rate movements, and levels of support and resistance. However, just as the object of Narcissus' desire, his own mirror image in the water of a pond, vanished whenever he attempted to reach for it, the real dynamics of foreign exchange cannot be grasped in mere *reflections* of the market. To understand the market, it is therefore essential not only to see what the outcomes of market decisions are, but also to understand how these decisions are actually formed.[i]

"Trading is psychological," one foreign exchange trader captures the nature of the process behind visible market movements. The decision-making portrayed by market participants is highly dynamic and takes place in the midst of a constantly vague market setting. Being actively involved in the market and feeling the actual risk of trading positions at stake is an entirely different experience to thinking about exchange rates from the outside, traders observe. This is especially true of market-makers[ii] who constantly trade and quote prices to others. In the words of one trader: "It is a big difference if you say, 'OK, what is the dollar tomorrow?'—you might be right. But if you have a real position, when you are in the market, people ask you for prices, bids, and offers. You lose dollars, you get dollars, your position varies . . . It's not easy to work under market conditions. It's very easy to have a view on the dollar . . . [But] if you have a position, you have to fight your own psychology, your own ideas, and weakness, and strength. You are too brave and too bold, and you are too shy, and that makes the trading so difficult." Thus a multitude of complex factors, including subjective expectations, current trading positions, trading limits, and the actions of other participants, influence trading decisions in real life. Because these factors often conflict with each other, trading involves constant ambivalence, where there are invariably reasons to buy and to sell at the same time. In the words of one trader, "Two contradictory pieces of news is actually good because at least they give you an argument for one side, whichever you believe in!"

Traders also stress that to simply keep one's status quo and to hold on to the current trading position is also a trading decision; however, often a less explicit and intentional one. As one trader observes, "not to decide can be a decision," and indeed it always *is* a decision. Consequences are painfully experienced, for example, by those corporations whose financial managers do nothing to cover the exposure of their business to foreign exchange risk. Whereas, from an internal reporting standpoint, these managers may view currency-hedging as

---

[i] "Much is reported on the technical procedures of the stock exchange, on the stock volume which is traded daily, and the importance of the stock exchange in the economy of a nation. However, we know little about the players, their motivation, their mutual dependencies and about what influences them," according to Peter Maas and Jürgen Weibler.[2]

[ii] For a definition of market makers, see Chapter 9, "The Basics."

taking a position and doing nothing as a less risky alternative, the exact opposite may be true: Doing nothing opens their business up to a permanent risk that is simply outside their area of expertise. "Basically you have three decisions available: you buy, you sell, or you do nothing," one trader summarizes. Another trader provides a vivid example of how even the third of these alternatives (i.e., taking no action) communicates to other market participants and influences their decisions. "If you make a price to someone and they don't deal, that can affect your position because you might have pitched it up. And you think, 'oh, that means it's a buy.' And you think 'I'll probably skew toward buy as well, so I think I'll buy some.' That's a decision!" Therefore, as it is impossible for market participants not to decide, it is also impossible for them *not* to communicate by what they do and by what they do not do.[3]

Thus, the social influence of others is a decisive aspect of trading decisions which is frequently highlighted in the interviews. "You talk to the other guys and if they have the same opinion, you do a deal. And if they have perhaps another opinion, then you wait a little bit and see what the markets will do," contends one trader. The influence of groups on foreign exchange decisions is substantial, and not always is the quality of decisions improved by the group, as the experience of another trader shows: "People definitely do things in a group that they would not do on their own, and usually to the detriment of the shareholders. We tried numerous times to take 'desk positions,' ones that were not tied to an individual trader but rather to a collective responsibility. The ratio of winning trades to losing ones was not good, and typically the discipline was more lax!"

So, how *do* foreign exchange traders try to achieve a winning ratio in their trading decisions? To answer this question, let us consider the European survey that asked hundreds of traders to systematically rate the various characteristics of their decisions according to their importance. To make answers more representative, traders rated all aspects separately (1) for their best and (2) for their worst trading decisions. Figure 2.1 compares the resulting two decision "profiles." Characteristics are arranged clockwise and in descending order of importance, with the most important characteristic located at the top. The distance to the center of the figure indicates the average importance of the decision characteristics.

Remarkably, traders rated the same three aspects as most important for both their best and worst decisions. Traders perceive *feelings* to be the most important aspect of their decisions by far. The importance of feelings in trading decisions was regarded as even more important than the decision outcomes (i.e., the loss of money in the case of unsuccessful decisions and

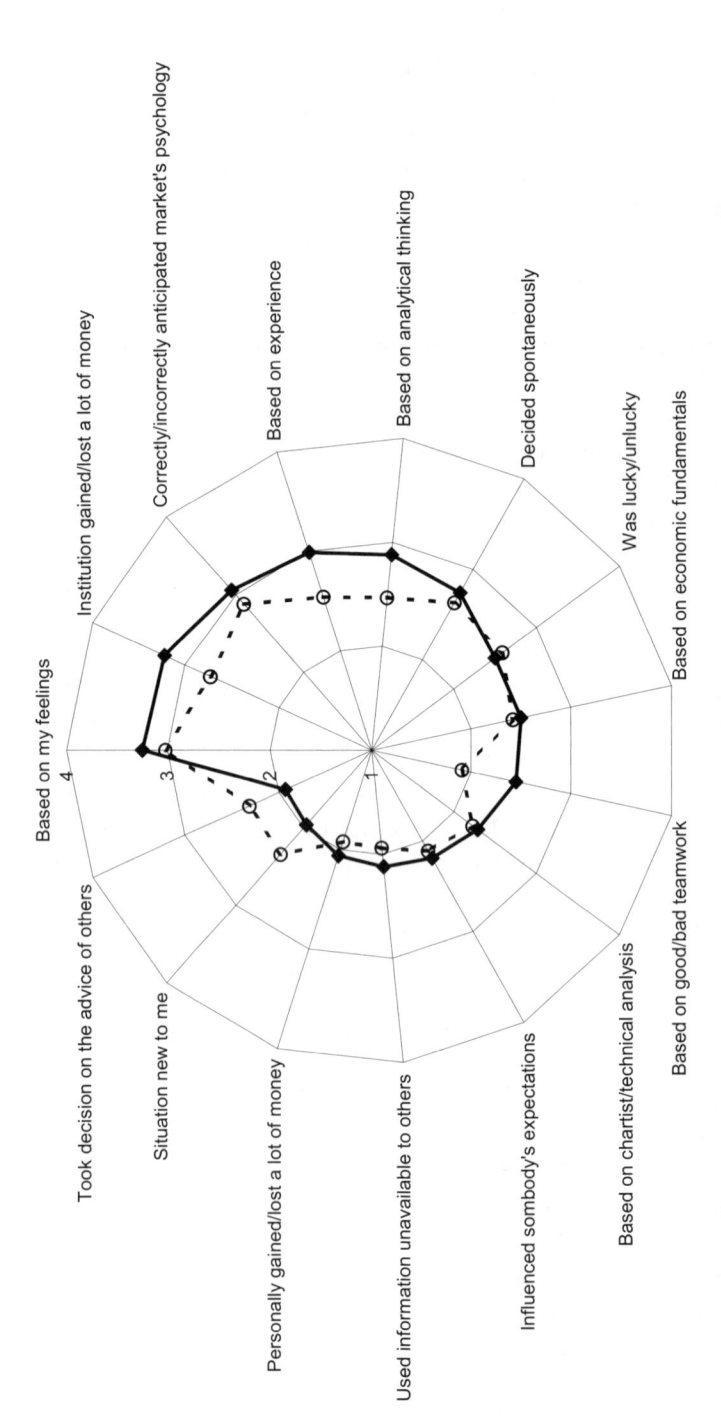

Figure 2.1 Psychological profiles of best (♦) and worst (⊖) trading decisions: 1 = Strongly disagree, 4 = Strongly agree.

the gain of money in the case of successful decisions). The third of the most important aspects, both in traders' best and worst trading decisions, is anticipation of market psychology: traders perceive their best decisions to be based on a correct anticipation of the market's psychology, whereas they perceive their worst decisions to result from an incorrect anticipation of the market's psychology. Thus, feelings and market psychology were perceived clearly as *more important* than such rational decision aspects as analytical thinking, fundamental economic data, or computer decision programs.

The distances between the two profiles in Figure 2.1 indicate characteristics that are perceived as differently important for best and for worst trading decisions. The considerable overall similarity in the two profiles implies that there are only few intrinsic characteristics which differentiate the good from the bad trading decisions. In other words, while making decisions, traders have little or no stable criteria on which to judge the quality of their decisions. Instead, decision quality is determined in retrospect by the result (i.e., by whether money was gained or lost as a consequence). Many traders explicitly commented on the fact that the quality of trading decisions is only defined in terms of the amount of money made or lost. Good decisions then are measured in terms of their profit alone—regardless of how the profit was achieved. In the words of one trader, "I made a lot of money. That's the only thing that defines a good decision from a bad decision, really."

A systematic analysis of differences showed that "teamwork" ranked significantly more important in best trading decisions. This finding reinforces the importance of social and group factors in successful trading. Moreover, the analysis also showed that in worst trading decisions, "I took the decision on the advice of others" and "the situation was new to me" ranked significantly more important. These findings might be explained away as self-serving tendencies on the part of the traders. Attributions are psychological judgments about the causes of behaviors or events: While somebody who forms an *internal* attribution holds the actor responsible, somebody who forms an *external* attribution thinks that situational causes are responsible for a certain behavior or event. Because both the advice of others and the novelty of a market situation attribute bad trading decisions to external reasons, traders' ratings might express a self-enhancing attribution bias that distorts their explanations for success and failure.[4]

However, these findings may well reflect the *reality* of poor trading decisions. As we will see in the section "Trading intuition: Bridging affects and cognition" in this chapter, missing experience and familiarity with market situations does not allow for trading intuition. Moreover, group dynamics among traders can indeed lead to the result that the advice of others produces bad trading decisions. Groups exert a potentially dangerous influence on the decision-making of individuals, as was shown by James Stoner.[5] His research presented persons with "choice dilemmas" that involved a cautious alternative with little but certain benefit and a risky course of action with a large potential benefit. In the area of investing, such a choice might be the decision between a government-grade bond and a volatile stock option. In foreign exchange, traders may ask themselves whether they should enter the risk of buying a currency for which they perceive a small possibility of a so-called technical break.[iii] Whereas the break is likely to be rebuffed and a trading loss is thus probable, on the rare time the technical level does break, potential profits could be huge. Stoner's research on how people react to such choices resulted in the formulation of the so-called "risky shift" phenomenon: after participating in a group discussion, willingness to take risk *increases*.[iv]

"In the event that you find the accused guilty, the bench will not entertain a recommendation for mercy. The death sentence is mandatory in this case," pronounces a line from Sidney Lumet's film *12 Angry Men*, in which a jury room hosts a group of 12 men who deliberate their verdict on a young defendant in an apparently obvious murder case. In the initial ballot of votes among the men, 11 are convinced of the defendant's culpability, while the juror played by Henry Fonda votes "not guilty." What follows in the film is hard to explain by the laws of statistical probability; however, knowledge of social processes in groups helps.[7] The implications of risky shift and group polarization phenomena are far-reaching, not only for the verdicts reached by panels of judges in juries,[8,9] but also for all trading and investment decisions in financial markets. Such decisions, too, are often the outcome of group processes, and they reflect systematically different levels of risk than the individual traders acting alone would have entered.[10]

Thus, rather than reflecting rational and detached decisions, accounts of traders portray a dynamic process that is defined by psychological and social factors. Expanding on topics that have materialized already in this first glimpse at participants' own view of market decisions, the following parts of the book explore the most relevant areas in greater depth. (1) Traders' initial observations have stressed the importance of social dynamics to their decisions (the

---

[iii] For a discussion of technical analysis as a method to predict exchange rates, see Chapter 4, "Expectations in the Foreign Exchange Market."

[iv] Refining these findings, later research determined that this shift toward increased risk is a manifestation of "group polarization," the decision-making tendency in groups in which *any* preference held by group members in the beginning becomes more extreme in the course of the group interaction.[6] Thus, depending on the participants, group decisions can also lead to systematically less risky solutions than individuals would have chosen.

section "Social herding dynamics" explores these dynamics and the collective outcome of traders' influence on each other). (2) Traders' initial insights into their decisions have underscored the importance of feelings (the section "Affects" examines the role of these feelings and of trading intuition). (3) Traders have observed the conflicting complexity of factors that influence their decisions in a dynamic and vague market setting (the section "Cognitions" explores some of the mental shortcuts that allow them to cope with this complexity). (4) Finally, traders have observed that in the real-life setting of the market, the actual experience of market risk has an impact on their decisions (Chapter 3, "Risk-Taking in Trading Decisions," explores the psychological aspects of such risky decisions). Before we continue to explore these vital areas of traders' decision-making, the following excursion describes some of the most important steps in the history of decision-making theory and contrasts the normative–economic view of decisions with a descriptive–psychological view. Readers who are familiar with this conceptual background and who are mainly interested in the first-hand accounts of foreign exchange decisions may directly proceed to the section "Social herding dynamics."

EXCURSION: UNDERSTANDING DECISION-MAKING IN FINANCIAL MARKETS

From objective prices to psychological theories of decision-making

In the course of the last centuries and especially over the last few decades, significant theoretical contributions have been made which shape the ways in which we think about decision-making in financial markets. More than two and a half centuries ago, a decisive first step toward understanding how people form decisions in the realm of wealth and money was undertaken by the Swiss physicist and mathematician Daniel Bernoulli. As early as 1738, on the eve of Frederick the Great of Prussia's meteoric rise to power and the War of the Austrian Succession (1740–48), Bernoulli was the first to introduce the concept of "utility" to decision-making and thus effectively set the stage for later theories of choice. Taking this step allowed Bernoulli to differentiate between the price of an object, which is a characteristic of the object and which is therefore the same for everybody, and the object's utility, which is dependent on personal factors for each individual. Thus, Bernoulli observed that the value of things is not based on their price but on their *utility*. Gaining $10,000, for example, is more important when one is penniless than when one is rich.[11] This property, which is referred to as "diminishing marginal utility" by economists, implies that if we were to graph utility against wealth, we would see an upward-sloping curve that gets flatter as wealth increases. The richer investors are, the less utility they gain with each incremental unit of profit. This definition of utility has a far-reaching consequence for the decisions of investors. It implies that people are fundamentally risk-averse (i.e., they prefer certain to uncertain prospects of equal expected value).[12] For example, people usually prefer $10 for sure to a wager where they win $20 if a coin comes up heads and gain nothing if the coin comes up tails.[13]

Today, Bernoulli's insight forms the basis of all decision-making theories that are based on the notion that, when people make decisions, they *maximize* value or utility. But how can one maximize utility in a *risky* choice, such as in investments, where uncertainty is part of the decision? While placing money in a bank account earns investors a predetermined interest and is therefore a riskless choice, the decision to take part in a lottery or to buy a certain stock or currency is a risky choice because it leads to an outcome that cannot be known in advance. Here people are assumed to maximize *expected* utility. In other words, expected utility theory postulates that decision-makers base their choices on comparing the expected utilities of the decision alternatives; they first weight the utility of each alternative with the likelihood of its occurrence and then choose the alternative that will return the highest expected utility.[14]

Expected utility theory is the leading economic theory of choice in such risky environments as financial markets; most economists who study decision-making equate the maximization of expected utility with rational behavior. This theory assumes that decision-makers have information about the likelihoods and the consequences of each decision alternative, and that they behave rationally by deciding according to what *maximizes* expected utility. John von Neumann and Oskar Morgenstern demonstrated theoretically that if a decision-maker fulfills certain basic axioms of rational behavior such as "transitivity" and "invariance," then his or her decisions indeed maximize expected utility.[15] For example, according to the principle of "transitivity," a home buyer who prefers house A to house B, and house B to house C, should also prefer house A to house C, and according to the principle of "invariance," the purchase should not be influenced by how the houses are advertised (i.e., how the alternatives are presented), but only by how the objective information given about them differs.

Within psychology, the systematic study of how people make decisions began when, half a century ago, Ward Edwards reviewed the theory of decision-making and acquainted psychologists with the economic literature on the topic.[16] What followed was an enormous expansion of decision-making research by psychologists who often found that how people actually form decisions *contradicted* expected utility theory, both in the controlled and systematic study of decisions in research laboratories and in the observation of real-life decisions.

A historic new step in decision-making theories was taken when the economic Nobel price laureate Herbert Simon disagreed with the very concept of maximization on which expected utility theory is based.[17,18] According to Simon, decision-makers do not maximize but they "satisfice" (i.e., they attempt to reach a satisfactory but not a maximal degree of accomplishment by their choices). For example, when deciding between alternative investments, market participants look for alternatives that appear to satisfy their most important needs rather than conduct an exhaustive analysis of all available investments. Simon also introduced the notion of "bounded rationality," thereby emphasizing people's cognitive limitations of perceiving and selecting information and of learning.

Some 20 years later, the psychologists' Daniel Kahneman and Amos Tversky's "prospect theory" provided convincing empirical evidence against the notion that the decisions of investors are governed by utility maximization.[19,v] While violations of expected utility maximization in decisions had already been described earlier (e.g., the decision paradoxes found by Nobel prize laureate Maurice Allais in 1953 and Daniel Ellsberg in 1961),[20,21] until then such violations had usually been discarded as merely theoretical exceptions. The concept of bounded rationality and the existence of simplifying heuristics in decision-making[22] could still be explained away by economists as optimizing efficient use of time and thus as ultimately being rational. However, prospect theory revealed psychological framing effects in decision-making which systematically violated the invariance axiom of expected utility theory.[vi] These findings could no longer be reconciled with the economic notion of rational behavior.[23] The insights of prospect theory resulted in an economics Nobel prize for Kahneman in 2002; today, the effects explained by prospect theory are widely documented not only in finance and psychology, but also in such areas as medicine and law.

Thus a growing literature on behavioral decision-making shows that psychological factors determine the way people take risk and form decisions in

---

[v] Translating basic psychological concepts into a mathematical model, Kahneman and Tversky's central article on prospect theory has become one of the most frequently cited sources in the economic literature. However, only few psychological insights into decision-making are equally formally conceptualized.

[vi] For an example of a framing effect, see the section "Normative–economic and descriptive–psychological approaches" in this chapter. For a more detailed description of framing, see Chapter 3, "Risk-Taking in Trading Decisions."

financial markets. Compared with utility maximization theory, more complex descriptions of how people make decisions have evolved.[24] Most importantly, many of the novel approaches to decision-making move from the classical focus on what decision-makers *should* do to observations of what they *actually* do in real life. New "naturalistic" decision theories describe how decisions take place naturally, as opposed to the theory-based and axiom-based view of decisions.[25] For example, narrative approaches to decision-making observe that people attempt to construct coherent *stories* to organize their knowledge of events and to form such decisions as those of jurors at court trials,[26] and that people imagine *scenarios* to predict the future course of events.[27] One especially relevant approach to the kinds of decisions made in financial markets is the "recognition-primed decision model."[28,29] This model describes the decision-making of experienced professionals who perform under such conditions as time pressure, ambiguous or missing information, dynamically changing situations, and the need to perceive and distinguish relevant patterns in the environment. It has explored the high-stakes decisions of firefighters, pilots, and military officers, who—like traders—make fast and effective decisions that are based on their experience. The model describes how these professionals recognize situations to determine appropriate interventions and evaluate possible results by imagining the outcomes of their actions.

Like the recognition-primed decision model, the following exploration of foreign exchange decisions also rests on interviews with the actual decision-makers. However, before we turn to the first-hand views of traders, the vital conceptual difference between normative and descriptive views of decisions is clarified. This difference lies at the very center of the current debate about financial markets between economists and psychologists.

Normative–economic and descriptive–psychological approaches

When economists and psychologists discuss financial markets, quickly differences between their basic understanding of the decisions of market participants surface and the disparities between a normative and a descriptive approach are guaranteed to stimulate controversy.[vii,viii] Often, the boundaries between

---

[vii] See Hogarth and Reder.[30]

[viii] Next to *normative* and *descriptive*, there are also *prescriptive* approaches to decision-making which establish guidelines and advice on how to make successful decisions. Their prescriptions are usually related to specific decision-making contexts (e.g., how to set up a retirement plan or how to allocate funds to various kinds of investments). Good examples of a prescriptive approach to decision-making are market newsletters advising their readers on where to invest their money.

these two perspectives are blurred in this controversy, creating confusion and leading to untenable claims.

Traditional economics uses a normative model, basing its approach of financial markets on the assumption that participants process information fully rationally. In contrast, the descriptive approaches of decision-making used in psychology attempt to explain how market participants *actually* form their decisions in experimental situations and in real life. These theories stress that all trading decisions represent a form of *human behavior* and that market results are the outcomes of cognitive, affective, and social processes. Thus, accurate descriptions of how decisions are actually made and of the participants' limitations to process information rationally—not only elegant and abstract modeling of the market—are necessary.[24,31,32] How does one achieve such descriptions? Asking study participants to choose between pre-formulated investment scenarios, observing traders' decisions in the market, and analyzing introspectively the factors that have led to a certain trading decision have all produced descriptive insights about decision-making.

There is no shortage of empirical research and market observations which show how substantially descriptive results and the outcomes suggested by normative models differ.[33] To give an example, in an experiment published in the prestigious *New England Journal of Medicine*, participants were asked whether they would treat lung cancer by radiation therapy or by surgery, and they were provided with information about the effects of each treatment.[34] For their decisions, participants received information about the effects of both treatments on 100 patients at three points in time (i.e., during treatment, after one year, and after five years). However, whereas for some of the participants this information was formulated in terms of how many of 100 patients were still alive, other participants received the same information formulated in terms of how many patients had died. Although objectively the information in both groups of participants was *identical*, the degree to which surgery was preferred to radiation therapy was dramatically influenced by the mere circumstance of how this information was formulated (i.e., in terms of the number of surviving patients vs. the number of patients who die). The attractiveness of surgery rose substantially when the outcomes were presented in terms of the probability of living rather than in terms of the probability of dying. Researchers found that this effect is present even among statistically trained graduate students and experienced radiologists.

Such framing effects (i.e., decisions are psychologically influenced by how problems are *formulated* and subjectively *perceived*) are in stark contrast to the normative model which is based on rational decision-makers who process information in a complete and unbiased way. Because decisions in the area of finance and investments are also full of framing effects,[ix] psychologically informed market observers duly notice that traditional economic models contradict empirical knowledge and show a complete neglect for the psychological factors involved in how people *actually* form decisions. Accordingly, because traditional finance simply assumes that market participants optimize their decisions and otherwise sees them as black boxes,[x] behavioral economists Werner De Bondt and Richard Thaler complain that traditional finance appears deserted by people, who are undoubtedly the most important ingredient of markets.[35]

Traditional economists reply that psychological critics overlook the essentially *normative* nature of economic market models. For example, when they establish models of how the foreign exchange market works, they are less concerned about whether the underlying assumption of rational decision-making on the level of individual traders is true than they are interested in whether the model allows them to make correct explanations and predictions on the market level (i.e., of exchange rates). Thus, the observation that individual market participants form their decisions quite differently to what economic theory postulates may ultimately be a nuisance to economists, but it does not impact the normative quality of their theories.

In other words, the difference between a normative and a descriptive understanding of the foreign exchange market is also about the contrast between (1) a static and result-oriented and (2) an adaptive and process-oriented approach. To visualize this contrast, imagine the metaphor of an unevenly shaped bowl into which a viscous liquid is poured, as suggested by Herbert Simon.[36] If the bowl is completely stationary and only the equilibrium result of the transfer of liquid is of interest, then nothing about the liquid needs to be known and the result can easily be determined. However, if the bowl is itself in rapid motion or if the question *how* the equilibrium is reached is important, then more knowledge about the characteristics of the liquid is needed. If we follow the lines of this metaphor, decisions of market participants are clearly poured into the foreign exchange market "bowl," which is in constant motion.

[ix] For further examples of framing effects, see Chapter 3, "Risk-Taking in Trading Decisions."

[x] According to the *Oxford English Dictionary*, the term "black box" was first used in the Royal Air Force for navigational instruments in airplanes and then extended to denote any automatic apparatus that performs complex functions. In psychology, the black box metaphor is often used to characterize behaviorist B. F. Skinner's approach to human behavior. This approach sees knowledge of inner psychological processes as unnecessary for understanding behavior that is determined by environmental antecedents and consequences.

"What makes a good trader—who should I hire?" "How can I outsmart my competitors in the market?" "Why do traders tend to cut their profits short and ride their losses?" "How can I train my traders not to be too overconfident in their trading decisions?" These questions are vitally important to market participants, and they cannot be addressed with a normative method. To predict the actions of adaptive actors (say, thinking and feeling market participants) in complex environments (say, today's foreign exchange market), knowledge of objectives is thus not sufficient. Market participants care less about the fictitious end state of the market than about the process of *how* the market moves on its way. To illustrate, in my interviews, traders frequently stressed that all trading decisions depended on the trading time horizon (i.e., whether the decision-maker took a short- or long-term perspective), and they emphasized that each decision was only right or wrong within a certain horizon. In the words of one trader, "Your decision is as good or as bad as it is right or wrong within a given time frame. And time always makes things relevant or irrelevant."

Economists often lose sight of the fact that a normative analysis is not descriptive and confuse their economic ideals with market reality and with the actual decisions of market participants. "Much as we typically deny it— it is because of this confusion on our part that we have trouble buying behavioral stuff," one economist vehemently expressed in a private conversation. Often, the problem is based on untested assumptions. For example, economists may believe that market participants are in fact purely motivated by profit maximization. Alternatively, they may assume that the fierce competition in the financial markets indeed ensures the survival only of optimal (i.e., rational) participants. Finally, they may think that such aspects of rational choice as invariance and transitivity are not only intuitively appealing on a theoretical level, but that they describe *actual* human choice behavior. However, each of these assumptions has been proven wrong, and the traditional economic view of decisions cannot and should not claim to be *both* normative and descriptive.[33,35-37] People often fall in love with the theory they were trained in and then spend the rest of their lives defending it, psychologist Arnold Lazarus once remarked about the discussion between the various schools of psychotherapy.[xi] The same insight may be true of the views taken by financial market theorists.[xii]

[xi] Presentation at the Evolution of Psychotherapy conference, Hamburg, July 27–31, 1994.
[xii] For example, Ariel Rubinstein examines theoretical economists' tendency to explain empirical data in a way that helps them justify their convictions.[38] Rubinstein concludes that what is needed is, "much more than citing experimental results and marginally modifying our models. We need to open the black box of decision making, and come up with some completely new and fresh modeling devices."

Observing that many market theories are merely directed at a theoretical long-term equilibrium, John Maynard Keynes once dryly remarked, "In the long run, we are all dead." In contrast, from a descriptive perspective, the market is always on the way and never arrives. The processes by which currencies are traded, and *how* the market moves, are not static and technical, but dynamic and driven by humans. Thus, for a better grasp of these processes, understanding the *actual* decision-making of participants is needed. Theories reflecting such an understanding do not emanate from hypothetical assumptions, but instead have to consider psychological and social market dynamics. A vital key to these dynamics is the mass psychology involved in social herding processes.

SOCIAL HERDING DYNAMICS

> Mass psychology really is the key to determine price action, at the end of the day.
>
> Foreign exchange trader

Like all human decision-makers in real life, foreign exchange market participants are influenced by social factors and do not make their decisions in a detached state of psychological isolation. Rather than thinking, feeling, and behaving merely as individuals, traders are members of a social collective.[39] Thus, any genuine understanding of trading decisions requires knowledge about how the decisions of traders *interact*.

We now turn to a discussion of herding processes and scrutinize some of the psychological motives for herding. Going far beyond such spectacular incidents as market crashes, the social dynamics of herding *pervades* decision-making in the foreign exchange market.

Herding and psychological conformity

In the foreign exchange market, herding results in behavior of market participants that is fueled by perceptions and assumptions about *other* participants' behavior. This sets in motion a homogenizing and self-regulating process of decision-making on the collective market level. In this social psychological process, perceptions of others' decisions become the basis for one's *own* decisions. As one foreign exchange trader observes, in herding, participants try to anticipate and mimic the behavior of other participants. Consequently, herding leads market participants to orient their own behavior according to perceived (or merely suspected) group norms.[32] Decisions then merely imitate the decisions of others at the expense, or even at the exclusion, of other information.[40]

Explanations of herding in financial markets often refer to *conformity*, a psychological phenomenon which can even be demonstrated in small groups: The decisions of people who interact with each other in groups have a tendency to converge, often until they are practically identical. Early evidence for the power of groups to affect the beliefs of their members was provided by social psychologists Muzafer Sherif and Solomon Asch.[41,42]

In Asch's classic experiment, participants formed decisions regarding a simple task—matching the length of an original line to one of three comparison lines of clearly different length. These supposedly straightforward decisions were made openly by each of nine people, in their order of seating. What participants in the experiment did *not* know was that the eight other persons in the group were actually confederates of the experimenter who were instructed to at times unanimously respond with a wrong judgment. The confederates then indicated that they perceived an obviously longer or obviously shorter comparison line, not the same length comparison line, to match the original line.

The others' responses turned out to have a decisive effect: whereas comparison estimates in a control group were virtually without error, being exposed to wrong judgments of others and publicly declaring one's own decision dramatically increased the number of distorted estimates. After the experiment, even those subjects who were strong enough to make dissenting judgments reported that they started to doubt their own eyes when other group members disagreed with them. Although Asch found individual differences in how prone people were to giving in to group pressure (some participants *never* conformed to the wrong group judgment, others went with the majority nearly *all the time*), overall findings clearly demonstrate how reluctant people are to dissent from a perceived group consensus, even if their individual judgment is in stark contrast to the group's.

While the subjects in Asch's experiment had the clear-cut task of matching the length of lines, participants in the foreign exchange market consistently face a more ambiguous demand: they need to turn highly complex market information into trading decisions. There is good reason to assume that in such unstructured decision settings, where there is plenty of evidence and data to support *many* market opinions, herding is relatively common.

One important reason for herding among foreign exchange participants is their *uncertainty* in a frequently changing and ambiguous decision environment. In such a climate, herding expresses the search for *any* kind of rule. Because this search, one trader says, is often based on thinking that "they are bigger, or better, than I am," big market players can especially take advantage of this uncertainty of others. Another trader remarks dryly, "[If] you have the advantage of roaming a big book and make the people in the market feel that you know where it goes ... they hop on the same train ... to push it even further!"

Accordingly, another explanation of herding in the foreign exchange market revolves around participants' *fear* and *anticipated regret*[xiii] if they decide wrongly. Both of these unpleasant feelings are intensified when they have to be endured alone (i.e., when they are not shared by others). Likewise, a wrong decision brings more self-reproach when one dissents from a group than when one is just as wrong as the others.[32] A wrong decision that is shared by the others at least provides the comfort that everybody was wrong.[xiv] Moreover, a wrong decision made alone may be more difficult to explain than a wrong decision shared by others. "Worldly wisdom teaches that it is better for reputation to fail conventionally than to succeed unconventionally," John Maynard Keynes observes.[44] One trader describes his problems in getting support for an unconventional trading decision: "This was difficult for me to present to my board. They said everybody is speaking about it and you did not do it, *why?*" Thus, in systematically unpredictable conditions, herding may be reasonable for foreign exchange participants who are concerned about their reputation, because it allows them to share the blame.[40]

Herding dynamics in the foreign exchange market

> A trend is your friend, and if everyone is going to go along (...) you better join the crowd rather than being against it.
>
> Foreign exchange trader

In the previously described experiment on social conformity, it was the consciously and cleverly designed set-up of a psychologist which triggered herding reactions in small decision-making groups. Similarly, in the complex environment of the foreign exchange market a number of agents can set off herding; these agents may do so both consciously and unintentionally.

One trader, for example, says that well-regarded people can trigger herding: "There are certain people in the market who are economists or who write for certain news wires, who have a fairly important role to play, what they have to say is very important. Just now there are several big funds that will wait until this guy writes his piece before they put out their positions." Other traders

---

[xiii] For a discussion of regret theory, see the section "Affects" in this chapter.
[xiv] "The herd minimizes risks and prevents loneliness," according to Norton.[43]

observe that leading banks can trigger herding through their trades: "The large banks are more or less opinion leaders. If they buy a large amount, then everybody says 'OK, let's buy because it seems the market is moving up.'" Leading banks can also initiate herding through the statements of senior officials which are widely disseminated by the news media. "Goldman Sachs had a seminar several weeks ago and their chief economist stood up and said that the Australian dollar is far too cheap, this thing has to appreciate. By the end of the afternoon, it was 2% higher. Now there was no other information out on the Australian dollar, there was no other reason why the Australian dollar appreciated other than the senior economist came out with that thing. That was reported on the news wire, and you know that certain people are going to be following that news wire service, and it becomes like a herd mentality. There is no point of me sitting here not trading it, not getting involved, if everybody else is buying it," says one trader.

Central banks and politicians can also initiate herding. "If a central bank comes to a commercial bank for an intervention and they sell $50 million, $50 million is nothing in the market. But the commercial bank which buys these 50 million knows it is an intervention, and of course they sell another 50 million, and so forth. So it is a snowball effect more or less, and that moves the market," according to one trader. Another trader notes that the statements of central banks and politicians are examples of news which should be followed, even if they are not personally believed, because of the *anticipated* reaction by the market which will inevitably follow: "Talking the dollar up is, literally, coming out with phrases like: 'We think the dollar is too cheap' ... People will react to that, if a central banker is saying that. Even if you think, at the end of the day, 'he probably doesn't believe it', there are enough people out there [who will react], like a herd mentality!"

Once set in motion, herding processes may oscillate between stages that are reinforced by self-fulfilling social dynamics.[xv] In the *building and integration* period, following the herd is advantageous and may result in trading profits, traders explain.[xvi] One trader describes this as a market environment in which "you get hurt if you go against the stream." At this stage, a quick recognition of "what influential others do" is important, even if it is contrary to one's own

---

[xv] For a discussion of self-fulfilling prophecies, see Chapter 4, "Expectations in the Foreign Exchange Market."

[xvi] The observation of herding dynamics has led to a number of sophisticated attempts to remedy the economic theory of information processing. For example, economists examined the role of informational cascades in financial fads where it is optimal to simply follow the behavior of others, and showed that optimizing decision rules may be characterized by market participants' herding behavior without using their own information.[45,46]

belief. During this phase, "No one is really sitting there and saying: No, I am against it, I keep this position and run against the rest of the world," as one trader explains. "Even if I am convinced that the market should go in the opposition direction, I will not go against the market," another trader agrees. Joining to the perceived consensus and to the actions of the others may be required, for example, when herding determines the market's reaction to a likely rumor; as a third trader states: "It doesn't matter if it is right or wrong. I have to take action on it because *the market* is." Yet another trader describes this feature simply, observing that in the short run one joins an irrational movement because one doesn't want to go against the market.

"Herding *dissolution* starts with the rapidly growing perception that building and integration has peaked. By definition, if everyone says it is going up, they all bought it or will buy it later. Once everyone has bought something, they can't sell it ... If everyone buys something, there is only one way it can go, at least in my logic. The other 99.9% of the foreign exchange population that has bought it will not understand why it is going down—*I* will understand why it is going down," reasons one trader.

Baseball legend Yogi Berra's line, "Nobody goes there anymore. It's too crowded," is also an apt description of this herding stage. This is reflected in many statements of traders such as, "If the obvious is too obvious, then it is obviously wrong," "[as] soon as all expect the same thing, it becomes null and void," and "if everybody thinks something, they are wrong." For their own trading, many traders attempt to actively anticipate this turn of the herding process. While it is difficult to determine a defined cut-off point between building and dissolution, one trader mentions that if nine out of the ten people he calls assert one thing, he becomes very cautious and tends toward the other opinion. Yet another trader remarks that often the general news media becomes interested in a certain development in the financial markets only at this turning point. However, attempts to take advantage of a development may come too late. "In the foreign exchange market, when you get the trade recommendation from everyone, saying 'this is what you need to do,' you get all the predictions from all the strategists, 'you know the euro is going to $1.30,' that is the time when you say 'OK, well if everyone is thinking this, everyone is doing it, then it is not a great idea anymore.' And that is when the smart money starts getting out," observes one trader. Once the smart money is out, traders who have held on their trading positions may find themselves on the wrong side of the market, left by the herd. Another trader remarks dryly: "We call it ... 'orphans' time'."

During a market crash, the importance of herding becomes particularly visible. For example, herding processes are likely to have propelled the

October 1987 crash in the stock market, when stock prices fell by a third although no important negative news had been released in the media.[32,40] Because market crashes are driven more by a sudden and dramatic change in collective perceptions than by the sudden and dramatic change of underlying economic fundamentals and concrete news stories in the media,[47] "economic models alone cannot describe real crash experience".[48] This change in the collective perception of the market dramatically increases the role of affects in the decisions of market participants,[xvii] and it leads participants to become even more dependent on each other in their decisions. In the aftermath of the 1987 crash, the ups and downs of various national stock markets became more linked to each other.[50] The shared recent experience of surprise and fear among market participants plays an important role in this intensification of co-movements among national markets. *Emotional contagion* leads people not only to synchronize their behavior with others, but also to converge on an emotional level, and to intensify the synchronization of their actions in the face of threat.[51–53]

Herding processes may also be fueled by the psychological tendency of human decision-makers to overweigh readily available information. Recency and a prominent position in panic-stricken public discourse can powerfully facilitate psychological availability. Systematically overweighing current affect-laden information then supports herding.[xviii]

In addition, herding is characterized by *self-reinforcing* decision-making mechanisms based on "information cascades." The dynamics of such cascades can be likened to the spreading of an infectious disease. However, while the diseases studied by epidemiologists are based on easily transmitted viruses, during an information cascade in the market it is *information about the behavior* of participants that leads others to actively copy their actions, which in turn stimulates even more participants to follow. Such cascades of information and ensuing behavior imply that herding not only works in a linear fashion, but that it also feeds back into itself, which may escalate initially small causes. Thus, a small leak will sink a great ship.

[xvii] The role of emotions in trading decisions is discussed in the section "Affects" in this chapter. The increased role of affects during market crashes is already observed in Turner and Killian's lucid description of crowd behavior: "The situation is ambiguous or unstructured; the participants do not share pre-existing, traditional expectations as to how they should behave; the outcome is uncertain ... [and there is] a sense of urgency, a feeling that something must be done now."[49] Thus during the emergence of crowd behavior, mood is communicated and an unspecific sense of what actions to take emerges.
[xviii] For a discussion of the so-called "availability heuristic," see the section "Cognitions" in this chapter.

Herding can also help explain exchange-rate volatility. When participants simply *mimic* the behavior of other participants, instead of processing market information independently, they promote existing market trends. "People tend to ... become more bullish as we go up, so therefore the market goes up, so therefore people become more confident, etc. ... Hence, we get the overshoots and the undershoots that take place," in the words of one foreign exchange trader.

Herding in the foreign exchange market is often nurtured by new trading and information technologies. These technologies provide participants with real-time market information, and virtually the same market information is available to all market participants today.[xix] This aspect of global financial news allows for *instantaneous* individual adjustments to collective market behavior. Moreover, the use of computer-aided trading decision systems may cause large parts of the market to react simultaneously and similarly, thereby intensifying herding behavior. "The system is trend-following," one trader explains. "If one fund begins to buy, other funds follow!"[xx]

Traders also perceive herding dynamics among the financial news services. They report that providers of financial news frequently follow the trends set by other news providers: "As soon as one firm comes up with a very particular product or gimmick, everybody else will catch up immediately," states one trader. Likewise, there is herding in traders' choice of financial news providers: "The market makes the decision for you on which information provider to choose," remarks one trader, while another trader observes matter-of-factly that, "You need Reuters because everybody else has it."

Herding dynamics among market participants can also be found in the selection of relevant news items. One trader generally states that regarding news selection, "Basically we look at things we think the market is going to focus on." Another trader rationalizes how he adjusts his selection of news and filters the available market information according to the choices of others: "I have to know what other parts of the market think." To foreign exchange traders, the *anticipation* of herding in the market is a reason rumors in the foreign exchange market should be taken seriously and acted on, even if one doubts them personally. Since "people just assume the news is correct," it then

---

[xix] "The recipient of mass communication ... often finds himself defining his experience as one that is extensively shared and he in some sense interacts with his image of the large body of fellow-viewers and listeners," according to one explanation of how mass media may foster the conditions underlying collective behavior.[49]

[xx] Similarly, the widespread use of so-called "portfolio insurance" (i.e., systematic loss-limiting strategies to sell stocks when they begin to fall) may have played a role in the 1987 crash in the stock market.[54]

becomes necessary to act *personally* as if a piece of news were correct, and not discard it as rumor. As Chapter 5, "News and Rumors," shows, this may be one of the reasons traders do not consider accuracy among the most important characteristics of news.

Chapter 4, "Expectations in the Foreign Exchange Market," continues to address the phenomenon of herding, illustrating that *market forecasts* are also influenced by a self-reinforcing dynamics. Traders observe that both the widespread use of "technical analysis" and the belief in the validity of "chartism" are based, at least in part, on herding.[xxi] In other words, traders use charts because they see that other traders use them. They perceive charts are a useful tool to predict currency fluctuation since they see that a large part of the market is doing so. Hence, as one trader tellingly observes, one main reason for the use of chartism is, "Because *you* can't ignore it if the others use it!" Thus, herding, far from being connected only to sporadic dramatic market developments, is a *regular psychological aspect* in the social dynamics of decision-making in the foreign exchange market.

AFFECTS

> You are emotionally up when you are making money. You feel that you can do no wrong.
>
> Foreign exchange trader

"Desire is irrelevant. I am a machine," declares the android who heroically returns from the future to save the human race in the blockbuster movie *Terminator 3: Rise of the Machines*. Likewise, most economic approaches to financial markets rest on an exclusively cognitive conception of decision-making. *Feelings* are perceived as irrational, and while they are believed to damage the interests of some market participants, they are not believed to have any influence on the market level, at least not in a lasting way.[55]

In contrast, a psychological understanding acknowledges the important role of *affects*[xxii] to market participants and may even consider affects to be at the heart of market decisions. Throughout the interviews, traders refer to feelings. One trader's view that trading decisions are a "feeling process" is confirmed by systematic survey ratings of hundreds of other traders. Traders rated "my

---

[xxi] For a definition of technical analysis and chartism, see Chapter 4, "Expectations in the Foreign Exchange Market."

[xxii] Affect is the generic term for a broad range of psychological phenomena which include feelings, emotions, moods, and motivation.[56]

decision was based on my feelings" as the most important characteristic of both their best and their worst decisions, which shows that affects play not only one but *the* central role in trading decisions.[xxiii] As another trader says, "Making money in foreign exchange comes down to a very basic thing. We tend to make it so esoteric, but you have to buy if you *feel* it is going up."

Thus traders are quick to recognize the role of affects in their decisions and in collective market processes. Indeed, they see personal greed as determinant of risk-taking, perceive the fear and hope in the participants' expectations as the biggest driving force behind exchange-rate movements, and hold these emotions responsible for overshooting market reactions. "If there is a collapse in a currency or a sudden movement, everybody has got the wrong position, so therefore there is *fear* they are going to lose a lot. And there are other times when you've got the right position and suddenly the market starts to move your way. And, therefore, people multiply their position, because, you know, 'it's going well, let's make sure we leverage up on it!' And they maximize, and basically they squeeze nearly everything they possibly can out of a move but still want to hold on to the position—because they now have *hope* that they are going to make even more money. And at those precise points ... the market will turn," one trader explains. For their own trading decisions, traders consider emotions a two-edged sword that is both helpful and hazardous. As one trader says, "Emotions are important and they are integral, but they are also very, very dangerous." Thus, while some traders observe that, for trading, emotions need to be under control and, in the words of one trader, "perhaps the best deal is where people don't have emotions, are quite unemotional," other traders believe that a good trader has to be emotional. Emotions may be needed, for example, in order to "feel" the market and to get an intuitive grasp on the current market situation. Emotions can also be a necessary source of feedback in risk-taking; as one trader observes, "The pain of losing is very important and yes, you do have to have fear, because not having fear makes you run your risk too far." Another trader succinctly illustrates his belief by saying that: "A good trader is an emotional trader."

In fact, affects influence decision-making in a variety of ways. Take moods, for example.[xxiv] Psychological research has found that information and stimuli

---

[xxiii] This finding is reported in the section "Trading decisions: The view of traders" in this chapter.
[xxiv] Moods, like emotions, refer to a non-cognitive feeling process. However, while emotions are more intensive and have a specific cause, moods last longer, are less intensive, and have no specific target.

which are compatible with a person's mood are learned better than incompatible stimuli.[57–60] Similarly, moods influence what kind of material can be retrieved from memory: stimuli congruent with a person's mood—negative stimuli if a person is sad, positive stimuli if a person is happy—are recalled more easily than are incongruent stimuli.[61] Moods also affect how people form expectations: When asked to estimate the probabilities of future events, happy people give higher estimates for positive events than depressed people do.[58]

To trading decisions, these findings are extremely relevant. Because people, and not machines, inhabit the foreign exchange market, affective, not detached and objective, processing of market information influences how traders perceive the market, whether they form positive or negative expectations, and how willing they are to enter risks.[62] Besides influencing individual market participants, mood also *links* them to each other. The mood of participants influences the dynamics of communication between them and determines their reaction to information from the financial news media.[xxv] For example, one trader recounted: "I saw on late T.V. last night how the Chinese fired up missiles into the direction of Taiwan, and you saw two U.S. aircraft carriers moving there, but the comment was very calm ... If they would have commented nervously and others would follow, then it easily could happen that a movement in the foreign exchange market would have come up."

Thus affects are at the very heart of market decisions, and not just involved in a peripheral or secondary role. Affects determine what alternatives are taken into account, what kind of information is collected, and how it is processed. They determine the *interpretation* of information and assign psychological meanings and weights to it.[64] As Chapter 7, "Surfing the Market on Metaphors" shows, traders' metaphorical conceptualizations of trading decisions and of the market abound with affective descriptors. For example, traders often conceptualize the market as "crazy" or "tired," as in the following case. "You've traded all day, it's been a nightmare day, you think I'm tired, the market's tired, the dollar's tired. How many times have I gone that way, 'Oh, the dollar's looking tired!' [However], the dollar is not ... tired. The dollar is either bid or it's offered. The dollar doesn't sit there and go: Phew, I'm really tired today." While this trader observes such affective market constructions with some irony, they express traders' psychological understandings of the market and assist traders in their affective decision-making. Thus affects not only "distort" the mechanistic decision-making typical of

---

[xxv] This connection between general market mood and the influence of the media is described by psychologist George Katona.[63]

Terminator androids (as can be argued for the status quo tendencies and the overconfidence phenomena discussed in the following); instead, as the last part of this section shows, affects are also *constructive* by allowing traders to translate their experience and knowledge of the market into trading intuition.

Status quo tendency

"I've worked with lots of people who just cannot [cut a losing position based on a decision they made once]: 'I love this position, the dollar is never ever going to go any lower.' And the dollar just carries on going lower," one trader observes in the interviews. The so-called "status quo bias" describes how market participants, once they have decided on a certain course of action, resist changing their mind even if new evidence surfaces that the chosen course of action is not optimal. For example, traders may hold onto their choices even if these choices have proven little successful, simply because changing them would mean abandoning the status quo.[32,37,65]

In foreign exchange trading decisions, the status quo tendency can lead traders to pursue a losing strategy even if the strategy has already caused losses for an extended period of time. Traders become emotionally attached to a certain trading position and market view, which they describe metaphorically as "being married" to a position. Such a trading position can become extremely difficult to abandon even after a large loss is accumulated because, as one trader explains, "you take a position for a good reason." Another trader echoes this sentiment, saying "Because you want to be right, you do not want to take the loss." In addition to the influence of the status quo tendency on single trading decisions, an even more comprehensive status quo tendency can be found in general trading styles and preferences. Foreign exchange traders observe that, while these trading styles are vastly different, traders usually base their approach on the trading experience they made early in their careers, and they are not likely to change this approach afterwards. The influence of personal trading styles and preferences may later work independently of, and even contrary to, present market conditions and current information. As one trader lucidly observes: "You have traders who are bulls and others who are bears ... You just tell them this Friday's closing price and say, 'You are not supposed to look at the screen, do not read the paper, just do something.' Then some will buy, and some will sell. Those who buy are not those who were selling two days ago because they always will buy."

A particularly strong form of the status quo tendency is represented by *decisional escalations* in trading decisions. Here, affects induce traders not only to keep but even to *expand* a losing position. In other words, traders not only refuse to reconsider their strategy and to finish the negative process started by a bad trading decision, but actively push their wrong course of action even harder. A vivid example is given by a trader who describes his reaction to seeing his position in U.S. dollars fall: "The dollar goes lower, so you are going to buy again and buy again just to show the people that 'I am sure! I am right!'"

From the viewpoint of economic utility maximization, the status quo tendency is irrational and leads to decisions that are clearly biased. Purely profit-maximizing decisions are based only on *future* outlooks and objective rates of return, not on holding on to the subjective reasons a strategy was initially chosen. However, affective and psychological dynamics can explain this phenomenon.[xxvi]

For example, sticking to one's decisions once they are made is often based on emotional commitment.[64,66] Once people are emotionally invested in their beliefs, it may become very difficult and even impossible to change them by means of information or other cognitive measures alone.[67] Two other important affective dynamics that underlie the status quo tendency are *anticipated regret* and the need to reduce *cognitive dissonance*.

Regret theory postulates that people base their decisions on how much unpleasant regret they are likely to experience.[68,69] Understandably, people do not like to feel regret. Thus, they attempt to anticipate the extent of possible regret involved in each decision alternative, compare the alternatives by the amount of anticipated regret, and then decide on a way that helps them limit future regret to a minimum.[xxvii] This theory translates easily into the experience of traders who succumb to the status quo tendency of holding on to a losing trading position. To decide to close one's trading position and to realize the resulting loss leads to a high degree of anticipated regret, especially if one considers the possibility that the market may turn around. In contrast, not closing the losing position immediately and risking the possibility of an

---

[xxvi] The status quo tendency can also be explained by general loss aversion. People experience any given difference between alternatives as more consequential if it is perceived as a difference between unfavorable alternatives than between favorable alternatives. Thus possible disadvantages of a change appear larger than its possible advantages. Hence the status quo bias can also be explained as a result of the generally asymmetric nature of risk-taking[37] (see Chapter 3, "Risk-Taking in Trading Decisions").
[xxvii] For example, a study by Zeelenberg et al. shows that decision-makers are "regret-averse" and choose regret-minimizing alternatives.[70]

even larger trading loss some time in the future only leads to a small amount of additional regret, and thus seems preferable.

Moreover, errors of omission are often experienced as invoking less regret than do errors of commission.[32] Take the example of a foreign exchange trader who simply keeps the trading position that has caused some loss already. If consequently the loss increases, the trader committed only an error of omission and is likely to experience less regret than a trader who committed an error of commission by actively closing a losing trading position that then starts to generate profits.

Another psychological explanation of the status quo tendency is the motivation of human decision-makers to reduce what psychologist Leon Festinger calls "cognitive dissonance."[71] Cognitive dissonance arises whenever decision-makers hold contradictory perceptions or contradictory attitudes toward some object. For example, people who like to smoke cigarettes may also know that smoking causes cancer and thus experience dissonance. In this example, the object is smoking, and a positive attitude toward smoking ("I like smoking") contradicts a negative evaluation ("smoking is bad for my health"). Because experiencing cognitive dissonance is uncomfortable, people try to reduce it or even get rid of it completely. Smokers, for example, may attempt to change their behavior and quit smoking. Another strategy that helps smokers reduce their cognitive dissonance is to change their conflicting perceptions and attitudes. Smokers may convince themselves that they actually don't really like to smoke or that smoking may not be so dangerous after all. Thus, unpleasant cognitive dissonance can be reduced by a change in behavior or by a change in attitude.[14]

In the foreign exchange market, cognitive dissonance often appears in the form of post-decisional dissonance, after trading decisions are made. One trader notices, "It's intriguing and very clear that people have a very different view on the market when they *don't* have a position than when they *do*. Conviction that the dollar will go up can be very strong before somebody buys dollars but after they have bought them ... they can very quickly doubt their judgment." Like the smokers in the previous example, traders who experience dissonance after entering a trading position try to reduce it. One of the easiest ways to do so is to form an overall evaluation of the market which focuses on information that is compatible with the new position. This, in turn, makes traders vulnerable to engage in the status quo tendency. "You forget your own rules so that you close your position at a certain loss because you know it is coming, it is coming," as one trader translates this finding into the foreign exchange market. Similar affect-driven dynamics to reduce post-decisional dissonance *after* decisions are formed have been found among sports bettors. People who just placed their bets at the racetrack think their chance of winning is better than people who are about to place their bets.[72]

In trading decisions, even the inflated version of the status quo tendency, which is apparent in striking decisional escalations, can be explained by an affective dynamics. Usually, such decisional escalations are observed when market participants have already made a substantial investment of money and efforts into a certain trading strategy. Although a detached and objective evaluation may clearly reveal the strategy's futility, traders feel psychologically *committed* to the money and efforts they have already invested. Traders and trading institutions alike may be affected by such dynamics and consequently throw good money (or good effort) after bad.[73,74,xxviii] Such dynamics could be observed during the development of the famous Concorde supersonic airplane, whose last flight was in 2004. Early in the process of its construction, when only a fraction of the development budget was spent, it became clear that operating Concorde would never be profitable. However, by that time the British and the French governments felt too committed to the project and did not want to "waste" the money they had invested already. "It would even have been more cost-effective to terminate the whole enterprise just before tightening the last screw," Hungarian mathematician Laszlo Mero writes.[77]

To summarize, the status quo tendency explains the psychological inclination of market participants to maintain and even to reinforce an initial trading strategy instead of changing it in light of new and better information that contradicts it. In foreign exchange trading, simply giving in to this tendency can be extremely costly. "People who are stubborn when they take a particular view that goes wrong, they are going to lose money," one trader remarks. Thus, as another trader remarks, "only when you *really* look at what you have done, then you can accept your own bad decision." As the next section shows, one of the psychological keys to traders' difficulties in considering relevant information and experience is overconfidence.

Overconfidence

> If you get too confident and too cocky, the market will just let you down.
>
> Foreign exchange trader

[xxviii] The phenomenon that people take past costs into account when making their decisions, and that they prefer those alternatives in which they have already invested money, effort, or time is also called the "sunk cost effect."[75,76]

A survey conducted among Swedish car drivers reported that 90% considered themselves above-average drivers.[78] Statistical reasons alone make it impossible for this result to reflect the *actual* level of their driving skills. However, a large number of studies show that decision-makers are generally inclined to be *overconfident* in their own abilities and in the accuracy of their judgments. "When people say that they are 90% certain that an event will happen or that a statement is true, they may only be correct 70% of the time," according to behavioral finance researchers Werner De Bondt and Richard Thaler.[35] "You may be *absolutely* sure that the dollar is going up, and [yet] it is going down," a trader translates this finding into the foreign exchange market.

Interviews with traders confirm that overconfidence plays a large role in trading decisions. Traders notice that this is especially the case after market participants generate gains for an extended period of time. The observation of one trader that, "The trader that's the *most* dangerous is probably the trader that's had a good run," is complemented by that of another who adds that, "If a trader makes good profits, he becomes more risky because he says, 'I can't fail! I'm like the Pope whatever I do.'" Other traders observe that this tendency to become overconfident after success is especially present among inexperienced market participants.

Overconfidence easily turns into a danger as people who are *too* sure of their beliefs may fail to consider important information.[79,80] As one foreign exchange trader notes regarding trading decisions, "If you make money ... you do not evaluate [the information] *that* carefully every time. Because you feel you are on a good run, you make money, so trust your feelings and trust the way you take your decision ... Otherwise I would maybe look at the chart, maybe speak with one or two more people. But if I'm on a good run, why should I?" Thus, overconfidence among market participants may lead them to *neglect* valuable outside information for their trading decisions, blindly insist on the correctness of their judgments, and enter too high levels of risk.

However, the amount of available information does not necessarily reduce or eliminate overconfidence in decisions, as a classic study by Stuart Oskamp demonstrates.[81] Clinical psychologists and students were provided with case study information about a patient and had to form clinical judgments about the patient. The more information participants received, the more confident they became of their judgments while the accuracy of judgments remained essentially *unaffected*. That more information may lead to increased overconfidence but not to increased judgment accuracy was also found in an unpublished study conducted by Paul Slovic and Bernhard Corrigan on how horse race handicappers set betting odds.[xxix] Increasing the amount of information on which the horse race handicappers could base their decisions also *increased* their confidence in their judgments but did *not* increase their prediction accuracy. Thus, the only effect of the additional information was to overload the handicapper with information, resulting in errors rather than in increased precision.[79] Overconfidence may also help explain the well-known preference of sports bettors for low-probability wagers on the outcomes of horse races or football games.[82]

Likewise, in a market setting more information may result in increased confidence, as a study on stock market forecasting demonstrates. For example, one study asked MBA students to make stock forecasts of companies publicly traded on the NASDAQ. Students based their forecasts on the information they received about the companies. Not surprisingly, they became more confident the more information they received. However, this increase in their level of confidence even took place when the added information had already been provided. Moreover, while added information (both redundant and new) increased participants' confidence, it actually *diminished* their forecasting accuracy, which led the authors of the above study to aptly identify the "harmful effects of seemingly helpful information."[83]

Overconfidence among market participants also helps explain excess trading (i.e., the phenomenon that market participants trade too much)[84,85] and that there is too much volatility in the markets.[54,86] Moreover, overconfidence may tempt participants to enter excessive levels of risk.[87,88] A number of characteristics make the foreign exchange market a particularly fertile environment for overconfidence among its participants. Participants in the foreign exchange market are provided with a continuous deluge of information, and the circular nature of news processing additionally leads to repetitions and redundancies.[xxx] Moreover, overconfidence has been found to be especially strong in those situations where it is difficult to form accurate judgments.[89] This difficulty *defines* decision-making in financial markets where predictions, at best, can only be made with accuracy close to chance. In the words of a foreign exchange trader, "the trader has to be in 51% of the cases right. If this is true, then he can be in 49% wrong." Lastly, overconfidence has been found to correlate with the degree of expertise persons think they have.[90]

However, perceiving only the danger and the possible negative consequences of overconfidence may not be enough. Using data from the North American

---

[xxix] For a description of the study, see Russo and Schoemaker.[79]
[xxx] See Chapter 5, "News and Rumors in the Foreign Exchange Market."

study, Brandeis finance professor Carol Osler and I compared traders' self-evaluations of their trading performance with the assessments provided by their supervisors, and we examined traders' confidence in their personal exchange-rate forecasts. Not only did we find that overconfidence had no negative effect on the trading profits generated by these traders, but we also found that overconfidence actually *positively* influenced such aspects of traders' professional success as their hierarchical rank in their bank and the duration of their trading experience.[91] These findings are supported by the interviews, in which many traders observed the importance of high confidence in oneself and in one's abilities. "It's a confidence ... a certain amount of ego," one trader explained. In the words of the trading manager of one of the world's leading foreign exchange floors: "If you are not that self-confident, you are not going to be a good trader." Another trader agreed, saying that, "One thing that all good traders are is they are confident in their own ability that they are making the right decisions." Thus, overconfidence can also be valuable by permitting traders to operate with conviction. "[T]he ability to gather conviction, to be decisive about something that most other people would not [...] and the willingness to take the risk when it's not conventional wisdom" are critical to success, according to one trader. Thus, as another trader stressed, traders need "strong confidence in themselves even though the market goes against them, [and to] have their own strong belief in their own scenarios." Moreover, strong self-confidence helps traders to cope with the negative psychological impact of losses. Only optimistic and self-confident traders can survive in a decision-making environment that confronts them with discouraging and stressful situations every day. As another trader remarked, "When you are in the trough, you have to come out of it very quickly because if you get caught in it, it's going to affect you."

Thus, our findings on overconfidence among foreign exchange traders correlate with the findings on overconfidence among Swedish car drivers. The European and the North American surveys asked participants how successful they perceived themselves as foreign exchange traders.

Figure 2.2 summarizes the results for 290 European traders. As the figure shows, two-thirds of the traders (66%) consider themselves as more successful than other traders. Only every 14th trader (7%) considers himself or herself *less* successful than other traders. If U.S. traders now triumphantly feel that they know better, their reaction might be a sign of overconfidence. Indeed, results were even *more* pronounced for 401 North American foreign exchange traders where almost three-quarters of the traders (74%) considered themselves to be above average! Yet overconfidence is not the only psychological

Psychology of Trading Decisions 51

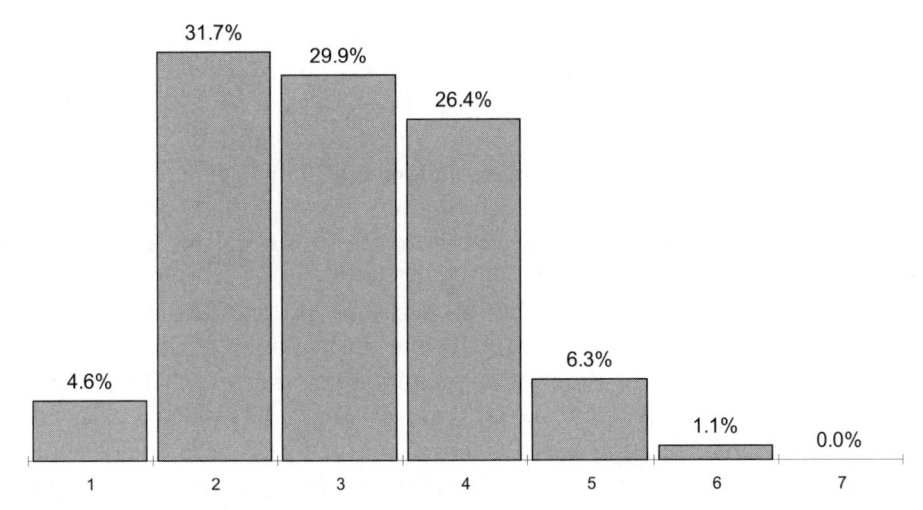

Figure 2.2 Overconfidence in foreign exchange traders: 1 = Much more successful than other traders, 7 = Much less successful than other traders.

Bar values: 1 = 4.6%, 2 = 31.7%, 3 = 29.9%, 4 = 26.4%, 5 = 6.3%, 6 = 1.1%, 7 = 0.0%.

characteristic shared by traders in the global market. Another common characteristic of their decisions, discussed in the next section, is intuition.

Trading intuition: Bridging affects and cognitions

> I sense when it gets dangerous. I see certain price movements that clearly tell me there is danger, and this is when I back off. It is experience, it is pattern recognition: "I have seen it before." And I all of a sudden deep down you remember: "Man, I've seen that before, and right after that thunder and lightning struck, and the world fell apart." You remember what if you are young you have never experienced.
>
> Foreign exchange trader

Why did you decide to buy yen? What made you sell your position in dollar? Ask foreign exchange traders to explain their decisions, and usually they will describe a rapid process in which a hunch (e.g., that a drop in the dollar–yen rate is about to occur) has crystallized without the simultaneous availability of knowledge (e.g., why exactly the exchange rate will drop). "I had a strong feeling over this weekend that we are going to see a devaluation. *Why* I had that feeling, I don't know," one trader says about a successful trading decision.

"My heart said it will move," another trader explained, describing a *feeling* that resulted from a tacit decision process he was not even aware of.

This implicit process to which these traders refer draws on a combination of information, knowledge, and experience (e.g., perceptions of other market participants, analyses of economic fundamentals, and memories of past market developments). When traders address the close link between such implicit cognitions and an experienced feeling in their decisions, they usually refer to *trading intuition*.

For example, one trader describes his decisions as, "intuitive based on ... what you see happening in the market. Your interpretation of the news, your interpretation of the way things are, your interpretation of what's going to happen, and then you *feel* that the odds are in your favor to take a particular position." In fact, intuition plays a dominant role in the accounts of actual trading decisions. In the words of another trader, "In foreign exchange decisions, intuition plays a larger part than anything else!" Yet another trader echoes this sentiment, adding, "I think every trading decision ultimately is still intuitive."

However, compared with decisions that are (or that at least *pretend* to be) based on logical analyses and explicit probabilities, trading intuition may still have a bad reputation.[28] Lowering his voice in the trading room, one trader confides, "Intuition, it's a very big part, if not even the biggest part in my decision taking. Yeah, I must say so, [but] don't tell it to my boss. It's ... exactly the thing you cannot explain rationally!"

From firefighters to court judges to sport coaches, intuitive decision-making is used by professionals from all walks of life. How then *can* the intuition in trading decisions be best understood? Neurological research shows that when people decide in situations they have some experience with, their explicit reasoning is preceded by a non-conscious process. The parts of the brain activated by this process are related to previous *emotional* experience of similar situations, and they differ from those neural systems involved in explicit and declarative knowledge. Thus people may decide advantageously even before they consciously know which strategy works best.[92] Psychology has also demystified the magic that is frequently associated with intuition, showing that intuition ultimately does not contradict analytical thinking and that it even can be learned.[93,94] Instead, market intuition includes a process by which traders recognize a *pattern* in the present market environment, based on their ability to access their memory of thousands of past market patterns already experienced. Thus the automaticity of trading intuition can be likened to chess masters who find ingenious moves in simultaneous games in a split second, without careful analysis of all the moves possible. While chess experts have access to a large number of possible board patterns that almost instantaneously bring to mind suitable moves at various stages and situations of the game, expert traders have a vast repertoire of stored market situations available, and, rather than calculating, they base their decisions on associations of the present with the past. Both the traders' and the chess masters' intuition requires *experience* and knowledge of numerous previous patterns of figures and positions, respectively.[95]

Though *building* market intuition requires experience, it does not necessarily require conscious learning. As one trader observes, "You have sort of a certain amount of experience and expertise, and you've seen things happen over time. You've seen how certain economic, social, or political factors have moved the market. You've seen markets that have been heavily oversold or heavily overbought. And then everything that you've learned and that you've seen over the years helps you to make a decision!"

Applying one's intuition to decision-making also does not require deliberation and conscious effort. "I do not have to do this thinking, it will be *in* me," one experienced trader describes how he processes market information. Research by Harvard psychologist Ellen Langer and co-workers demonstrates that knowledge acquired latently and without intention may later be activated without any efforts to consciously understand the new situation.[96] Making trading decisions then, in the words of another trader, can be likened to, "Sitting down as a surgeon with a series of instruments in front of him, deciding on how he is going to do the operation *today*. The truth is, the operation in foreign exchange—to buy or to sell—is never the same, and the information set is never the same, and the circumstances are never identical. And it's a question of deciding ... subconsciously which tools am I going to take out of my tool kit today in order to conduct the operation? And that's a subconscious process."

Thus, while traders are regularly unable to give an exact account of the reasons for their decisions, intuitive decision-making should not be mistaken as being accidental or irrational.[xxxi] Rather, market intuition builds on experience and the recognition of market patterns. This allows trading experts to quickly identify the dynamics of the current situation and to leapfrog ahead where novices need to proceed in small steps.[28,95] Numerous quotations from

---

[xxxi] The difference between rational (i.e., logical), nonrational (i.e., intuitive, emotional, psychological), and irrational (i.e., illogical and unreasonable) decisions is important in this context. In rational decision-making, the specific objectives and the outcomes of each alternative are clarified, and then the decision is made. Intuitive decision-making, by contrast, happens too fast to permit objective analysis. Intuitive decisions are also characterized by an inability to explain how the decision was made.[95]

the interviews show that trading intuition is indeed rooted in market experience and the ability to access tacitly a large repertoire of different market situations. "If you are out there like 10 or 11 years, it looks like gut feel but it's actually your experience," observes one trader. "If you drive a car for 20 years ... and the car makes a noise, you can pretty much tell what this noise is emanating from. Trading is the same," concurs another.

The insights of traders also shed light on *how* trading experience translates into the ability for intuitive trading decisions: Experience helps them to establish which aspects of the current market situation are significant and to compare these aspects to their memory of relevant market situations in the past. "The older you get, the more you mature, the more experienced you are ... the entire decision-making process is much more along the lines of 'have I seen that before, have I not seen, do I remember something, do I not?'" says one trader. "It's like I have been wearing this T-shirt a couple of times before," thus one trader recounts the kind of intuitive insight to which experience can lead, described by another trader as a sudden *"déjà vu."*

Experience and the memory of past market patterns also suggest decision and action strategies. Among chess players, "The grand-master's memory holds more than a set of patterns. Associated with each pattern in his or her memory is information about the significance of that pattern—what dangers it holds, and what offensive or defensive moves it suggests. Recognizing the pattern brings to the grand-master's mind at once moves that may be appropriate to the situation," Herbert Simon argues convincingly.[95] The same kind of resulting aha! feeling about which action to take surfaces in a trader's account of his decision-making—listening to various information sources, summing up pros and cons very quickly, not "think it to death [and then] all of a sudden you just say: 'right'!"

The results of the European survey highlight the importance of intuition for successful foreign exchange trading. Analyzing the perceived characteristics of trading decisions, I compared (1) traders who regarded themselves as more successful than other traders, and (2) traders who regarded themselves as less successful than other traders.[xxxii] A systematic comparison of *best trading decisions* between the two groups resulted in three statistically significant

---

[xxxii] While traders were grouped on the basis of self-reported trading success, these groups also reflect objective trading abilities. Self-ratings of trading success correlate to a statistically significant degree with supervisor evaluations of trading ability and trading profits, as findings from the North American survey show. In other words, traders who perceive themselves as more successful are also rated as better by their supervisors, and traders who perceive themselves as less successful are also rated as less successful by their supervisors.

differences; each of these differences underscores the role of intuition in profitable trading decisions. Not only did the "successful" trader group report that their best decisions had led to *higher gains* for their institution than did the "less successful" trader group, successful traders also reported that they had acted considerably *faster* and that their decisions had been more *based on experience*. In other words, the best trading decisions of successful and less successful traders differ in what lies at the heart of trading intuition: the ability to quickly process and react to information, based on a vast pool of experienced situations. Conversely, in traders' reports of *worst trading decisions*, the only statistically significant difference between the "successful" and the "less successful" group of traders was that less successful traders reported to a considerably higher degree that the decision had been made *in a situation new to them*. These systematic findings certainly provide excellent support for the importance of intuition in successful trading.

These findings also correspond with the interview accounts of experienced traders who describe that they back off taking a trading decision in situations for which they need more experience. Regarding such intuitive backing away from dangerous situations, decision researcher Gary Klein provides an example that is *strikingly* reminiscent of the quotation at the beginning of the present discussion of trading intuition. It is about a fire lieutenant in charge of a group of firemen. The crew is busy in a house, spraying water on a kitchen fire. "Then the lieutenant starts to feel as if something is not right. He doesn't have any clues; he just doesn't feel right about being in that house, so he orders his men out of the building—a perfectly standard building with nothing out of the ordinary. As soon as his men leave the building, the floor where they had been standing collapses. Had they still been inside, they would have plunged into the fire below."[28]

COGNITIONS

In the dynamics of real-life trading decisions, the distinction between affective and cognitive processes is arbitrary and blurred. To give an example, traders' overconfidence about their professional skills and about the precision of their forecasts (see the previous section) can be explained in affective terms (e.g., by an effort to protect their self-esteem or by social and professional demands to appear assertive). However, overconfidence can equally well be explained in cognitive terms by the so-called availability heuristic (see the present section): To traders, those market developments that they correctly predicted personally may simply be more easily available in memory than predictions that failed to materialize.[64]

Thus, the psychology of trading decisions is best understood as a complex interplay of affective and cognitive factors. Instead of separating these factors, only understanding their interaction leads to a comprehensive understanding of decision-making in the foreign exchange market, both for individual traders and on the collective market level.[55]

In trading practice, such interplay of affect and cognition can clearly be observed when seemingly purely *cognitive* elements of the trading situation, which on the surface appear to be only about a difference of numbers, determine trading decisions via *emotions*. A case in point is the risk-taking of market participants. Traders observe that merely the *size* of a trading position emotionally influences their decisions, and that they experience a subjective emotional limit to the amount they can trade in one single transaction. "Everyone has their own comfort level, as far as risk is concerned and the degree of loss they can live with," says one trader; "I think the most important advice is that as trader you should restrict your taking of risk to a level that you feel comfortable with on an emotional basis," adds another. Therefore, it is impossible to replace two traders by one, simply doubling the trader's position. One trader explains: "There are very profitable traders who are very good at taking relatively small positions and who make more money doing it than if they try to increase the size of their position because their manager said: 'Today, you made this much—if you double every position you took, you'd make twice as much. And we hire two more people that look just like you and they are just as good as you, at what you are doing, and they take twice as much risk as you are taking, then between us we are going to make ten times more money than you made!' [It sounds] logical, but it does not work that way. People respond differently to different levels of risk." Consequently, a trader who simply doubles his trading position "is always quicker to get out and quicker to get in at good or bad levels, and overall his business therefore becomes much less efficient. Because he is just responding differently as a consequence of the *anxiety* of a bigger position!" Thus, the cognitive aspects of trading decisions discussed in this section show a close relationship to affects, and the dividing line between the two areas is often arbitrary.

Moreover, like affects, the cognitive phenomena in trading discussed in this section often lead to decision outcomes at odds with expected utility theory. For this reason, they are sometimes called "biases," "fallacies," or even "errors." These labels have the unfortunate implication that widespread characteristics of decision-making are aberrations. Nonetheless, I will occasionally use the term "bias" to be consistent with the literature.[xxxiii]

Heuristics

"It is your own judgment and you have to be very fast. It only lasts a few seconds, of course, and you have to make up your mind either to close your position or to open a position," one trader observes regarding his daily decision-making. This sentiment is echoed in the statement of another trader: "You have no time to think about what you do next, you have to decide within two seconds."

Thus traders are quick to comment on their need to reduce and simplify the vast amount of relevant market information they are flooded with each trading day. When asked about his decisions, one trader responded by first admitting the simple fact that, "Most of them are based on just a few [bits of] information, not too much and out of the feeling and the guts. Let's take an example, we have seen the yen moving quite well, seen that there is a problem in the banking system, there is unemployment picking up, one could see that something has to happen with the yen. You choose the currency against which it is most interesting to play and that's it ... Sometimes you have too much information, so take a few logic things and go into it."

This clearly indicates that traders do not process information in the fully rational way defined by traditional economics. Instead, for their decisions, they need to reduce and simplify the amount of information surrounding them. To do so, they use psychological short cuts and simplifying rules of thumb which help them to process market information in a quick and competent way.[98] These information-processing short cuts are called *heuristics*.

Because heuristics simplify and reduce the amount of information that needs to be processed, they are particularly important in environments that are complex and that require rapid decision-making.[99] Thus the foreign market is guaranteed to activate the use of heuristics in the decisions of market participants: Heuristics do not require the kind of computation of utilities and probabilities that rational *Homo economicus* is supposed to perform. Instead, they allow traders to realistically manage the cognitive tasks involved in processing market information and to form trading decisions using limited information in little time.[97] In the telling words of one trader,

---

[xxxiii] Psychologists Gerd Gigerenzer and Peter Todd criticize that in the course of the "heuristics-and-biases" research agenda the use of the term "bias," which implies error and inability, has become attached to the term "heuristic," which actually stands for a useful cognitive process.[97]

in currency trading, "You really haven't time to figure it all out. For important decisions in your life you tend to get a little piece of paper and say pros and cons. But you haven't got time to do that. You've got to get 20 pros and 19 cons in your head in the split second that it takes to react."

Heuristics usually determine decisions without people being consciously aware of them. Studies have shown that even such experts as highly experienced chess masters habitually base their decisions on heuristics.[100,101] More often than not, a heuristic allows people to make high-quality judgments and decisions within little time. For example, a study conducted among pedestrians and graduate finance and economics students in the U.S. and in Germany has shown that a simple heuristic based on mere recognition ("if a company is recognized among people, include its stock into your portfolio, if they do not recognize a company, omit the stock") can lead to returns exceeding those of professionally managed mutual funds and the market index.[102,xxxiv]

However, from the traditional economic viewpoint of rational and complete processing of information, heuristics often lead to biased decisions. Heuristics thus have both functional and dysfunctional aspects.[104] While they expedite and simplify the decision-making process, they may also lead to systematic and predictable mistakes.[22] As the following discussion of the representativeness heuristic, availability heuristic, and anchoring-and-adjustment heuristic shows, heuristics are systematic psychological phenomena and not random errors of single individuals. Thus, their use in trading decisions can lead to collective market outcomes that are substantially at odds with what traditional economics considers to be rational.[xxxv]

Representativeness

"I don't like to read too much, I think there comes a stage where you can overload yourself with information which is often quite contradictory," one trader observed in the interviews. How then do traders form trading decisions, relying only on restricted information that is not too complex? Often, the answer is provided by the representativeness heuristic. This heuristic reduces the amount of information that traders need to process, for example, in subjective estimations of probabilities (e.g., of a certain market development such as a weaker yen tomorrow than it is today) and

---

[xxxiv] However, a later study shows the limitations of this simple heuristic and finds that, in a bear market environment, the name "recognition heuristic" may lead to poor choices and may even be outperformed by pure ignorance.[103]

[xxxv] This has led behavioral economists to write about "quasi-rational" economics.[76]

in predictions of future outcomes (e.g., of the decision of the Federal Reserve Bank to cut interest rates). While it is somewhat tricky to understand the representativeness heuristic in theory, practical examples help demonstrate how it works among decision makers in *any* kind of setting where information abounds.

The use of the representativeness heuristic leads market participants to base their inferences simply on the *apparent resemblance* between two situations, at the expense of other information. The likelihood of alternatives is simply judged by using representativeness as a yardstick, rather than by conducting probability calculations in a statistically correct way. Representativeness, or resemblance, is used as the psychological criterion to answer such questions as whether something in the market (e.g., the current market conditions, the possibility of an interest-rate cut, the value of the dollar at the beginning of the next trading day) is part of a certain category or group of phenomena (e.g., market conditions that lead to a crash, economic climates in which the central bank decided to cut interest rates, currencies that depreciated dramatically overnight). Representativeness is also used to judge the likelihood of a specific outcome stemming from a certain action rather than from other actions (e.g., whether a downward movement of the yen was initiated by the Bank of Japan or by other market participants).

While the representativeness heuristic often allows for quick and correct assessments of such questions, it can also lead to flawed and erroneous conclusions because representativeness (i.e., the mere similarity between phenomena) does not take into account a number of other important factors that are required for correct assessments of probability.[22] Furthermore, often the representativeness heuristic is based only on apparent first-sight similarities of phenomena and *not* on an in-depth analysis of all their characteristics. Hence, it has been noted that what is produced is instead, "a natural tendency to draw analogies and see identical situations where they don't exist ... Give people a little information and click! they pull out a picture they're familiar with, though it may only remotely represent the current situation."[98]

One important manifestation of the representativeness heuristics is the so-called "base-rate fallacy," where important statistical information about the likelihood of events is ignored at the expense of psychologically more impressive but actually irrelevant information. This irrelevant information becomes the basis for the decision merely because it suggests representativeness. In a study conducted by Daniel Kahneman and Amos Tversky, participants were told that a total of 100 brief personality descriptions had been established for 30 engineers and 70 lawyers and that one of the 100 descriptions was randomly chosen. Participants received the description of this person and were asked to indicate their subjective probability estimate that the person described was one of the 30 engineers:

> Dick is a 30-year-old man. He is married with no children. A man of high ability and high motivation, he promises to be quite successful in his field. He is well liked by colleagues.

After reading this description, the average participant in this study thought that the probability that Dick is an engineer is 50%. This conclusion is based on the representativeness heuristic: people conclude that because Dick's depiction is *equally representative* of lawyers and of engineers (which is correct, no piece of the description suggests that he is either a lawyer or an engineer), his chances of being an engineer are 50–50. However, in doing so they neglect important *base-rate information*; we also know that the description is randomly chosen from a pool of 100 descriptions of which 30 are for engineers and 70 for lawyers. No relevant piece of information whatsoever is added by Dick's description; the correct probability of Dick being an engineer is therefore 30%.[105]

The engineer-and-lawyer example shows how the representativeness heuristic in decision-making can be triggered by vivid information: When people are provided with no specific information about Dick, they make correct use of the relevant base-rate probabilities (i.e., they think that Dick has a 30% chance of being an engineer). To summarize, when confronted with complex decisions about the probabilities of alternatives, people usually use information that seems to *distinguish* a given alternative, even though this differentiating information may have little or no influence on the overall likelihood of the alternative. Thus, the much more important base-rate information about the basic possibility of the alternative is overlooked.[99]

Another manifestation of the representativeness heuristic is the so-called "conjunction fallacy," which occurs when people perceive the co-occurrence (i.e., the conjunction) of two events as more probable than the probability of either one of these two events alone. Think, for example, of next year and the possibility of the various market events. Which of the following scenarios do you consider most likely and which one least likely?

1. The U.S. Federal Reserve will change interest rates at least three times.
2. The U.S. dollar will appreciate against the euro.

3. The U.S. Federal Reserve will change interest rates at least three times *and* the U.S. dollar will appreciate against the euro.

Considering that the third scenario ("the U.S. Federal Reserve will change interest rates at least three times *and* the U.S. dollar will appreciate against the euro") is more likely than any of the single events described in the first scenario ("the U.S. Federal Reserve will change interest rates at least three times") and the second scenario ("the U.S. dollar will appreciate against the euro") illustrates the conjunction fallacy. The explanation is deceptively simple: The combined probability of two events cannot possibly be greater than the probability of either of these two events alone. However, when people imagine events, actions, or scenarios, they generally do so quite specifically. Detailed descriptions of a scenario are therefore more *representative* of the way people imagine events, and the representativeness heuristic may lead decision makers to judge specific and detailed descriptions as being more likely than general scenarios.[106] "As the amount of detail in a scenario increases, its probability can only decrease steadily, but its representativeness and hence its apparent likelihood may increase. The reliance on representativeness, we believe, is a primary reason for the unwarranted appeal of detailed scenarios and the illusory sense of insight that such constructions often provide," Tversky and Kahneman explain.[107]

The European study investigated if traders use the representativeness heuristic in the form of the conjunction error: Judging detailed and specific foreign exchange market scenarios as more likely than general scenarios. Participants were asked to rank-order the following developments from the most likely to the least likely:

1. The [U.S.] dollar will rise against the mark.
2. The Swiss franc will be stronger in December than in July.
3. The dollar will rise against the mark *and* the Swiss franc will be stronger in December than in July.
4. The dollar will rise against the mark *or* the Swiss franc will be stronger in December than in July.

Answers indicated the strong presence of the conjunction fallacy in the forecasts of market participants. Three-quarters (75%) of the foreign exchange traders considered that "the dollar will rise against the mark *and* the Swiss franc will be stronger in December than in July," as more likely than either of the single events "the dollar will rise against the mark," and "the Swiss franc will be stronger in December than in July" alone, or than the probability that "the dollar will rise against the mark *or* the Swiss franc will be stronger in December than in July." This conjunction fallacy was also committed by almost three-quarters (74%) of the financial journalists.[xxxvi]

These results demonstrate clearly that foreign exchange participants are certainly not immune to being influenced by the representativeness heuristic. While this psychological aspect of decision-making allows them to quickly process information and assess likely market developments, it is also a source of bias in their decisions and forecasts: It may lead them to base their decisions on irrelevant information, not on important information such as probabilities that are based on statistical and historical evidence. Consequently, it may lead them to overrate the likelihood of descriptively highly detailed market scenarios.

Moreover, psychological research has identified another decision dynamics that is based on the representativeness heuristic. A visit at any casino in Las Vegas provides one with ample opportunity to observe roulette players who commit the so-called "gambler's fallacy." This fallacy is displayed in the belief that after a run of several black numbers, the next number is more likely to turn out red than black. This erroneous assumption can be explained by the representativeness heuristic, which leads many gamblers to believe that *chance* sequences are "locally representative"; in other words, that every small sample of a random sequence resembles the characteristics of the infinite sequence. Many roulette players believe that every part of the sequence of black and red numbers is representative of the proportion of red and black numbers produced by chance, and that any deviation from the overall proportion produced by chance will self-correct itself in the other direction.[108] In the foreign exchange market, the gambler's fallacy may lead traders to assume a reverse in the development of an exchange rate after a certain previous devel-

---

[xxxvi] Comparable with probability estimates based on the conjunction fallacy, there is also a disjunction fallacy which concerns the probability of *alternative* events. The likelihood that either event A happens or event B happens is necessarily greater or equal to the likelihood that event A happens alone or the likelihood that event B happens alone. Thus, assuming that "the ECB will decide to lower interest rates tomorrow" or "U.S. unemployment rates will be up next month" is more likely than "the ECB will decide to lower interest rates tomorrow *or* U.S. unemployment rates will be up next month" means committing the disjunction fallacy. In the European study, 85% of the traders and 86% of the financial journalists made disjunction errors, considering "the dollar will rise against the mark *or* the Swiss franc will be stronger in December than in July" as less likely than either of the single events "the dollar will rise against the mark" or "the Swiss franc will be stronger in December than in July" alone or their joint probability (i.e., that "the dollar will rise against the mark *and* the Swiss franc will be stronger in December than in July").

opment or influence traders' assumptions about the next exchange-rate quote appearing on the trading screen.

Availability

The use of the availability heuristic leads decision-makers to judge the likelihood of an event based on whether information about the event is psychologically available. Events that are psychologically more accessible (i.e., events for which it is easy to bring to mind an instance or an occurrence) are judged to be more likely and more frequent than events that are harder to imagine.[109]

This heuristic plays an important role in trading decisions. When traders rely on availability, they will judge market events as possible and probable if these events are easily available from *memory*. Moreover, they will base their likelihood estimates on how easily the events can be *imagined*. In the words of cognitive psychologists Richard Nisbett and Lee Ross: "When people are required to judge the relative frequency of particular objects or the likelihood of particular events, they often may be influenced by the relative availability of the objects or events, that is, their accessibility in the process of perception, memory, or construction from imagination."[110]

Often, the availability heuristic allows traders to judge the probability of market events fairly accurately since often the subjective availability of events correlates well with their actual frequency. Because frequent market events are more easily remembered and imagined than rare ones, basing decisions on availability usually leads traders to valid estimates.[109]

However, psychological availability can also be a completely inadequate way of judging the likelihood of market events because the subjective availability of events is also based on factors that have little to do with their *actual* frequency. For example, improbable news may be easily available to traders simply because they were prominently announced in the news. "When there is something going on [in the market], you have a headline. This, the headline, is the thing. And very, very rarely the story behind that headline moves the [exchange rate]," one trader observes.

Thus, to traders some market events may be more available simply because the traders perceive them as emotionally relevant, and not because these events are indeed more frequent. As we have seen, *how* financial news is reported is important: In comparison to information that is presented in a pallid, theoretical, and statistical form, vivid and sensational information remains more available and is easier to recall.[106] A striking case in point is a study on the perceived causes of death. The study found that the public regards death from fire as more likely than death from drowning and accidental death as more likely than death from stroke, although statistics prove the opposite.[111] How can this be? General news coverage is more likely after catastrophic causes of death whereas diseases are less interesting to report. This journalistic focus on sensational events makes certain causes of death more psychologically available to readers.[112] Also, the timing of events plays an important role in psychological availability: recently reported events are more readily recalled than events that happened in the remote past.[99]

Thus, a number of subjective factors influence psychological availability in the foreign exchange market and consequently the decisions of market participants. For example, recency effects lead participants to overemphasize recent market news and trends, and to underestimate or even completely ignore other relevant information, such as historical data and statistical averages. Traders are guided by how vivid and sensational a certain news report is when evaluating the report's information and forming expectations. Emotional interest in a certain topic and the concreteness and proximity of a certain news item (i.e., its temporal, spatial, and sensory closeness) determines how vividly traders perceive market information and to what extent it affects their trading decisions.[110] For example, one trader comments on the importance of vivid market information reported on financial television. In contrast to newspapers, with financial television news, "You have the possibility to *be there and listen* to a press conference ... Now you can listen to Mr. Greenspan when he is at the testimony and [listen to] *how* he said it."

Anchoring and adjustment

Similarly, the anchoring-and-adjustment heuristic is another implicit rule of thumb that decision-makers use for subjective predictions and estimates. Anchoring and adjustment works in two stages: first, decision-makers form an initial estimate by perceiving and selecting some anchor value that is endowed with psychological significance; and, second, they arrive at the final decision (i.e., their *actual* prediction or estimate) by an adjustment from the previously chosen anchor. Once the anchor is chosen, usually the following adjustment is only small.[99] For example, traders may recall that an exchange rate was at about 1.60; then they form a more precise estimate of the actual exchange rate by choosing a number that is fairly close to this initial number.[113] In the words of the well-known fund manager David Dreman, anchoring "is a simplifying heuristic that people adopt in attempting a difficult quantification. Rather than calculate from scratch, they take some starting point and make adjustments."[98] Decisions based on anchoring and adjustment can be unreliable because the chosen anchor may be based on irrelevant information. Moreover, since the adjustment is usually small, decisions that are affected by this heuristic may end up insufficiently adjusted.

In the foreign exchange market, anchoring-and-adjustment phenomena determine estimates of forthcoming economic figures and affect predictions of exchange rates. The workings of this heuristic suggest that market participants form such estimates and predictions not by processing market information and calculating probabilities independently, but by perceiving certain psychologically important market anchors and forming subjective adjustments. In fact, there is no shortage of anchors provided by market experts (e.g., the predictions of economists and market analysts). "The dealing room economists have the most influence on the markets, on what the market actually focuses on. Because if they tell the dealers 'this is an important number,' then the dealers will look no further than that," one financial journalist observes. Certainly, the financial news media play a fundamental role in providing anchors to the market participants. "Without us, they don't know where the market is," another financial journalist concludes.

While anchoring phenomena happen constantly both inside and outside the markets, they can even be actively induced by deliberately exposing decision-makers to a value that then serves as an anchor for their decision. In an insightful study by Tversky and Kahneman,[22] a wheel-of-fortune was spun before participants were asked whether the percentage of African countries in the United Nations was higher or lower than the number indicated by the wheel-of-fortune, and what they believed the actual percentage of African countries in the United Nations was. The wheel-of-fortune was manipulated to indicate 65 in one group and 10 in another group of decision-makers. Even though people assumed this was a purely random number, the results in both groups were markedly different. When the number on the wheel (i.e., the introduced anchor) showed 65, participants estimated on average that the percentage of African countries in the United Nations was 45. When the number on the wheel showed 10, the estimated percentage of African countries in the United Nations sunk to 25. Even when participants were paid for giving accurate estimates, anchoring effects did *not* change in both groups.

Finally, the anchoring-and-adjustment heuristic is not only relevant for quantitative estimates but also for decisions that involve *qualitative* results.[79] Indeed, empirical studies show unmistakably that even experts rely on anchoring-and-adjustment processes to arrive at decisions. For example, in one study, experienced, professional real estate agents toured houses for sale and were provided with comprehensive information about the houses. However, various agents were provided with different information about the listing price of the houses. The real estate agents, many of them veterans in their field, were then asked to appraise the values of the houses. Although they consciously did not rate the listing price as an important piece of information, their appraisal values differed significantly. Agents who had seen a higher listing price perceived the houses as more valuable and consequently gave considerably higher appraisal values of the homes than did others.[114] Such findings suggest that also in the foreign exchange market, experience and expertise do not eliminate the powerful influence of the anchoring-and-adjustment heuristic on the decisions of traders.

Hindsight bias

"How many times have I sat there thinking: 'Oh, this dollar, it's very bid, and this dollar is going to go up,' and not done anything. And then watched it go up and not have made any money, because I didn't *do* anything about it," one trader reflects on the great trades he missed out on executing. From a psychological perspective, we might add "he *seemingly* missed out on executing," because when people remember events and developments, they do not simply retrieve information from storage the way a computer processor does with information saved on a hard disk. The hindsight bias demonstrates that to remember is to *psychologically reconstruct*. Hindsight bias describes the inclination of such decision-makers as this trader to perceive retrospectively their past anticipations and predictions as more accurate than these anticipations and predictions actually were at the time they were made. Once people are familiar with the actual outcomes and know the course of history, hindsight leads them to believe that such events as the outcomes of parliamentary elections, the recent burst of a stock market bubble, and the sudden appreciation of a currency were obvious and inevitable even *before* they happened. This "I knew it all along" tendency can be found among laypeople and decision-making experts alike. It works automatically; decision-makers are usually unaware that their current judgments of the past are influenced by retrospective knowledge.[106]

A well-known example of the hindsight bias is provided by psychologists Baruch Fischhoff and Ruth Beyth about U.S. president Nixon's visits to China and Russia in 1972. Before Nixon's departure, participants in a study were asked to rate the probabilities of various events or outcomes, such as a meeting between Mao and Nixon or a joint U.S.–Russian space program. After Nixon's return, participants were asked to recall their original predictions. Results showed hindsight bias as most participants thought they had given higher probabilities for events that had *actually* occurred and lower probabilities for events that had not.[115]

The hindsight bias has been shown to affect economic expectations,[116] and interviews with traders provide ample evidence for the hindsight bias also among foreign exchange market participants. "Why didn't I do what I had known all along?" is one trader's query regarding a recent trading decision, while another trader observes that there is hindsight bias in the evaluations of trading decisions by others. If trading decisions turn out badly, the criticism from other members in the trading team and the supervisor is likely to be colored by hindsight: "You decide to go long—[if] it's fine, you will never hear anything about it. [However, if] you go long [and] the price goes down, you make a loss, then [with a certainty of] 100% the remark comes, 'Yeah, I had another opinion.'"

"To analyze the reason for your losses ... is I think very important. To digest it, to analyze what was wrong," says one trader. Hindsight in the evaluation of trading decisions makes such an analysis difficult because it leads decision-makers to believe that, in the words of another trader, they "knew it better anyway." Financial markets provide participants with frequent possibilities "to convince themselves that they could (should) have made the right choices had they tried harder, or that they will be able to do so in advance in the future."[32] In the foreign exchange market, the hindsight bias provides past market developments with an illusory logic and predictability which makes appropriate learning from experience difficult. This illusory logic is likely to affect participants' future interaction with the market and the quality of their trading decisions (e.g., when it keeps participants from openly analyzing past trading strategies and from learning from mistakes they *might* have made).

Thus, learning about the hindsight bias offers not only consolation to the trader quoted at the beginning of this part, it also provides him with more realistic insights for his future trading decisions. As another trader reflecting on what he learned about trading aptly remarks: "I found this hindsight bias to be most prevalent in terms of trades that I didn't make ... it always seemed that one reflected on the good trades one didn't make, as opposed to saying," '*well good thing I didn't do that.*'"

ABBREVIATED REFERENCES

See the reference chapter at the end of the book for full details.

1 Yates, F. J. (1990)
2 Maas, P. and Weibler, J. (1990)
3 Watzlawick, P. (1967)

4 Mullen, B. and Riordan, C. A. (1988)
5 Stoner, J. A. (1961)
6 Moscovici, S. and Zavalloni, M. (1969)
7 Brown, R. (1986)
8 Bray, R. M. and Noble, A. M. (1978)
9 Isozaki, M. (1984)
10 Maital, S. (1982)
11 Bernoulli, D. (1738/1954)
12 Kritzman, M. (1998)
13 Baron, J. (2000)
14 Starmer, C. (1993)
15 von Neumann, J. and Morgenstern, O. (1947)
16 Edwards, W. (1954)
17 March, J. G. and Simon, H. A. (1958)
18 Simon, H. A. (1957)
19 Kahneman, D. and Tversky, A. (1979)
20 Allais, M. (1953)
21 Ellsberg, D. (1961)
22 Tversky, A. and Kahneman, D. (1974)
23 Frey, B. S. (1990)
24 Slovic, P. (1990)
25 Beach, L. R. (1997)
26 Pennington, N. and Hastie, R. (1992)
27 Jungermann, H. and Thüring, M. (1987)
28 Klein, G. A. (1998)
29 Klein, G. A. (1993)
30 Hogarth, R. and Reder, M. W. E. (1987)
31 Lopes, L. L. (1995)
32 Zeckhauser, R. et al. (1991)
33 Tversky, A. and Kahneman, D. (1988)
34 McNeil, B. J. et al. (1982)
35 De Bondt, W. F. M. and Thaler, R. H. (1994)
36 Simon, H. A. (1959)
37 Thaler, R. H. (1992)
38 Rubinstein, A. (2003)
39 Newcomb, T. M. (1972)
40 Scharfstein, D. S. and Stein, J. C. (1990)
41 Sherif, M. (1936)
42 Asch, S. E. (1951)
43 Norton, L. P. (1996)
44 Keynes, J. M. (1936)
45 Bikhchandani, S. et al. (1992)
46 Banerjee, A. V. (1992)
47 Shiller, R. J. (1989)
48 Ferguson, R. (1989)
49 Turner, R. L. and Killian, L. M. (1957)
50 Lee, S. B. and Killian, L. M. (1957)

51 Hatfield, E. et al. (1994)
52 Hatfield, E. et al. (1993)
53 Gump, B. B. and Kulik, J. A. (1997)
54 Shiller, R. J. (2000)
55 Pieters, R. G. M. and Van Raaij, W. F. (1988)
56 Wertlieb, D. L. (1996)
57 Forgas, J. P. and Bower, G. H. (1988)
58 Bower, G. H. and Cohen, P. R. (1982)
59 Bower, G. H. (1981)
60 Bower, G. H. et al. (1981)
61 Bower, G. H. and Forgas, J. P. (2000)
62 Van Raaij, W. F. (1989)
63 Katona, G. (1975)
64 Etzioni, A. (1988)
65 Samuelson, W. and Zeckhauser, R. (1988)
66 Steiner, I. D. (1980)
67 Berelson, B. and Steiner, G. A. (1964)
68 Bell, D. E. (1982)
69 Loomes, F. and Sugden, R. (1982)
70 Zeelenberg, M. et al. (1996)
71 Festinger, L. (1957)
72 Knox, R. E. and Inkster, J. A. (1968)
73 Staw, B. M. and Ross, J. (1989)
74 Garland, H. (1990)
75 Arkes, H. R. and Blumer, C. (1985)
76 Thaler, R. H. (1991)
77 Mero, L. (1998)
78 Svenson, O. (1981)
79 Russo, E. J. and Schoemaker, P. J. H. (1989)
80 Russo, E. J. and Schoemaker, P. J. H. (2002)
81 Oskamp, S. (1965)
82 Golec, J. and Tamarkin, M. (1995)
83 Davis, F. D. et al. (1994)
84 Barber, B. M. and Odean, T. (2000)
85 Barber, B. M. and Odean, T. (2001)
86 Daniel, K. et al. (1998)
87 Kyle, A. S. and Wang, F. A. (1997)
88 De Long, J. B. et al. (1991)
89 Pulford, B. D. and Colman, A. M. (1997)
90 Bradley, J. V. (1981)
91 Oberlechner, T. and Osler, C. L. (2004)
92 Bechara, A. et al. (1997)
93 Myers, D. G. (2002a)
94 Hogarth, R. M. (2001)
95 Simon, H. A. (1987)
96 Langer, E. et al. (1978)
97 Gigerenzer, G. and Todd, P. M. (1999)

98 Dreman, D. (1995)
 99 Duchon, D. et al. (1991)
100 Reynolds, R. I. (1991)
101 Reynolds, R. I. (1982)
102 Borges, B. et al. (1999)
103 Boyd, M. (2001)
104 Hogarth, R. (1981)
105 Kahneman, D. and Tversky, A. (1973)
106 Plous, S. (1993)
107 Tversky, A. and Kahneman, D. (1982)
108 Tversky, A. and Kahneman, D. (1971)
109 Tversky, A. and Kahneman, D. (1973)
110 Nisbett, R. E. and Ross, L. (1980)
111 Slovic, P. et al. (1976)
112 Combs, B. and Slovic, P. (1979)
113 Hastie, R. and Dawes, R. M. (2001)
114 Northcraft, G. B. and Neale, M. A. (1987)
115 Fischhoff, B. and Beyth, R. (1975)
116 Hoelzl, E. et al. (2002)

3
Risk-Taking in Trading Decisions

> *The conflict I experience every day is to balance risk and expectation. To take calculated risk, that's the real conflict. To bet $100 to make $500 rather than bet $100 to make $100.*
>
> Foreign exchange trader

"Everything is risk," one trader comments on the fact that risk forms the very center of decisions in the foreign exchange market. In fact, their search for profits confronts traders with the changing faces of risk all the time. For example, they may sell options in the foreign exchange derivatives field and pick up a small and certain premium while exposing themselves to the small chance of unlimited loss—"like picking up nickels in front of a steamroller. Sooner or later you will get *squashed*!", as one trader vividly explains.

Risk, defined by the *Oxford English Dictionary* as "hazard, danger; exposure to mischance or peril," is usually perceived by market participants as the variability of returns from their investments; for example, investing a government-grade bond with a fixed and guaranteed annual rate of return is less risky than investing in the new stock of a highly volatile technology company. Uncertainty about future events and developments is an inevitable part of trading decisions. Thus, traders weigh risks constantly while they attempt to form possible scenarios of the market future and embark on decisions whose outcomes are uncertain. As one trader remarks, "I would not enter a position where the [potential] profit is very tiny and the [potential] loss could be very big. Of course that is one simple thing which would affect any position, so that is the first question: 'Can I make money out of my position, and is the risk that I enter not tremendous?'"

Risk is about the *future*, and indeed the efforts of humankind to understand and master risk methodically by means of such sciences as mathematics, history, statistics, and economics have become cornerstones of the modern age.[1] In the foreign exchange market, what are the psychological characteristics of risk-taking? And what explanations are there for some of the striking risk-taking phenomena among foreign exchange market participants?

ASYMMETRIC RISK-TAKING

We tend to cut losses too late and to cut the profits too quickly.

Foreign exchange trader

Some of the most remarkable answers regarding the question of risk-taking in financial markets have been provided by psychology. Accordingly, when psychologist Daniel Kahneman was asked about the origins of the name of the decision theory he and Amos Tversky had developed, Kahneman replied that they chose a name that was easily noticed and recalled.[2] However, a fancy name is not the only remarkable characteristic of "prospect theory"; its most valuable merits are the insights it offers into the way people actually take risks.

While expected utility theory assumes that people are generally risk-averse (see Chapter 2, "Psychology of Trading Decisions"), prospect theory explains that there is a fundamental difference depending on whether the perception of gains or the perception of losses is involved. When the alternatives of a risky choice involve gains, people are risk-averse; however, when the alternatives of a risky choice involve losses, people are *risk-seeking*.

This can easily be demonstrated by the following example. Imagine a real decision involving real money.

Which of the following do you prefer?

A   A gamble with an 80% chance to win $4,000 and a 20% chance to win nothing.
B   A gain of $3,000 for sure.

Facing a choice involving gains, most people (four out of five in Kahneman and Tversky's study) prefer the certain gain offered by alternative B to the risky gamble offered in alternative A. However, results are different if the choice involves loss.

Which of the following do you prefer?

A	A gamble with an 80% chance to lose $4,000 and a 20% chance to lose nothing.
B	A loss of $3,000 for sure.

Here, most study participants (more than nine out of ten in Kahneman and Tversky's study) prefer the risky gamble in alternative A over the certain loss in alternative B; in other words, they become risk-seeking in the face of loss.

Participants in Kahneman and Tversky's study consisted of university students and faculty, not of financial experts. The European survey in contrast investigated whether professional foreign exchange traders also display this tendency to become risk-seeking when possible losses are involved, as prospect theory suggests. To make traders' choice more realistic, the amounts at stake were increased. Traders were asked whether they would be more willing:

A	To accept a certain loss of US$30,000.
B	Or to enter an 80% risk of running a loss of US$40,000.

More than two-thirds (71%) of the traders preferred the risky alternative B, which shows that also among foreign exchange traders—veterans in decisions involving real money in the face of risk—there is a *propensity to seek risk in the face of possible loss*.

How can this tendency to become risk-seeking when losses are at stake be explained? According to prospect theory, decision outcomes are not evaluated by their impact on overall wealth, but by the change they bring from a *subjective reference point*. In other words, decision-makers judge the outcomes of decision alternatives not in absolute terms but by considering the resulting deviation from a subjectively determined status quo. For example, when they decide whether they should go for a luxurious or an inexpensive dinner, people do not think about their objective overall net worth. Instead, people simply determine a psychological reference point (e.g., the amount of money currently in their wallet or the amount of money they usually spend on dinner). This reference point is not objectively predetermined but *subjectively* chosen; most of the time, its choice is not a deliberate act but occurs implicitly. In fact, the choice of this reference point can be psychologically influenced both by the decision-maker and by others.[i] In any case, once the reference point is

---

[i] This variable nature of the reference point forms the basis for the so-called framing phenomena discussed in the section "Framing and mental accounting" and for the psychological strategies to manage trading risk discussed in the section "Managing trading risk: Institutional and personal strategies."

established, people consider the effect of the meal purchase relative to the reference point, and their willingness to take risks depends on whether they perceive a choice between gains or between losses.

Take the example of somebody with an overall net worth of $200,000 who usually spends $15 on dinner. This person's reference point for dinner meals is probably the $15 usually spent on dinner. Financially, she does not experience the choice between an expensive $200 meal at an exclusive restaurant and skipping dinner altogether as the difference between the resulting $199,800 vs. $200,000 of her overall net worth. Instead, she perceives her choice as the difference between the extra expense of $185 for the exclusive restaurant meal vs. the saving of $15 if dinner is omitted altogether. The cost of the meal is not determined *objectively*, in terms of its effect on her net worth, but *subjectively* (e.g., with respect to the average cost of a meal, as in the above example, or maybe with respect to the amount of money currently in her wallet).

Thus, comparable with the utility function provided by Bernoulli's insights (see Chapter 2, "Psychology of Trading Decisions"), prospect theory provides a so-called "value function" of the effects of losses and gains for human decision-makers.[ii] However, whereas the utility function is based on an individual's objective wealth level and considers only positive utilities, the value function is based on a subjectively determined reference point from which it considers both the positive value of gains and the negative value of losses. This value function looks *different* for gains and for losses, as Figure 3.1 shows.

Because its slope increases in the area of gains, when possible decision outcomes are perceived as gains of different degrees, the value function leads the decision-maker to be *averse to risk*. Because its slope decreases in the area of loss, when possible decision outcomes are perceived as losses of different degrees, the value function induces the decision-maker to become *risk-seeking*.[iii]

The implications of the asymmetric nature of risk-taking for foreign exchange trading decisions are enormous. The different shape of the value function in the area of gains and losses can lead traders to dramatically different risk-taking, depending on whether gains or whether losses are at

---

[ii] Next to this value function, which concerns subjective perceptions of *utility*, prospect theory also explains subjective perceptions of *probability*. For a discussion of this "probability weighting function," see Brandstaetter et al.[3]

[iii] The so-called "reflection effect" implies that, when the signs of decision outcomes relative to the reference point are inverted, preferences are reversed: Risk aversion regarding positive outcomes turns into risk-seeking regarding negative outcomes. Evidence for this effect has already been found by Harry Markowitz[4] and Arthur Williams.[5]

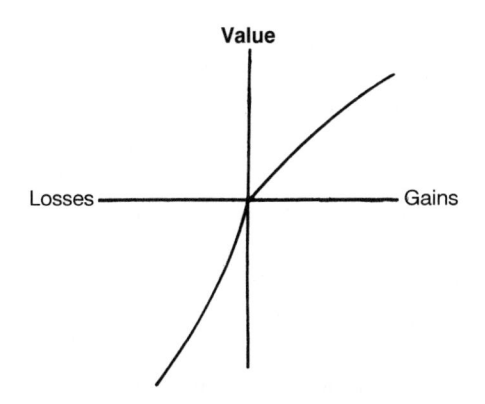

Figure 3.1 Prospect theory: The value function.
Reproduced from "Prospect theory: An analysis of decision under risk", D. Kahneman and A. Tversky, 1979, *Econometrica*, **47**(2), p. 279, with permission from The Econometric Society.

stake. For example, it explains the tendency of market participants to close winning trading positions too early and to let losing trading positions ride too long.[6] After a successful trade, traders perceive the decision of when to cut their trading position and when to realize their trading profit, as a decision between different degrees of gains. As we have seen, in the area of gains, decisions tend to be risk-averse. This leads traders to realize their profit early. Here, they feel that a bird in the hand is worth two in the bush, and they would rather not wait for further possible gains. In contrast, in the area of losses, decisions tend to be risk seeking. This is why traders, after a transaction that has generated a loss, hesitate to close their trading position and rather wait with the decision to cut their loss. Consequently, while traders realize gains too early and while they are still small, they allow losses to accumulate and close losing trading positions too late, often because of some irrational hope that the loss will reverse. "A trader will behave differently in his decision-making process if he is going into profits than if he is going into a loss. Having a profit, he is going to grab it much too fast, and having a loss, he will have a tendency to wait," one trader explains. Another trader echoes this sentiment, saying, "We take profits too early and cut losses too late."[iv] However, traders also observe that the tendency toward asymmetric risk-taking in the face of possible losses decreases with trading experience. In the words of one trader,

---

[iv] One way to cope with asymmetrical risk-taking is automated trading by mathematical models. In the words of a trader, "A model is not more clever and does not know any better than a trader, but it is going around that irrationality that a trader behaves differently in his decision-making process when he goes into profits to when he goes into losses."

"One of the differences between a junior and a senior trader should be that he [the senior trader] just acts opposite to what is human. And human is to take quicker profits than losses because you always think that this cannot be true and that you are right, so you let the losses run and you take the profits away too quickly."

Not only is the value function described by prospect theory different in the areas of gains and losses, it is also *steeper* for losses than for gains. This means that equally large movements from the reference point in the direction of gains and of losses are experienced with different intensities; the choice between winning and losing an identical amount of money from the status quo contrasts a relatively larger amount of pain for a possible loss to a smaller amount of pleasure for a possible gain.[7] In the words of Kahneman and Tversky, "Losses loom larger than gains. The aggravation that one experiences in losing a sum of money appears to be greater than the pleasure associated with gaining the same amount."[2] Thus, traders hate losing $100,000 more than they love to win $100,000. Because losses are psychologically weighted roughly twice as much as gains,[8] their risk-taking is characterized by marked *loss aversion*. "Taking losses is quite difficult," admits one foreign exchange trader.

A striking example for the psychological aversion to realizing a trading loss is provided by the following account of one trader: "I never wanted to declare or record a profit on an options trade until I had paid for the premium of acquiring that option." In fact, loss aversion makes any decision to realize a trading loss and close a losing trading position difficult. In the words of another trader, "It's fairly easy to run a position that is profitable, but the hardest decisions are those when to take a loss." Some traders even define their most valuable trading decisions not in terms of the ones where they made their highest profits, but of the ones where they made the emotionally more difficult decision to close a losing trading position in time. "The more important decisions are those where you actually reduced or cut losses, because they are much more difficult to make," says yet another trader. Thus the loss aversion expressed by the value function of prospect theory may also be the reason traders frequently report a disproportionally strong emotional reaction after losses, which by far surpasses the intensity of emotions after gains.

In order to avoid an imminent loss, traders may become highly risk-seeking and engage in courses of action they would otherwise clearly consider as too dangerous. "Some people take on more risk because they've lost yesterday, which is definitely the worst thing you can do," one trader observes this dangerous consequence of loss aversion After a trading loss, trades offering the opportunity to break even may become particularly attractive.[9] Indeed, traders often describe how after losses they chase the lost amounts in an effort to win them back.[v] "If a trader loses money, he tries to get it back," in the words of one trader.

However, not all traders equally succumb to the risk-taking dangers involved in loss aversion. As Chapter 6, "Personality Psychology of Traders," explains, experienced traders resist loss aversion. Instead of giving in to this natural risk-taking tendency of letting their losing positions run or even increasing their risk level, they are disciplined and controlled about taking their losses. As one trader observes knowingly, "A good dealer is not the dealer who instantly makes a few million bucks. A good dealer is one who knows where to cut his position." Another trader agrees, "I think trading isn't necessarily about making money because *anybody* can make money, anyone. I could get my mom to come in today and say, 'Away you go, mom,' and she could trade dollar–mark and she could [take a position that would] make money, because anybody can do that. But it isn't about making money; it's about losing the least amount of money as possible when you are wrong."

Thus, managing the psychological asymmetry in risk-taking and the aversion to loss explained by prospect theory is key to successful trading. As one trader remarks, "A good trader is differentiated from a bad trader not by how he makes money, but how he *loses* money. I would say it's easy to be happy when you make money; it's the easiest thing in the world. But it's really difficult to continue thinking objectively and make rational decisions after you lose money because that's a totally different ball game."

FRAMING AND MENTAL ACCOUNTING

> If the market is range trading and you sell at the bottom or you buy at the top, you're bound to run after the market the whole day.
>
> Foreign exchange trader

The previous discussion of asymmetric risk-taking described how traders evaluate the outcomes of their decisions based on the difference from a subjectively chosen reference point. This section shows that influencing the subjective reference point may have a dramatic influence on risk-taking in trading decisions. The reference point can be psychologically *influenced* and even manipulated—by the trader himself or herself as well as by others through framing and mental accounting.

---

[v] "When new traders look at the market and set their sights on contracts making a price move, they typically want to get a position at yesterday's close," according to Clasing and Craig.[10]

Framing is about selecting and influencing reference points for decisions. It takes place whenever decision-makers are influenced by how a situation and the alternatives involved in a decision are described, and by how decision-makers subjectively perceive the situation. The process of framing can be likened to looking at one and the same landscape from various viewpoints: just as a scenery seems different to a spectator from several viewpoints, the psychological meaning of a problem and of alternatives changes according to how the problem and the alternatives are *perceived*. Different perceptions of one and the same decision problem can then lead decision-makers to prefer different solutions.[7] Thus the same problem (in terms of its contents and the factual information provided) may lead to radically different decisions depending merely on the way the problem is described.

Likewise, the willingness to take risk in a trading situation depends on the *framing* of the situation. Prospect theory predicts that for risk-taking whether the decision is "framed" (i.e., presented by the environment or perceived by the decision-maker) as a choice between losses or as a choice between gains is decisive. Take the following example of such a framing effect in risk-taking.[11]

Problem 1

Imagine that, in addition to whatever else you have, you have been given a cash gift of $200. You are now asked to choose between:

A   A sure gain of $50.
B   A 25% chance of winning $200 and a 75% chance of winning nothing.

Problem 2

Imagine that, in addition to whatever else you have, you have been given a cash gift of $400. You are now asked to choose between:

A   A sure loss of $150.
B   A 75% chance of losing $200 and a 25% chance of losing nothing.

From the perspective of the results, both problems are ultimately *identical* and describe a choice between exactly the same alternatives: Alternative A leads to a certain gain of $250, whereas alternative B offers a gamble between a 75% chance of winning $200 and a 25% chance of winning $400. However, despite the fact that the outcomes of the two alternatives are *identical* in both decision problems, most people choose alternative A (which involves no risk) over alternative B in the first problem and B (which involves risk) over A in the second. This difference is intriguing and can only be explained as a framing phenomenon. The "gain frame" in the first formulation of the problem, where the decision is *perceived* as a choice between two gains, leaves decision-makers *averse to risk*. The loss frame in the second problem, where the decision is *perceived* as a choice between two losses, usually induces decision-makers to *seek risk*. Merely the different presentation of the same problem (i.e., different framing) leads to altered decisions.[7] Another remarkable example of a framing effect in medical decision-making has already been given in Chapter 2, "Psychology of Trading Decisions." Experienced physicians' decisions between surgery and radiation therapy of cancer was determined by how the choice between the two treatments is formulated (i.e., as the number of surviving patients vs. the number of patients who die).

Decision-makers experience framing effects in *all* kinds of environments where risky choices are made. Trading and investment decisions are particularly relevant examples, but they are by far not the only ones. For instance, to lose weight, one person I know stores food in two separate refrigerators, with different rules about what may be eaten and when. Similar *mental accounting* is used in financial decisions, when people mentally separate different parts of their money into various accounts for which they have different risk-taking attitudes.[6,12,13] Mental accounting thus also refers to the differences in individuals' subjectively chosen reference points for various decisions. As the section "Asymmetric risk-taking" in this chapter has shown, decision alternatives are evaluated by the change they bring from some reference point (i.e., whether an outcome is perceived as gain or loss relative to the reference point is decisive).

In trading, mental accounting may determine the influence of *prior* decision outcomes on current decisions. Whether a trader frames those outcomes as gains or as losses can dramatically influence the amount of risk the trader is willing to take in a subsequent decision.[9] Consider the situation of a trader who, after a series of unsuccessful trades, finds herself $90,000 in the red at the end of an unsuccessful trading day. The trader can either stop trading or take the risk of a last trading opportunity: to invest $10,000 in a risky trade with a 5% likelihood chance of gaining $100,000 and a 95% likelihood of losing the investment of $10,000.

In this situation, the trader can adopt one of several possible reference points, and her decision whether or not to take the risk of the last trading opportunity is determined by her mental accounting (i.e., by the way she *frames* the situation and consequently which *reference point* she chooses for the decision). From an economically rational viewpoint, optimal investment and trading decisions should not be influenced by mentally accounting for what was. To maximize profits, decisions should be based purely on the future value offered by alternatives. One potential reference point would thus have the trader consider the last trading opportunity as *independent* of all the previous trades on that day. In this case, she might decide against the last risky trade. However, a second potential reference point (which is often more persuasive for psychological reasons) would have the trader consider herself as $90,000 "in the hole." She then perceives the last trade as an *attractive opportunity* to finish the day even and happily decides to conduct the last risky trade. This example shows that mental accounting may influence decision-makers' risk-taking to the extent that they enter risks they would usually consider unacceptable.[14,15] This type of decision scenario is not merely a theoretical possibility, it can be observed in countless everyday situations, such as betting at race tracks. When people place their bets on the last race of the day, they indeed often attempt to regain their losses by choosing longer odds than they normally would.[16]

In the foreign exchange market, mental accounting can tempt traders to take unreasonably high levels of risk after a series of losses and put them in danger of entering a spiral of higher and higher losses. However, as the following advice of a head trader shows, the reference points involved in trading can be actively influenced to manage personal risk-taking: "If my dealers make losses, I ask them 'How many years do you have to go up to your retirement?' There are thousands and thousands of days. Then you tell them you have thousands of additional chances in your life. Forget about [the loss]!"

Whereas prospect theory predicts that in the area of loss people usually turn risk-seeking, the choice of a new reference point by way of mental accounting can actually make foreign exchange traders seek to *avoid* risks after a trading loss. One trader gives an example of how this may occur: "For instance, you had a good year and you are in December. If you made an excellent profit, and then you lose a little bit, then you say 'OK, I'm off for this year. So what, I had a good year, I will get a good bonus, so why should I risk anything?'" Here the event of a small trading loss after a long profitable trading period effectively triggers and reinforces the gain frame of overall profits accumulated over the year. The chosen reference point is the overall gain accumulated over the trading year; because gains are at risk, the trader turns more risk-averse and decides not to risk anything.

Conversely, mental accounting in trading decisions can also take the form of the so-called "house money effect," where prior gains *increase* rather than decrease the willingness to accept higher risks. Gamblers in Las Vegas are familiar with this phenomenon; as this effect may have caused them to quickly lose the money they just won. Now, how does the house money effect lead people to increased risk with the money they just won? The underlying reason for this effect is that people are more likely to take risks when the money they gamble with (or the money they invest) is not yet perceived as their *own* money (i.e., when the gains they just made are not yet psychologically incorporated into their own assets).[9,15,vi] The house money effect thus leads casino gamblers and traders in financial markets alike to subjectively perceive newly gained money as not really theirs but as money "of the house." They subsequently take higher risks with the house money and endure losses more easily. The following anecdote, told by financial journalist Gary Belsky and psychologist Thomas Gilovich, is a vivid account of the house money effect:[19]

> By the third day of their honeymoon in Las Vegas, the newlyweds had lost their $1,000 gambling allowance. That night in bed, the groom noticed a glowing object on the dresser. Upon closer inspection, he realized it was a $5 chip they had saved as a souvenir. Strangely, the number 17 was flashing on the chip's face. Taking this as an omen, he donned his green bathrobe and rushed down to the roulette tables, where he placed the $5 chip on the square marked 17. Sure enough, the ball hit 17 and the 35-1 bet paid $175. He let his winnings ride, and once again the little ball landed on 17, paying $6,125. And so it went, until the lucky groom was about to wager $7.5 million. Unfortunately, the floor manager intervened, claiming that the casino didn't have the money should 17 hit again. Undaunted, the groom taxied to a better-financed casino downtown. Once again he bet it all on 17—and once again it hit, paying more than $262 million. Ecstatic, he let his millions ride—only to lose it all when the ball fell on 18. Broke and dejected, the groom walked the several miles back to his hotel.
> "Where were you?" asked his bride as he entered their room.
> "Playing roulette."
> "How did you do?"
> "Not bad. I lost five dollars."

[vi] Therefore, the dynamics of the house money effect and the so-called "endowment effect"[17,18] are closely related to each other. A series of research findings shows that human decision-makers value money which they perceive to be *in their possession* more than the same amount of money which they do not perceive themselves to own.

Interviews with foreign exchange traders abound with ample evidence for the house money effect in trading decisions. In the words of one trader, "[After gains], it's easier for me to take high risks, for sure. It's like in the casino, you made 10 [thousand dollars], you had expected to make 5, but you have 10, so if you lose 5, you don't worry." Traders frequently observe that they take *more* risk because of a good trading performance on previous trading days. "If a trader makes good profits, he becomes more risky," observes one trader. Another trader echoes this sentiment, adding that it is, "Much easier to make money if you have already a good profit." House money is perceived differently and invites changed risk-taking; as one trader remarks lucidly, "You definitely go easier when you have a profit already and you can invest part of that in a new strategy." To put the house money effect in the form of a metaphor, in the terminology of one trader, "When things are going well one can, you know, put forward the accelerator a little bit!"

Similarly, the European survey showed a considerable influence of previous gains and losses on the willingness of foreign exchange traders to take risks. Traders indicate that previous successful trading days made them significantly *more* likely to take risks, whereas previous unsuccessful trading days made them *less* likely to take risks (Figure 3.2).

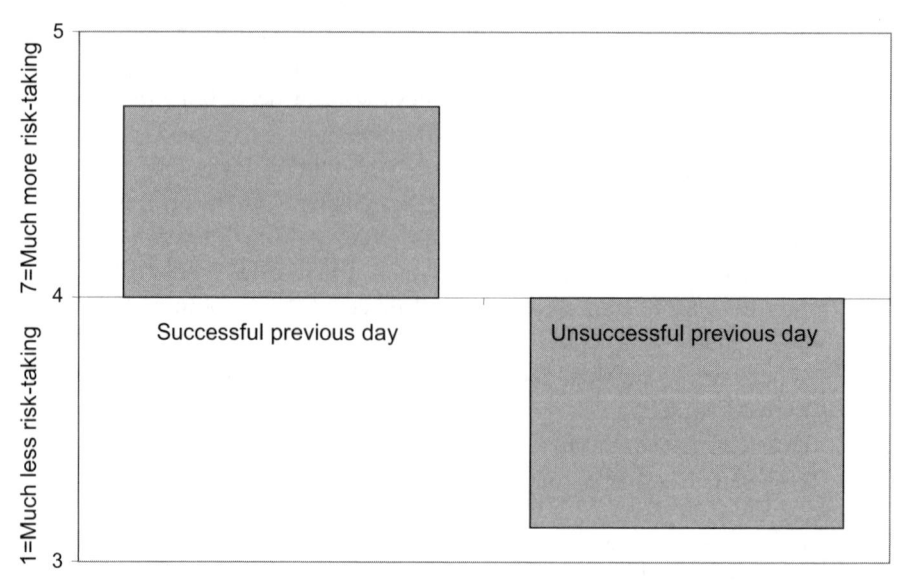

Figure 3.2 Effects of previous trading gains and previous trading losses on European traders ($n = 302$).

The effect of previous profits and losses on current risk-taking is eloquently underscored in the interviews. "You turn extremely risk-averse after defeat, and you turn extremely risk-taking after success," declares one foreign exchange trader. Interestingly, unlike commercial and investment bank traders who report becoming more willing to take risks, central bank traders see their risk-taking as *unaffected* after successful trading days with large gains. This significant difference in the level of risk-taking after gains indicates that the psychology of the house money effect is influenced by the goals and the motivation of decision-makers. While the goal of commercial and investment bank traders is to generate profits, central bank traders are not primarily profit-oriented but translate their institution's policies and strategies (e.g., to maintain a stable currency) into market reality.

MANAGING TRADING RISK: INSTITUTIONAL AND PERSONAL STRATEGIES

> This emotional involvement can get much too deep. And we say you get sort of married to a position; you just can't let go of it. You cannot let go of it, and even when it is going wrong, you just can't let go of it. "I know I'm right. I know I'm right." What happened to Nick Leeson, it's exactly the same thing: he just couldn't let go of it.
>
> Foreign exchange trader

In 1995, the English Barings Bank, considered at that time one of the most prestigious financial institutions in the world, collapsed after more than two centuries of operation. A single trader in Singapore, Nick Leeson, had accumulated more than £800 million of loss, trying to extricate himself from previous trading losses by more and more frenetic deals. Leeson was jailed and later recounted his story in a tell-all book, entitled *Rogue Trader: How I Brought Down Barings Bank and Shook the Financial World*.[20] Shortly afterwards, after a film based on Leeson's experience was released, it became public that another foreign exchange trader, John Rusnak at Allfirst Bank in Baltimore, had lost nearly $700 million in extremely large speculative trades on the U.S. dollar–yen exchange rate.[21]

How, one may well ask, can individual traders accrue such astronomic amounts in foreign exchange trading losses? The stories of Nick Leeson and John Rusnak illustrate that they ran up their dramatic losses over a period of time in which they had actually tried to *recoup earlier losses* and that they had done so by entering a lethal spiral of ever-larger trading risk. However, these stories also show that trading institutions and supervisors had failed to appropriately regulate the risk-taking of their traders and to recognize their losses in time. It is to such institutionally and self-managed aspects of limiting foreign exchange trading risk that this section now turns.

Institutional trading regulations establish a number of policies for taking trading risk which aim at controlling and reducing the amount of loss traders can accumulate. For example, daylight and overnight *position limits* regulate the sheer size of trading positions a trader is entitled to (i.e., the maximum amount of foreign currency a trader may have at any given point in time). While usual daytime position limits for individual traders are somewhere between $5 and $50 million, they may occasionally exceed several $100 million for some traders and for certain currencies. Most foreign exchange traders do not require an overnight position limit because they close their trading positions in foreign currency by the end of the trading day. However, traders at large international banks with offices in trading centers around the globe may shift their holdings in foreign currency to a different center at the end of the trading day in order to retrieve them the next morning (Figure 3.3).

Large positions in foreign currency can lead to substantial gains and losses

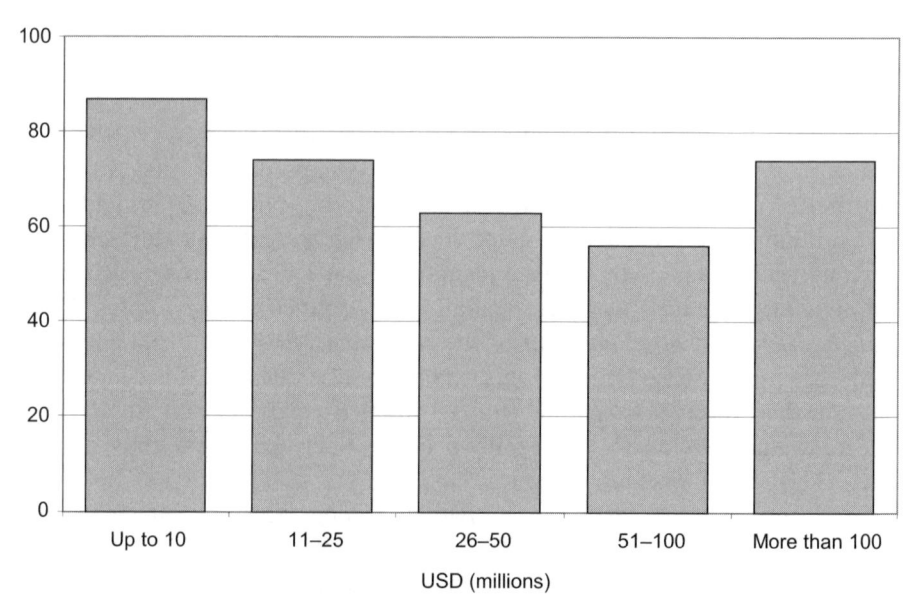

Figure 3.3 North American traders' daytime position limits ($n = 354$).

in short periods of time; for example, with a position of $100 million an aversive exchange rate movement of 1% in the course of one trading day (not an unlikely development even for leading currencies such as the U.S. dollar, euro, or Japanese yen) can translate into a relatively quick loss of $1 million.

"You lost one million, then you are quoting, your emotions paralyzed, all of a sudden it was two million. Maybe it is going to go on, maybe you lose three, nothing system-wise will stop you," one foreign exchange trader explains what may happen to an already sizeable trading loss without external controls. *Loss limits* provide traders with an additional external framework for risk-taking. They may be established for a trader's daily or monthly trading performance and regulate the amount of loss a trader is allowed to accumulate. Once the loss limit (also called a stop-loss limit) is reached, traders are forced to close their trading positions and "realize" their loss. One trader describes his own stop-loss: "You do whatever you want, but you are not allowed to lose more than one million. If I lose the million, I *have* to take the loss." Another trader explains that stop-loss limits can be especially valuable for more inexperienced traders who are still in training, recounting that, "On the younger guys in the foreign exchange we put a trigger level. Boom, if the position hits $20,000, if you've lost $20,000 on a position, cut it out. Don't really care, what you think doesn't matter, you were wrong. And you may be proved right 10 seconds later. Unlucky."

Traders perceive that the institutional rules that limit trading losses are reinforced more tightly in today's market than in the past. "You could look longer before someone intervened and said 'now you have to cut.' But these days... you have to run smaller risk, so if you are in a loss you cut the position earlier than you used to," one trader comments. While these measures of management control on trading risk have brought a general tendency toward less risk-taking among market participants, as one trader observes, they may also introduce more volatility into the market by influencing exchange rates. One trader observes, "Increasingly it's stop-loss limits which tend to build up in very large volumes, which have influenced what the market has done; not so much in the liquid markets in Europe but when it is a [an illiquid market in the afternoon] New York market or an Asian market early in the morning, the stop-loss levels almost always act like magnets." Likewise, while individual traders feel restrained in their risk-taking by institutional risk regulations, they also observe that feedback and supervision helps them counterbalance hazardous risk-taking tendencies. "Otherwise [we] would risk too much and [we] would say, 'well, I am coming back. I am over my limit and nobody knows it'," in the words of one trader.

Leading banks have established sophisticated feedback systems in an effort to monitor the performance and control their traders' risk. Trading institutions not only establish and monitor risk regulations for traders, they also determine periodically their overall exposure to foreign exchange market risk. Computer systems help trading floors and trading desks regularly determine their positions as well as current profits or losses.

The external risk management framework established by the management of trading institutions is complemented by personal risk-taking rules that traders themselves impose on their trading. "Banks have certain rules, they have certain guidelines, there must be for regulations—credit limits, loss limits, and things like that. Within that set of rules, each trader should have his own set of rules. Especially when it comes to taking a loss on a position," one trader explains.

Often, the risk-taking principles established by traders themselves reflect the ideal of rational traders not to be influenced by the outcome of previous decisions but to base the risk they enter solely on the prospects of the *current* trading decision. "That is the worst you can ever do, try to make up the previous day's damage," observes one foreign exchange trader. Another trader adds: "You say, 'OK, I lost $100,000 today, I have to make that $100,000 back'—it doesn't work. You may try it once, but then the day ends definitely with a loss of $200,000." Thus, traders recognize the need to take trading risks without being influenced by the outcomes of previous decisions. They observe that a successful trader always needs to start "from point zero," *unbiased* by previous gains and losses. As one trader spells out, "This is what makes a difference between an average trader and a good trader. On the following day, just forget what happened, start as from zero, and this makes the difference." However, as another trader's account of experiencing extended losses shows, choosing this reference point is not always easy: "You are in a very negative row, you make losses constantly, each day ... You do not sleep well enough, come to the office, and sit down: 'Today we'll make it!' [However, you make] another loss, and another loss. And that is *terrible*, you do not find yourself in a position on the fifth day ... to enter and say, 'Now forget about the past, now we make money!' "

To counterbalance the psychological tendency to increase risk-taking after losses, traders may use personal precommitment techniques.[vii] For example, they may enforce the realization of trading losses as soon as these losses amount to a certain percentage of the purchase price.[6] Other traders define the profits they can earn in one trading day as the limitation of their daily

---

[vii] For a discussion of loss aversion, see the section "Asymmetric risk-taking."

trading losses. "Never lose more than you can make," in the words of one trader.

However, in the face of actual losses all techniques to ensure disciplined risk-taking may be psychologically difficult to adhere to. "A lot of traders go through that planning process and they define a trading plan. Yet, they do not stick to it because then *hope* comes in, and they say, 'Ah, it's going to turn here,' and they do not take the loss. The problem is that it should not hurt to take that loss because it was planned, but if you don't have the discipline, and the willingness, and the readiness to work your plan you are not going to be a good trader," one trader remarks cogently. Thus, depending on the market situation, traders sometimes view rules for managing trading risk-taking as open to exceptions. One trader compares the rules he sets for himself with the resolution to go to the gym every day, admitting honestly, "One day you might rather go for a drink." However, as traders like Nick Leeson and John Rusnak know, going out for a drink can easily turn into several drinks, and what was supposed to be an enjoyable experience can also lead to a hangover and ultimate regret. As one trader declares, "Leeson, it is not working. You can't risk more and more and more to earn back losses!"

ABBREVIATED REFERENCES

See the reference chapter at the end of the book for full details.

1 Bernstein, P. L. (1996)
2 Kahneman, D. and Tversky, A. (1979)
3 Brandstaetter, E. et al. (2002)
4 Markowitz, H. (1952)
5 Williams, A. C. (1966)
6 Shefrin, H. and Statman, M. (1985)
7 Slovic, P. (1990)
8 De Bondt, W. F. M. and Thaler, R. H. (1994)
9 Thaler, R. H. and Johnson, E. J. (1990)
10 Clasing, H. and Craig, R. (1990)
11 Kahneman, D. and Tversky, A. (1982)
12 Thaler, R. (1985)
13 Kahneman, D. and Tversky, A. (1984)
14 Bazerman, M. H. (2002)
15 Tversky, A. and Kahneman, D. (1981)
16 Snyder, W. (1978)
17 Frey, B. S. (1990)

18 Thaler, R. H. (1992)
19 Belsky, G. and Gilovich, T. (1999)
20 Leeson, N. W. (1996)
21 Gotthelf, P. (2003)

4
Expectations in the Foreign Exchange Market

> *We grew up to anticipate what you think. It's sometimes fairly easy—when you start saying something I know what you want to say and I give you the answer before you have even completed the question.*
>
> Foreign exchange trader

"Prediction is very difficult, especially about the future," Niels Bohr, the famed Danish physicist and developer of quantum theory, once commented astutely. One old adage even has it that there are indeed only two kinds of prophets: those who know that they are wrong, and those who do not. While this saying may not *always* be true, it reflects that often people not only take aspects of the past for granted and are convinced about the present situation, but they also feel certain about a future course of events. However, there is no such thing as a *fact* about the future, a truism in financial markets as much as it is elsewhere. "Nobody can look into the future," says one foreign exchange trader frankly. Thus, rather than representing knowledge and certainty, market expectations are inherently unsure and they can only be held with varying degrees of confidence. In the words of one trader, "Taking a [trading] position you have risk. There is *no* absolute way to know that something is going to happen." Exploring how traders attempt to grasp the unknowable, this chapter demonstrates that the nature of the expectations driving market dynamics is psychological.

When asked what causes currencies to fluctuate, one trader responded matter-of-factly that, "It's the *anticipation* of an eventual change in the current status." Indeed, at any point of time, expectations determine what happens in the foreign exchange market as they trigger trading decisions, causing some currencies to appreciate and others to depreciate. "It's sort of a scientific process, all the time there are hypotheses that are being formed and the whole market concentrates on one, and each incoming piece of data sort of justifies it or proves it wrong, increasingly, until one thing really totally disproves or proves it right," another trader explains. However, while expectations may be conceived of in a highly formalized way that requires the expertise of specialists and complex computer models, predicting and forecasting are as common to market participants as they are to people in everyday life. Statements as varied as, "The Fed is going to lower interest rates soon," "The yen will become stronger against the dollar," and "Dinner at Domenici's is going to be tasty tonight," exemplify such expectations both in and outside the foreign exchange market. Accordingly, another trader comments bluntly that foreign exchange decisions are made, "By *human beings*. When you feel it in your guts!"

Because all participants' activities in the foreign exchange market such as investment decisions and trading behavior are related to the future,[1] one central question that arises is *how* participants form expectations about the market future and outlooks on the development of exchange rates.

As Chapter 2, "Psychology of Trading Decisions," has demonstrated, traditional economic theory approaches this question in a normative way; its view of rational expectations simply assumes that participants adjust them to a hypothetical fundamentally true value. However, the assumption of rational expectations is directly contradicted by a large number of empirical studies on real-life market participants. For example, a systematic analysis of yen–dollar exchange-rate expectations held by such foreign exchange institutions as banks, brokers, and international companies resulted in considerable differences among these participants, and revealed that their expectations were influenced by wishful thinking.[2] While Japanese exporters expected a relative yen depreciation that would boost their business due to increased international demand for cheap Japanese products, importers expected a yen appreciation that would allow them to buy their goods cheaply abroad. Such wishful thinking, also called "desirability bias," reflects the tendency of people to over-expect advantageous outcomes. This tendency has been confirmed among a variety of market decision-makers, ranging from business managers in a variety of industries to professional investment managers.[3,4]

Thus there is empirical proof for the impact of *psychology* on market expectations, and this evidence suggests that we need more knowledge of the actual processes involved in the expectations of participants. The importance of expectations and their role in human behavior is widely acknowledged in psychology.[5] For instance, the famed personality theorist George Kelly suggested that psychological processes are fundamentally controlled by people's anticipations.[6] In contrast to the traditional economic approach, a psychological understanding of expectations aims to show how they are *actually* formed.

The importance of descriptive psychological insights into (rather than normative economic assumptions about) expectations is also underscored by first-hand accounts of market participants who continuously anticipate imminent market trends and predict market outcomes (i.e., how these trends will affect exchange rates). As Chapter 5, "News and Rumors," shows, when doing so, participants base their expectations on a broad spectrum of information ranging from political to economic to financial. However, figures and facts alone are not sufficient in forming exchange-rate expectations. In the words of one trader, "I don't believe anything anymore ... Before, if a figure [i.e., economic release] was this and that, you bought or sold instantly. Now you think, 'what does it mean?' You are not so enthusiastic anymore of some figures and news." To form expectations, market information needs to be interpreted; a change in governmental policies, interest and inflation rates, and trade balance figures may only constitute the backdrop against which traders establish *other* participants' perceptions and interpretations, their likely change of expectations, and what trading strategies they embark on. "You are saying, 'I'm really thinking that Citi is looking to go long the currency,' for whatever reason," one trader observes.

Thus, the expectations of market participants are directed less at an objective economic future than at how others *perceive* the future and how they will *react* to it. As one trader observes, "I don't care what the numbers are. I don't care what the numbers might be ... What I care is if everyone was thinking it was going to be good, and therefore they were all long, [because then] it is going to go down; if everyone thought it was going to be bad, they will be short, and it will go up!" In addition, market participants do not form their expectations of the market in a detached way. Instead, they actively play on each others' expectations about the movements of exchange rates and try to influence the expectations of other participants to their own advantage. "The good traders also use psychology in steering the market ...: 'I know how other people think. We use that to our advantage by moving exchange rates in the short-term.' Short-term exchange rates can be manipulated, there is never a real rate of foreign exchange," he further explains.

The beginning of this chapter has stressed that the expectations that connect market participants to a possible future of the market are always uncertain; the remainder shows that they are *psychological* in nature. "It's an entirely intuitive process: What will other people think about it? What do I think about it?" one trader inquires. To answer these questions, this chapter compares the nature of expectations in the foreign exchange market to a metaphorical time machine. It examines the use of fundamental and technical/chartist analysis by foreign exchange participants, two approaches to predicting exchange rates which are based on different kinds of market information. Moving beyond this separation, the chapter explores aspects of market expectations which liken these to the psychological notion of attitudes and shows that subjective attitudes determine the expectations of market participants. These attitudes emerge in the social dynamics of the market, as the importance of participants' expectations about other market participants and the influence of the financial news media show.

EXPECTATIONS: A MARKET TIME MACHINE

In H. G. Wells' novel, *The Time Machine*, a traveler's desire to find out what will happen to the human race ultimately leads him on a tremendous expedition into a terrifying and perilous future. Metaphorically, the expectations of market participants also function like a time machine, as they allow participants a glimpse into the market's future. Foreign exchange traders stress that expectations play one, if not *the*, leading role in the dynamics of the market. "It is the expectation of the market which is most important," says one trader regarding exchange rates. "*Everything* is expectation," another trader concurs. Also market observers (i.e., financial journalists) underscore the vital role of expectations in the foreign exchange market. "Markets deal on expectations and the future. If you didn't have news of expectations and expectations of the market then what would traders deal on?" one financial journalist asks. "When a market goes from being golden to being rotten, like Mexico [i.e., the Mexican peso] goes from one day to another, not because anything fundamental has changed, it's because all of a sudden expectation went one way or the other," another journalist adds in support of this view.

Similar to travel in a time machine, market expectations change not only the views but also the behavior of participants, both among individuals and on the level of the collective market. Indeed, the foreign exchange market may be the most rapid of all financial markets to translate and integrate expectations of the future into the present market behavior. One trader observes lucidly that, "Especially the currency markets tend to run ahead. We have seen that over the last few years, especially the currency markets tend to focus very much on the future. We often had discussions with our economist in which he said, 'All the figures currently would point to such and such trend.' And then all that was already priced in!" Thus, in their present evaluations of currencies and trading decisions, market participants include their expectations of future events and discount the probable effects of yet-to-come developments. Consequently, on the aggregate level of the market, collective expectations about future events are integrated into the current level of exchange rates. "The market is always expecting some events ... and the thing is before this event happens, the market moves in that way ... Everyone said, 'OK, the dollar is coming up because there are interventions, there is some especially good big figure ... and the market is expecting that and buying dollars, and of course dollar–mark is going higher'," according to one trader. Thus the foreign exchange market creates an anticipatory reality that turns the expected future into the present in advance. "The market positions itself beforehand," another trader declares. As expectations about future events are built into the market, a trader's shrewd observation that, "If the news has come out, it is old for us: it is the past, it is already built into the prices," is hardly surprising.

Like a time machine, market expectations allow individual participants to turn the wheel of time ahead, and the collective market to preempt the likely future of the market. This journey in time, however, transforms the meaning and impact of market news and information. Effective news is the difference between the market's expectation and the actual published figure. Pointing to his massive, wooden trading desk, one trader explains that, "Information that comes out that is expected is not really information. It just confirms something you already know. You know, this table is made of wood. I don't need to know that [news] comes out that this table is made of wood. Because we know that—fantastic. [However, news that] this table is made out of gold, that's something different. If people don't know it, it is going to move [the market]!" Expectations thus determine the market's reactions to news by turning news into a check of already acted-on expectations. "What makes the market move is *the delta between the expectations and the news*. It's not the news itself," one trader explains. Thus, news that merely confirms expectations does not change the already created status quo of the market, independent of how positive or negative the intrinsic content of the news may be. Only *unanticipated* news, such as economic indicators deviating from what was expected, will move the market.[i] Accordingly, as one trader observes, "Some figures are coming. If the figures are good or bad does not make any difference. [However], it makes a big difference if you expect a bad number and a good one comes." Another trader echoes this sentiment, saying, "The final event gives just the conclusion and tells the people if their expectations were right or their positions were right. The *expectations* move the market, *not* the event."

According to traders, because expectations are already integrated into the market before the corresponding information confirms them, the arrival of anticipated news may even trigger a *paradoxical* move—in the opposite direction of what identical news would have triggered normally. "If the market has positioned itself beforehand, then you could get a totally adverse reaction to a certain event. You might get a positive number for the American economy, nevertheless the market reacts to the contrary because people were already long, and they are just going out of it," one trader observes. Another trader explains this shift with a pertinent market example: "Five percent inflation is a bad figure, and that would under normal circumstances hurt any bond market. But if the market's perception was the figure should be 5.5%, although 5% is still a bad figure the market could actually react the other way because what is expected is different from what the actual figure is." Thus, traveling in the time machine of expectations, participants not only catch a glimpse of the foreign exchange market's future; doing so actually *changes* the future they finally encounter.

FUNDAMENTAL AND TECHNICAL/CHARTIST ANALYSIS

> If you enter a position, you have many possibilities how you do it: One dealer says, "I look only at charts." Another says, "It doesn't matter to me, I'm dealing out of my feeling, out of the market. If you have the brokers only, you have a kind of feeling: are there more offers or bids?" Or you say, "I trade only on fundamentals because

---

[i] For example, "The relationship between a deficit in the balance of trade and the exchange rate depends crucially on whether the deficit was expected or not. A deficit that was expected may have no effect on the exchange rate, since the latter already reflected these expectations. In contrast, an unexpected deficit in the balance of trade may contain significant new information that is likely to be accompanied by large changes in the exchange rates," according to economist Jacob Frenkel.[7]

I don't believe in any chart; I don't believe in any rumor; fundamentals is what I trade." In reality it must be a mixture of all of that.

Foreign exchange trader

In the literature of financial markets, participants are often classified into groups according to two different approaches as to how they form their expectations: "fundamental analysis" and "technical/chartist analysis."[8,9] This section discusses some of the differences between the two approaches which reflect different assumptions about what kind of market information is predictive.[ii] In the words of one trader, Some people are working with charts, and according to the charts they make forecasts about the price movements. "Some others believe rather in the fundamental analysis, they say that something has to have a certain value: 'If the price is under this value, I buy it, and if it is overpriced, I sell it.'" This is the theory that everybody learns in the university. This section demonstrates that there are different "styles" in how traders use the two approaches over time and that the importance of the two approaches varies in different parts of the market. While the present section also illustrates that traders' expectations are generally influenced by *both* fundamental and technical/chartist approaches, the following sections in this chapter will show that additional psychological factors need to be considered. "Actually," in the words of the trader quoted above, "the prices are made by the dealers because they feel if it should go up or should go down. It is very simple; it is nothing magic."

In the financial literature, the term fundamental analysis is applied to all exchange-rate forecasting approaches that are based on some kind of economic theory (e.g., the analysis of such economic data as interest rates, inflation, economic growth, balance of payments, or money supply).[iii] In other words, fundamental analysis is used by market participants who form their expectations about currencies by considering the economic conditions on which they believe exchange rates rest. Fundamental market forecasters assume that

---

[ii] This section is reworked from material in *International Journal of Finance and Economics*, 6(1), pp. 81–93, T. Oberlechner (2001), "Importance of technical and fundamental analysis in the European foreign exchange market,"[10] with permission from John Wiley & Sons Ltd.

[iii] Money supply indicates the amount of money in the economy and is measured in various ways. M1 expresses cash and checking account bank deposits (i.e., money regularly used to purchase goods and services), M2 additionally considers savings accounts bank deposits, and the most comprehensive M3 measure also includes money market accounts. Traders considered money supply data to be very important to exchange rates in the 1970s and 1980s.[11]

superior understanding of relevant economic conditions (i.e., knowing these conditions *better* than other market participants or knowing them *before* other market participants do) allows one to successfully predict exchange rates.

Technical analysis, by contrast, is used by those market participants who base their expectations solely on exchange rates themselves and on patterns of previous exchange-rate developments.[12] Technical analysis does not rely on any assumptions about the economic basis of exchange rates. On the contrary, participants who employ technical analysis work on the implicit or explicit assumption that all underlying economic and financial information relevant to exchange rates is *already incorporated* into the exchange rates and that therefore analyzing this information does not help in predictions. In other words, technical forecasters believe that any analysis of economic factors cannot produce a better and more precise result than is already provided by the actual exchange rate. Instead, they see the basis for predicting exchange rates in the history of past exchange-rate developments because they assume that there are *recurring patterns* in how exchange rates develop over time. Underlying these patterns, they see changes in the attitudes of market participants which, in turn, may be based on economic, political, and psychological factors.[13] The goal of technical forecasters is to identify these patterns in order to predict future exchange rates. Probably the most important variety of technical analysis is its visual application: Chartist analysis is the search in exchange-rate charts for repeated patterns across time. Also called chartism, this branch of forecasting aims at identifying visible exchange-rate patterns (e.g., cycles, levels of resistance and support, and such chart formations as the well-known "head-and-shoulders" pattern).[14,iv,v]

Distinguishing between fundamental and technical/chartist market fore-

---

[iv] In practice, participants' forecasting mechanisms often cannot easily be classified as either fundamental or technical; see the short-term trading strategies based on information about money flows or purely quantitative approaches which explore mathematical associations in market data. With the help of computer programs, so-called neural network techniques build mathematical models that identify possible connections underlying extremely large sets of observation data. Such quantitative models appear technical in so far as they simply establish historical connections among a variety of variables; however, they may also be translated into assumptions about the effects of macroeconomic indicators on exchange rates. Regarding the role of these computer-assisted forecasts, one trader observes: "We are using machines to formalize the decision-making processes. And the ultimate outcome—this is at least what people claim—is that we will have systems making these decisions, so any trading decision is a totally emotion-free thing. There is one machine that tells you: 'now you buy and now you sell.' And you, the human, will follow it, and the trading decision will be based upon the data you feed into that big machine. You make that machine think like a brain and

casters has helped economists to explain the existence of heterogeneous expectations in the foreign exchange market.[8,18] There has been great need for such explanations in the field of economics because many studies have shown that, especially in the short term, predictions and models of exchange rates on the basis of fundamental economic data have little success.[19,20] For instance, economic analysis of such figures as growth rates or trade numbers often fails to predict short-term exchange-rate changes:[8] in 1984/85, the value of the U.S. dollar was dramatically higher than what was suggested by fundamental analysis. In response to such evidence that fundamentals alone are not enough to explain exchange rates, economists have started to develop theoretical models that duly consider the interaction of fundamentalist and chartist expectations.[21,22]

Thus the theoretical separation between fundamental and technical/chartist market forecasters has increased economists' awareness of non-economic factors in the expectations of market participants. However, people who study financial markets, "cannot just rely on assumptions and hypotheses about how speculators and other market agents may operate in theory, but should examine how they work in practice, by first-hand study of such markets," economist Charles Goodhart aptly observes.[23] Indeed, little is known about the *actual* use of fundamental and technical/chartist forecasting approaches by market participants. Precious evidence is provided by a small number of empirical studies conducted on this question[vi] which found that the importance of fundamental and technical/chartist forecasting methods depended on the forecasting horizon (i.e., for how long in the future foreign exchange traders form their expectations) and that technical/chartist analysis was used mostly for short-term forecasts. However, first-hand evidence from

---

then you feed it all the data, the news, the economics, the fundamentals, the GNPs, the political information; you just put all into it, and you add information about flows: who is buying, who is selling, with what volatility, and the computer will constantly try to tell you what to do. I think this is the utmost formalization." Tellingly, the trader adds that, "We have always tried to capture that. So far it has never worked."

[v] The financial literature also differentiates between "arbitrageurs" and "noise traders". According to this distinction, arbitrageurs are the so-called smart money investors who process market information fully and who decide rationally. Noise traders, as the name implies, rely on economically irrelevant information.[15] The groups of arbitrageurs and noise traders are closely related to market participants employing fundamental analysis and market participants employing technical/chartist analysis. Economists see fundamental analysis as the basis for the trading decisions by arbitrageurs, whereas technical analysis leads to noise trading because it is not based on valid economic market information.[16,17]

[vi] For the London foreign exchange market, see Allen and Taylor[24] and Taylor and Allen[25]; for Hong Kong, see Lui and Mole[26]; and for Germany, see Menkhoff[27].

market participants continues to be scarce; therefore, the remainder of this section presents my own findings from the European survey.

In the interviews, traders expressed a broad spectrum of diverging opinions on the relative value of fundamental and chartist approaches. For example, one trader dryly comments, in support of chartism, "There are a lot of people who have lost a lot of money by believing in fundamentals ... When you turn around and somebody says, 'Fundamentally, this should not happen,' it means that they had the right position but they were losing money on it." However, another trader retorts, "The dealer as Pavlov's dog exists, especially for people who work with charts. I know some people who work purely according to charts, and if the chart makes a certain movement, they buy or sell, whatever they feel: they have no intuition. Some people work with [chartism] and some people are successful with it. I always make fun of these people because there is an old saying: No chartist has ever died rich."

In contrast to the economic market model reflected by fundamental analysis, traders connect chartism to a behavioral and psychological view of the market, as can be seen in the definition of charts by one trader as, "Visual representations of mass psychology."[vii] Moreover, traders' accounts illustrate the importance of market participants' interaction with each other in two striking ways. On the one hand, traders observed that market participants have psychological *motives* for using chartism. For instance, one trader related the growing use of chartism to the experienced loss of personal contact with other trading agents caused by the use of electronic-trading devices. Anonymous numbers on the trading screen cannot replace the voices and conversations with other market participants; in an effort to make up for this loss, traders turn to charts in order to regain a sense of togetherness and psychological safety in their decision-making. This observation was confirmed by some traders who reported that they used charts in order to subjectively gain more confidence in the correctness of their trading judgments. As one trader observes, "Traders need to feel, perhaps more than most other decision-makers, that they are right, and charting helps create that confidence."

On the other hand, traders observed that trading decisions were affected by

---

[vii] This view is supported by literature on market "psychology" which is actually a discussion of technical forecasting methods. Because of its focus on the outcomes of trading behavior rather than on economic conditions, chartism can indeed be seen as an acknowledgement, even if superficial, of psychology. However, chartism represents only a quasi-psychology of the foreign exchange market: remaining on the level of observable and collective trading outcomes, it is purely behavioristic in nature and does not examine the underlying motivation and decision-making processes of market participants.

knowing about others who use chartism. Thinking about other market participants who employ chartist forecasting methods can generate self-reinforcing trading patterns that are clearly psychological in nature. On the collective market level, such trading patterns endow charts with the power to control exchange rates by way of *self-fulfilling market prophecies*.[viii] Self-fulfilling prophecies influence human interaction in various settings; they actively manage to bring about the predicted result, as a consequence of the sheer fact that they were made. They can govern the behavior of groups, as was strikingly demonstrated by the situation that arose in California in 1979, when newspapers reported the imminent danger of a fuel shortage.

Panicked car owners reacted by storming petrol stations to safeguard themselves and to fill up their tanks while fuel was still available. Despite the fact that the reason reported for the gas shortage ultimately turned out to be wrong, the *prediction* worked out to be correct: It triggered behavior among motorists which brought about the very shortage of gas which had been its initial message. Almost overnight, all reserves in California were depleted by frightened motorists. Thus, as the example shows, for a self-fulfilling prophecy to work, it has to be *believed*. Predictions that actively fulfill themselves and that affect future outcomes are based on people who are convinced of their veracity.[29]

Evidence for such kind of self-fulfilling dynamics in financial markets can be found in economist Robert Shiller's investigation of investors' motives during the dramatic price drops of crashes in the stock market. Following the record-breaking crash of October 19, 1987, investors were asked about how important they perceived various news stories that had been published at the time of the crash. Strikingly, the most important news items in the ratings of the investors were not economic or political news by nature, but rather those about the market's price drops in themselves.[30] In other words, investors were selling because they perceived the market as going down, thereby confirming their perceptions and turning these into an even stronger market reality![ix]

[viii] The concept of a self-fulfilling prophecy was first defined by American sociologist Robert K. Merton (the father of economic Nobel laureate Robert C. Merton) as an initially incorrect definition of a situation, which nevertheless triggers new actions that ultimately verify the initially false conception.[28] In other words, the prediction involved in a self-fulfilling prophecy confirms itself by *causing* the expected outcome to occur, and not by correctly foreseeing it, at least not in the beginning.

[ix] These results can also be seen as evidence for psychological information and feedback loops among the market participants[31,32] which are discussed in Chapter 5, "News and Rumors."

The argument of economist Lukas Menkhoff that chartism may be seen as a form of self-fulfilling prophecy is confirmed by foreign exchange traders' observations. As one trader notes, traders use chart analysis as "insurance" against the large number of other traders who are known to use charts, thereby providing an even stronger reason for other traders to use charts themselves. "Without the chart system you can't deal anymore because everybody uses it," another trader remarks of its prominence. As a consequence, in the words of one trader, "If a hundred people believe in something, these hundred people will move the market. So they confirm the chart."[x,xi]

To analyze the significance of fundamental and technical/chartist analysis more systematically, the European survey asked traders and financial journalists to rate the importance of the two forecasting approaches for a series of different time horizons.[xii] Figure 4.1 summarizes the importance assigned to the forecasting methods across seven time horizons, ranging from intraday forecasts to forecasts made for periods longer than one year.

The forecasting period has an important influence on the use of fundamental analysis and of technical/chartist analysis: the *shorter* the forecasting horizon the more important technical/chartist analysis is, and the *longer* the forecasting horizon the more important fundamental analysis becomes for foreign exchange market participants,[xiii] both for traders and for financial journalists. However, traders and financial journalists rated the importance of the forecasting methods differently; on each horizon, traders attributed a larger role to technical/chartist analysis than did financial journalists, and, conversely, on

---

[x] "Many trading strategies based on pseudo-signals, noise, and popular models are correlated, leading to aggregate demand shifts," according to economists Andrej Shleifer and Lawrence Summers.[16]

[xi] Similar observations may have led the influential hedge fund manager George Soros to observe that supply and demand in financial markets are not independent economic givens; in other words, the events at which market expectations are directed do not simply happen but are instead actively *shaped* by market participants' expectations.[33] Soros refers to this interdependency between the market and participants' expectations as market *reflexivity* and maintains that financial markets are not able to discount the future correctly because, while attempting to do so, they simultaneously influence and change the future. Since financial markets also influence the fundamentals they try to predict, market developments may greatly differ from economic models on which they are supposed to reflect.[34]

[xii] Because the financial news media play an important role in market expectations (see Chapter 5, "News and Rumors"), financial reporters' views were also examined.

[xiii] These findings are consistent with previous survey results from London,[25] Germany,[27] and Hong Kong.[26]

Figure 4.1

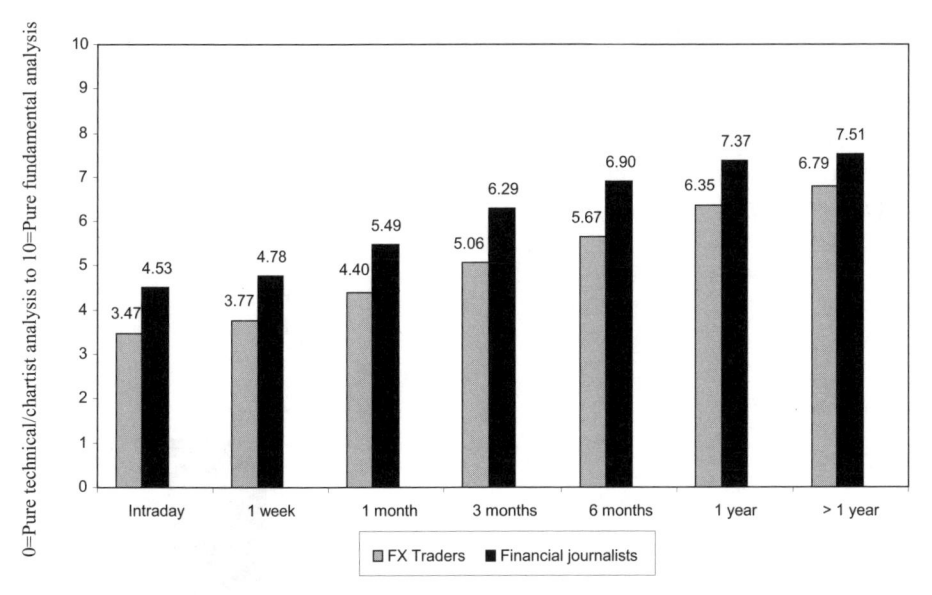

Importance attached to technical/chartist and fundamental analysis by foreign exchange traders ($n = 282$) and by financial journalists ($n = 49$).

each horizon, financial journalists placed comparatively more emphasis on fundamental analysis.

This striking difference between the two groups can best be explained by the different nature of their daily professional tasks: Unlike traders, journalists do not directly engage in trading decisions but provide the trading decision-makers with news and analysis *about* the market. One important aspect of this work consists of providing reasons for past market developments (i.e., attributing these developments to plausible explanations and developing a rationale for possible future market trends). To make financial news understandable and interesting, they are embedded in stories that suggest understandability and logic. To financial journalists, the task of weaving market news into a simultaneously interesting and plausible story implies the use of explanations and forecasts which are more often than not grounded in economic fundamentals. Thus, the functional difference between market reporters and trading decision-makers involves a more *analytic and academic* orientation toward the market on the side of financial journalists and a more *action- and result-oriented* involvement in the market on the side of traders, which is focused more on immediate perceptions (as reflected in the use of chartism) than on fundamental economic explanations.

In order to further explore the differences between the two group's basic approaches to forecasting, the European survey asked traders and journalists to indicate how important they perceived "feelings" and "rationality": first, in their own decisions and, second, in the collective foreign exchange market. Answers revealed one remarkable similarity as well as one consequential difference (Figure 4.2).

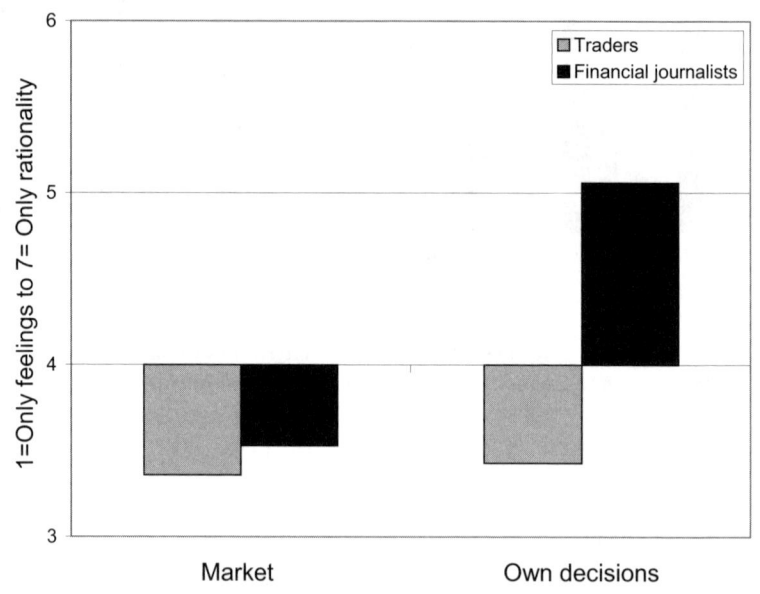

Figure 4.2 Perceived rationality and feelings: the market vs. own decisions.

For the collective market, traders and financial journalists alike rated feelings to be slightly more influential than rationality. This striking finding shows that *both* groups of market participants attach a larger importance to subjective feelings than to objective rationality in collective market movements. Hence, despite their different roles in the market, traders and financial journalists identically view the market as being more emotional than rational. In stark contrast, traders and financial journalists hold opposing views regarding the role of feelings and rationality on the individual level of their own decisions in the market. In their *own* trading decisions, foreign exchange traders consider *feelings* to be more influential than rationality, whereas in their own reporting, financial journalists consider *rationality* more important than feelings. These differences in how own decisions in the market are perceived may well explain why financial journalists make more use of fundamental analysis than do traders. Journalists need to purposefully find rationality and economic reasons when reporting on the foreign exchange market. Thus, whereas financial journalists likewise consider feelings to be more influential on the market level, they differentiate between this more "emotional" nature of the market and the more "rational" character of their individual reporting decisions. In contrast, foreign exchange traders rate feelings as more important than rationality both for the collective market and for their own trading decisions.

Over time, the relative importance of these two different forecasting approaches has undergone change, according to recent studies on the use of technical/chartist and fundamental analysis. For example, economists Jeffrey Frankel and Kenneth Froot show that a notable shift took place among the foreign exchange forecasting services surveyed by *Euromoney* magazine in the period from 1978 to 1988.[8] For while during 1983–1985, the percentage of forecasting services employing technical analysis reached a maximum, this percentage has decreased somewhat in subsequent years. The European survey indicates that the role of technical/chartist analysis among foreign exchange traders may have increased in recent years. Figure 4.3 compares ratings of traders in London with a survey conducted by economists Mark Taylor and Helen Allen among chief foreign exchange dealers in London.[24,25]

The comparison indicates that technical/chartist analysis has become *more* important to the foreign exchange market in the period in-between the two surveys.[xiv] Already, Allen and Taylor's data led them to extend a word of warning to economists who narrowly consider only fundamental factors when studying the foreign exchange market. Results of the European survey not only reiterate this warning, they may even indicate a further rise in the importance of technical/chartist analysis for market participants. On all trading horizons, the importance of technical/chartist analysis has grown among London traders in the period from 1989 to 1996. This finding is supported by another survey among foreign exchange traders in the U.K. which was conducted by economists Yin-Wong Cheung, Menzie Chinn and Ian Marsh. The results of their study indicate that technical/chartist-based trading increased as a preferred trading forecasting method between 1993

[xiv] This comparison should be interpreted with some caution. Unlike Taylor and Allen's survey, the questionnaire used in the European study did not offer an answer category that no particular view was held over a certain time horizon. The observed shift toward chartist analysis may be influenced by the different question format. Moreover, whereas Taylor and Allen surveyed chief foreign exchange traders in London, the European study included traders on all hierarchical levels. However, the majority of London traders included in the European study were actually senior traders (73%).

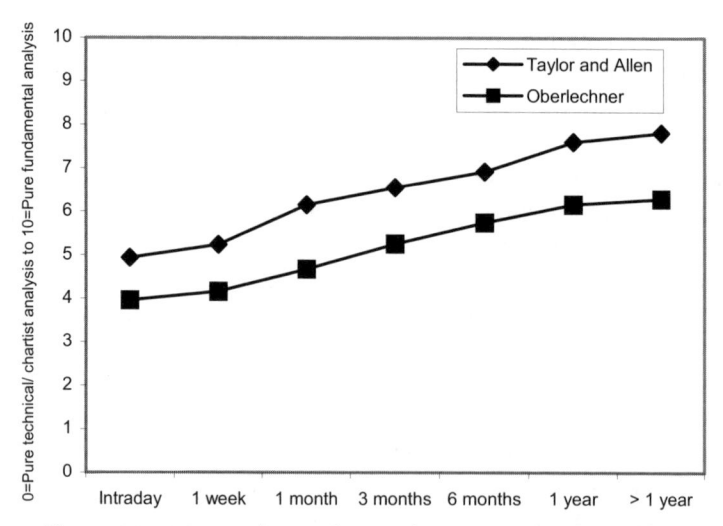

Figure 4.3 1989 and 1996 forecasting approaches in London.

and 1998, while trading based on the analysis of fundamental economic data remained almost unchanged.[35] All these findings suggest that the importance of non-economic approaches to predicting foreign exchange rates and trading currencies have even risen.

Regarding the forecasting approaches of traders in the European survey, for each trader, averaging his or her ratings on the various forecasting horizons results in one overall forecasting approach. Figure 4.4 presents the distribution of these overall approaches to predicting exchange rates among 289 traders.

The bell-shaped distribution indicates that usually both fundamental and technical/chartist forecasting techniques are *mixed*, and that the majority of traders are somewhere in the middle of the continuum. The figure thus clearly

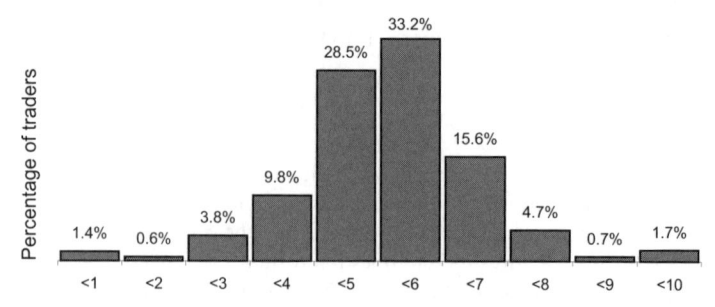

Figure 4.4 Overall forecasting approaches of foreign exchange traders ($n = 289$): 0 = Pure chartist analysis; 10 = Pure fundamental analysis.

shows that a strict distinction between foreign exchange traders who rely either only on fundamental analysis or only on technical/chartist analysis does not exist. On the contrary, traders do not see fundamental analysis and technical/chartist analysis as mutually exclusive; most use a more or less equally balanced overall forecasting approach.[25,26] Only a small minority use an exclusively fundamental or exclusively technical/chartist approach. Thus, rather than being a second-rate forecasting method that is employed by a subgroup of badly informed market participants who either do not possess relevant fundamental economic information or do not know how to interpret it, technical/chartist analysis emerges as a commonly used forecasting approach. Usually, this approach is mixed with the analysis of economic fundamentals. In the words of one trader, "Most foreign exchange traders are surprisingly enough inhabiting the middle ground. I would say that most of them are further to the continuum of being based upon event-driven and flow-driven and market-driven and size-driven and rumor-driven and all of the other intangibles and irrationals ... But I would also say that the majority of the foreign exchange trading population is more towards the mish-mash of a bit of economics, of a bit of politics, but then there is an awful lot else that gets involved as well!"

In order to obtain an even better understanding of traders' forecasting styles, their ratings across the various forecasting horizons were cluster-analyzed.[xv] The results showed that traders can be grouped in four main forecasting styles (Figure 4.5).

I have called the first of these forecasting styles, which was used by 43% of the traders, *ascending chartist*. Traders with this style use pronouncedly technical/chartist forecasts for their intraday forecasts. Then, they use progressively more fundamental forecasts on longer time horizons and end up using a highly fundamental forecasting approach for very long-term predictions of longer than one year. The second forecasting style, used by 17% of the traders, was termed *ascending fundamental*. The profile of this forecasting style proceeds parallel to the first group; however, it begins with even more fundamental forecasts for intraday forecasts and ends with an almost exclusively fundamental forecasting approach for periods longer than one year. In other words, the first two forecasting styles both show a linear trend from technical/chartist forecasts for short-term periods to fundamental forecasts for long-term periods. At all forecasting horizons, traders using the ascending fundamental style attach more importance to fundamental analysis than do traders using the ascending chartist style.

[xv] This statistical procedure identified groups of traders with similar forecasting profiles across the various time horizons.

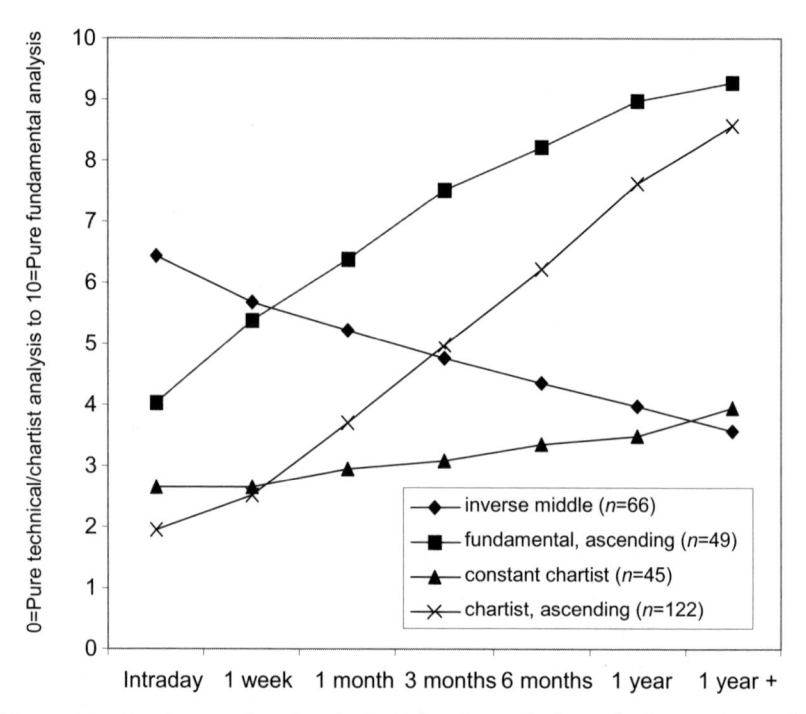

Figure 4.5 Fundamental and technical/chartist analysis: main forecasting styles.

The third style, used by 16% of the traders, was termed *constant chartist*. Traders with this forecasting style clearly use more technical/chartist than fundamental forecasts across all time horizons, and have a tendency to become somewhat more fundamental for longer forecasting periods. The fourth forecasting style was termed *inverse middle*. Used by 23% of the traders, this style reflects a balanced mix of fundamental and technical/chartist forecasts on all forecasting periods. However, unlike the other three styles, this forecasting style begins with slightly more fundamental forecasts for intraday forecasting periods and ends with slightly more technical/chartist forecasts for long-term forecasting periods. These various forecasting profiles across various time horizons among traders shed an even more differentiated light on the use and the importance of fundamental and technical/chartist analysis in the foreign exchange market. Not only do participants move beyond the dichotomy of purely fundamental and purely technical/chartist groups of foreign exchange forecasters, there are also different styles in how participants vary in their use over several forecasting horizons.

As traders vary in the extent to which they include fundamental and technical/chartist elements in their exchange-rate forecasts, the question arises of what the factors are which determine traders' preferences. Detailed analyses have revealed that overall forecasting approaches were not connected to such individual trader characteristics as age, gender, traded foreign exchange instruments, hierarchical position, and whether traders worked in the interbank market or as salespeople. However, trading location turned out to have a significant influence: When traders from the larger trading centers of London and Frankfurt were compared with traders from the smaller trading centers of Zurich and Vienna, results showed that trading location mattered, particularly on shorter forecasting horizons.[xvi] Traders from the larger trading centers had a notably more fundamental overall forecasting approach than traders from small trading centers who had a more technical/chartist overall trading approach.[xvii]

Reasons for these divergences may include such factors as training, cultural differences in what type of information is perceived as important, and different access to information in various trading locations. In the interviews, some market participants observed that the large trading centers (primarily London but also Frankfurt) are closer to the heart of foreign exchange information than smaller trading locations, such as Vienna or Zurich. Whatever the explanation for these differences, these findings clearly show that participants' expectations are not based only on economic information and that, when forming expectations, participants do not process information homogeneously. Thus, a more differentiated understanding of how exchange-rate expectations are formed clarifies why currency forecasters are heterogeneous and why information is interpreted differently by different forecasters.[2,36] As the next section illustrates, precisely such a better understanding of expectations is offered by the psychological concept of attitudes.

[xvi] Professionally relevant forecasting horizons of the majority of foreign exchange traders are considerably shorter than some months. It is on these professionally relevant shorter forecasting horizons that local differences in forecasting approaches were found. The convergence of forecasting approaches on longer trading horizons may therefore be explained by traders' lower exposure to these trading horizons.

[xvii] This difference was also visible when forecasting styles across time were compared for different trading locations. Specifically, the *ascending fundamental* style was over-represented in the relatively larger centers of Frankfurt and London and the *ascending chartist* style in the relatively smaller trading centers of Vienna and Zurich. The *ascending fundamental* style was under-represented in Vienna, whereas it was over-represented in Frankfurt and in London. Conversely, in Frankfurt and in London the *ascending chartist* style was under-represented. In Zurich, the *inverse middle* style was significantly under-represented.

PSYCHOLOGICAL ATTITUDES AND MARKET EXPECTATIONS

This section moves beyond the distinction of technical and fundamental forecasting approaches and demonstrates that expectations in the foreign exchange market can and should be *psychologically* understood as participants' attitudes toward future market events and developments.[xviii]

Shortly after the end of World War II, social psychologists Jerome Bruner and Cecile Goodman studied how subjective values and needs influence seemingly straightforward perceptions by asking 10-year-old kids to estimate the sizes of various objects.[38] The children adjusted the size of a circle of light to the perceived size of cardboard disks and judged the disks correctly. However, when coins were estimated, the children *overestimated* them proportionally to their value; children from a poor background overestimated the sizes of the coins even *more* than did wealthy children. Thus children's attitudes actively influenced their attitudes: to a poor kid, the same coin may have a very different subjective meaning than to a kid raised in an affluent family. While foreign exchange participants may never estimate the size of coins—in fact, the money they trade is reflected only by numbers on screens—they estimate *currencies* when forming expectations and predicting exchange rates. The question arises: Are traders, like the children in the experiment, also influenced by subjective attitudes? To answer this question, we need to explore the link between attitudes and expectations.[xix]

First: Most fundamentally, like attitudes, expectations about exchange rates are not inborn, but *learned*. Likewise, they are not stable, but rather change over time and vary among market participants. Foreign exchange traders learn to form their expectations in their *subjective interaction* with a complex market environment; their expectations change over time, and they differ from the expectations of other traders at any point of time. Foreign exchange expectations are indeed heterogeneous, as, for example, economist Ito has shown.[2] For example, the physical context of trading has a systematic influence on how market participants form expectations. As the previous section, "Fundamental and technical/chartist analysis," has demonstrated, traders use fundamental and technical/chartist forecasting methods to different degrees, depending on where they are geographically located. Even among supposedly homogeneous subgroups, such as traders who clearly follow a chartist forecasting approach, the actual expectations differ considerably.[24]

[xviii] Parts of this section are reworked from material in *Zeitschrift für Sozialpsychologie*, **32**, pp. 180–188, T. Oberlechner (2001), "Evaluation of currencies in the foreign exchange market,"[37] with permission from Verlag Hans Huber.

[xix] The list of aspects linking expectations to attitudes is based on Vanden Abeele.[39]

Second: The October 2003 election of Austrian actor Arnold Schwarzenegger as governor of the state of California refuelled the discussion as to whether violent movies make people more aggressive in real life; many of the movies in which Schwarzenegger has starred, such as *Terminator*, have certainly not been devoid of violent content. Although there is evidence that violent models in films indeed increase a tendency among viewers to resort to aggressive actions in everyday life, psychologists know that the effects of movies on viewers' behavior are mediated by *intervening variables*.[40,41] For example, a person's emotional maturity and the context and the company in which a film is seen influence whether and how movie violence affects aggressive behavior beyond the screen.

Similar to previous attitudes in the information-processing of *Terminator* viewers, the expectations of market participants are also intervening variables that affect trading decisions on all stages, from the way the market is perceived to what trading action is taken.[xx] Attitudes focus attention toward information that confirms what is already believed; they influence how events are interpreted, and affect behavioral reactions.[46,47] Like attitudes, expectations influence whether and how traders transform market information into buying and selling decisions. For example, the subjective expectation of a U.S. dollar appreciation may induce a trader to pay particular attention to speculative news reports about an impending interest-rate cut by the European Central Bank while disregarding information about growing U.S. unemployment figures. Divergent expectations among market participants may lead them to different interpretations of and reactions to identical information. "Two people can take the same bit of analysis and the same bit of news and have totally opposite positions. You can get two spot traders and one might say buy, one might say sell," according to one trader. This aspect of foreign exchange decision-making also contradicts the "black box" models of decisions found in traditional economic models which bypass psychological mechanisms and which assume that information is directly translated into trading behavior. In the words of one foreign exchange trader explaining how trading reactions to news depend on traders' expectations, "You've got confirmation of what my action was supposed to be and then you execute or

---

[xx] A large number of empirical studies which demonstrate that subjective attitudes bias how people process information and news exist.[42–44] For example, psychologist George Katona observed that, "human beings do not react to stimuli as automatons. Their motives and attitudes, even their tastes, hopes, and fears, represent intervening variables that influence both their perception of the environment and their behavior."[45]

you hold back and you don't do anything. But I have never seen a guy being surprised by the news and then go [in] reverse."

Third: Like attitudes, foreign exchange expectations are complex psychological processes that incorporate cognitive, affective, and behavioral elements.[xxi] The *cognitive* aspect of expectations includes a trader's opinions of what will happen in the market. It represents knowledge, perceptions, and judgments which are directed at future facts and events. An example for the cognitive aspect of foreign exchange expectations is a trader's analytic conclusion that concerns about falling exports will lead the European Central Bank to lower interest rates and that consequently the euro will depreciate. The *affective* aspect of foreign exchange expectations expresses personal and emotional evaluations of expected market events (e.g., whether the anticipated euro depreciation is good or bad, and whether it is personally liked or disliked). The high risks involved in trading decisions guarantee strong affective components in the expectations of market participants. As one trader declares, "The biggest mover of all, I would say, is fear in general. You know, people are *afraid* that something is going to happen." Lastly, market participants do not stop short at simply forming and holding expectations, but instead continuously adjust their decisions to their expectations of the future. Thus, expectations play a crucial role in individual trading behavior and in collective market movements; the *behavioral* aspect of foreign exchange expectations causes traders to take action. For example, a trader expecting the European Central Bank to lower interest rates might sell a large euro position in order to avoid the loss that would result from a depreciation of the euro.

The following account of a trader provides a lucid description of the interplay of cognitive, affective, and behavioral elements in foreign exchange expectations: "First of all, you build up your own opinion. Then you look at the fundamental data and rates, if they are also going into the same direction as you think [*cognition*]. If yes, you get more convinced of your opinion [*affect*]. And if then you talk to other guys and if they have the same opinion, you do a deal [*behavior*]."

Fourth: Some of the most attention-grabbing aspects of hypnosis are so-called "post-hypnotic suggestions" (i.e., commands to hypnotized persons to behave in a certain way once the actual hypnosis is finished). For example, a post-hypnotic suggestion might elicit a certain reaction in response to an external signal (e.g., to open a window when the clock strikes two). When people are asked *why* they opened the window, they quickly find a seemingly

---

[xxi] According to the "ABC" tripartite model of attitudes, they consist of an affective, a behavioral, and a cognitive component.[48–50]

reasonable explanation—however, without remembering the suggestion—such as that they suddenly felt warm and needed fresh air. Such external post-hypnotic suggestions are examples of the workings of the unconscious. But while the phenomena they produce are rare and spectacular, one's own subjective expectations subliminally influence decisions and behavior in a more constant way; foreign exchange expectations occupy a broad range from those formed deliberately and to those held without conscious thinking. One trader remarks of the fact that market participants typically cannot give a complete account of their expectations, and of the perceptions and reasoning on which they are based that, "Even information which is not even consciously perceived is information. When you go out and it is 20 degrees below zero for three weeks my experience will tell me that may have an impact on oil prices, and impact on the dollar. But I do not have to *do* this thinking; it will be in me. So, in fact, anything which is happening, me walking in the park with the dog, is a piece of information."

Fifth: Akin to attitudes, the manner of expectation formation also has repetitive and self-reinforcing characteristics. In the foreign exchange market, this repetitive aspect of expectations saves traders the arduous task of constantly having to figure out new ways of how to forecast; being able to rely on a routine process allows them to screen market information and to adjust their expectations more quickly, and to accelerate appropriate reactions. Both unconscious expectations and the more explicit cognitive processes involved in expert forecasting show a considerable automaticity and tendency to become routine.[39,51] Fundamental and technical forecasting approaches are good examples of how market participants use mechanisms that help automatize their expectation formation. They provide market decision-makers with routine mechanisms for forming their expectations, and they offer a set way of selecting and organizing market information and translating it into expectations.

All these characteristics demonstrate that, like attitudes, foreign exchange expectations organize participants' knowledge, evaluations, and behavior toward the future (i.e., toward future exchange rates). The link between expectations and attitudes suggests that expectations can best be explored by traders' *attitudes toward currencies*. Whereas the expectations of participants in the foreign exchange market gather around a variety of economic, political, social, and psychological factors, currencies are always at the heart of the action. However, how can these attitudes best be analyzed?

A classic psychological technique to study attitudes involves using so-called "semantic differentials" (i.e., scales that address potentially meaningful dimensions of an object and that are defined by bipolar adjectives, such as attractive–unattractive).[52,53] With the help of semantic differentials, psychologists have shown that neurotic persons have different attitudes toward loneliness than do others,[54] and that the connotative meaning of the word "anxiety" and of the color grey is nearly identical.[55] Thus, in the European and the North American surveys, I employed such semantic differentials to examine traders' perceptions and attitudes of various currencies. The following are some of the relevant European findings.

At the time the European survey was conducted, the euro had not yet replaced national currencies in the European Union; therefore, traders' pre-euro national home currencies (i.e., the Austrian schilling, the German mark, the Swiss franc, and the British pound), and the U.S. dollar, as the leading foreign exchange currency, were included in the semantic differential assessments.[xxii] These currencies were rated by traders on the following scales:

Good	1	2	3	4	5	6	Bad
Stable	1	2	3	4	5	6	Unstable
Unimportant	1	2	3	4	5	6	Important
Fast	1	2	3	4	5	6	Slow
Weak	1	2	3	4	5	6	Strong
Optimistic	1	2	3	4	5	6	Pessimistic
Passive	1	2	3	4	5	6	Active
Successful	1	2	3	4	5	6	Unsuccessful
Complex	1	2	3	4	5	6	Simple

A comparison of ratings by traders in different trading locations resulted in striking findings. For example, take the "polarity profiles" of the U.S. dollar which are based on averaged ratings of traders from various trading locations (Figure 4.6).

As the figure shows, the U.S. dollar was rated extremely homogeneously; on all nine scales, no differences between trader subgroups from Austria, Germany, Switzerland, and the U.K. were found. However, results look different for the European currencies, where the "home currency" is involved for parts of the European traders. As Figures 4.7 and 4.8 show, the trading location had a considerable influence on the ratings of these currencies.

Figures 4.7 and 4.8 demonstrate that Austrian traders rated the schilling significantly better than traders from other trading locations and that Swiss traders rated the franc significantly better than traders from other trading

---

[xxii] While such currencies as the Austrian schilling and the German mark no longer exist as national currencies, this development does not impact the psychological relevance of these findings.

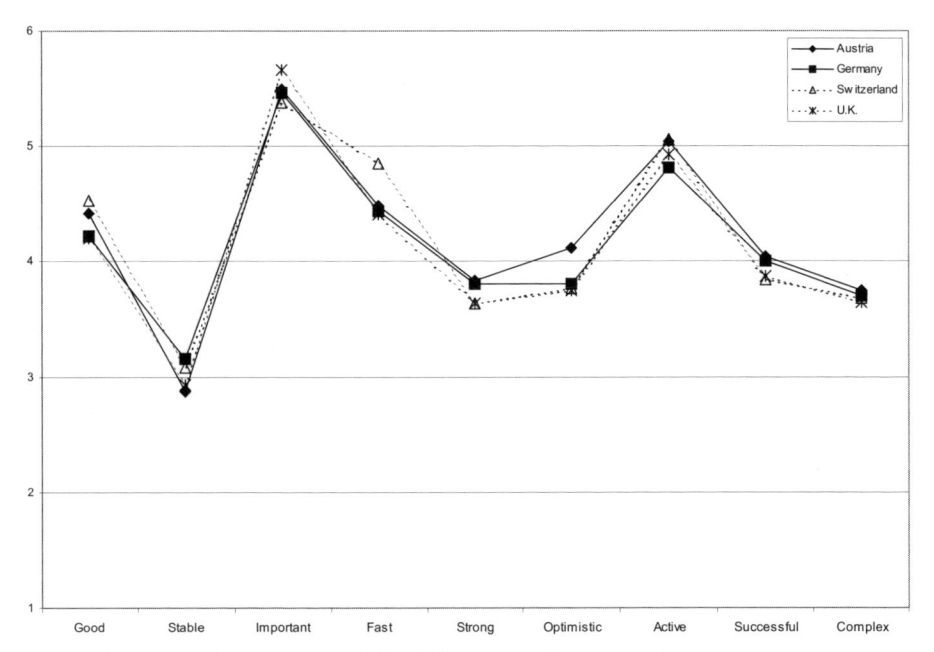

Expectations in the Foreign Exchange Market 113

Figure 4.6 Perception profile of the U.S. dollar: 1 = Negative perception; 6 = Positive perception.

locations.[xxiii] In fact, each of the European currencies was rated differently by the traders who rated their *home currency*; whenever the currency of an in-group was involved, conspicuous differences were present. In stark contrast, the U.S. dollar, likewise an external currency, was rated highly homogeneously by various geographic groups of traders in Europe. Thus, the perceptions of currencies were consistently characterized by systematic disparities between domestic and non-domestic traders.

A socio-psychological explanation for these differences is offered by the social identity theory of inter-group relations.[56-60] This theory assumes that people obtain *social identity* from their membership in groups. According to social identity theory, such group categories as nationality provide important self-definitions to people's identity. Moreover, a social and cognitive

---

[xxiii] Austrian traders rated the schilling as better, more stable, more important, faster, stronger, more optimistic, more active, more successful, and more complex than did other traders. Swiss traders rated the franc as better, more stable, more important, faster, stronger, more optimistic, more active, and more successful than did other traders.

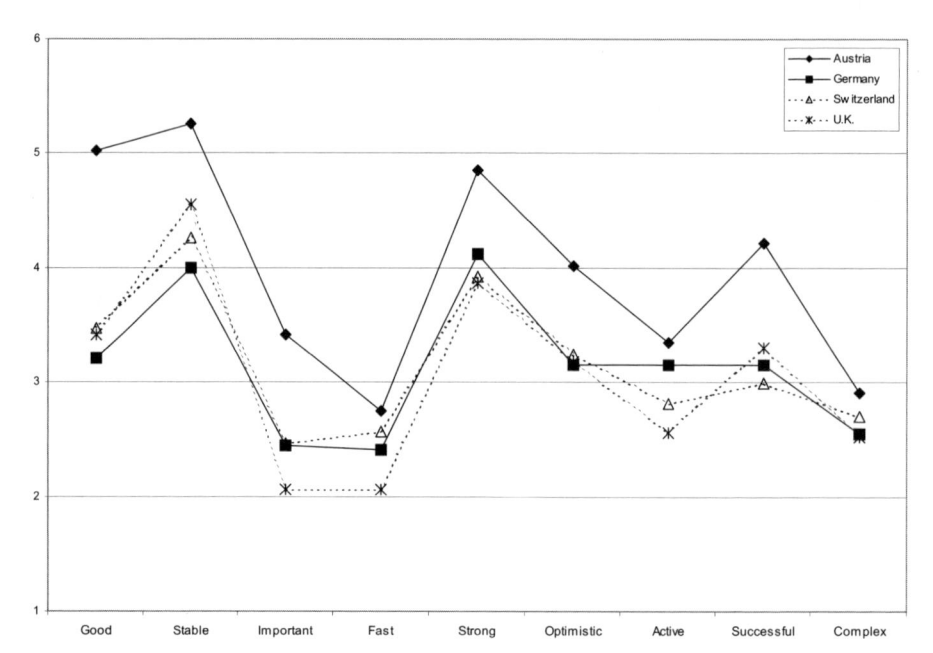

Figure 4.7 Perception profile of the Austrian schilling: 1 = Negative perception; 6 = Positive perception.

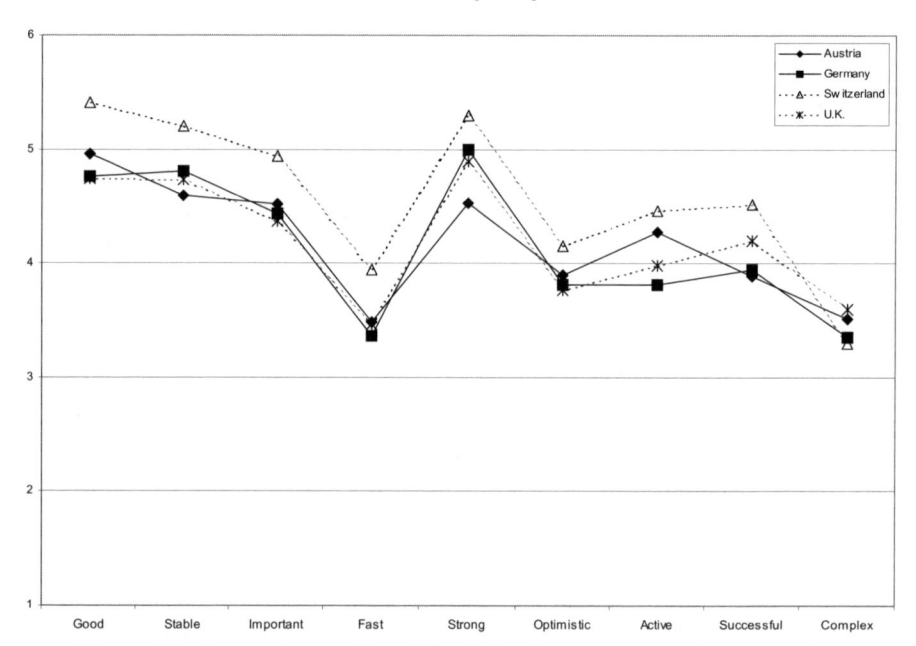

Figure 4.8 Perception profile of the Swiss franc: 1 = Negative perception; 6 = Positive perception.

self-enhancement process is centrally involved when people form social identity; this process expresses the human need for positive self-evaluations. However, what happens when groups and self-enhancement are important to people's identity?

Self-enhancement may lead people to introduce *differences* in their comparisons between the in-group and out-groups, and to evaluations that *favor* the in-group at the expense of out-groups. In other words, favorable comparisons help people achieve a positive social identity.[61–63] For instance, the need for social identity and positive self-evaluations can be witnessed in conflicts between groups. This need can lead to out-group bias even in the absence of external causes.[64] Thus, in the foreign exchange market, national identity influences attitudes toward currencies,[65] and social identity theory helps explain the home bias in traders' attitudes.[xxiv]

When the ratings of all currencies were factor-analyzed, the outcomes revealed three fundamental dimensions on which traders perceive currencies. These factors are *currency evaluation* (this aspect is determined by how good, stable, optimistic, and successful a currency is perceived), *currency potency* (determined by how important and how active a currency is perceived), and *currency activity* (determined by how fast and complex a currency is perceived). In other words, the traders differentiated between the psychological aspects of how good (currency evaluation), how strong (currency potency), and how active (currency activity) they consider a currency. Traders used these three factors very homogeneously: For each single currency, traders' ratings showed the same underlying three factors and, across the various currencies, the same aspects contributed to each of the factors.

The semantic differential technique has yielded these three factors of *evaluation, potency*, and *activity* in numerous studies on a variety of topics. From a psychological perspective, it is important that these factors do not only refer to merely theoretical and semantic phenomena, but that, on the contrary, they capture the essential underlying dimensions of people's experience. For example, the factor evaluation addresses such questions as: Is the rated object good or bad for me? Should I strive to attain it or keep at a safe distance?[74] It is easy to imagine that such questions also play a central role in the expectations of foreign exchange participants when deciding on which

---

[xxiv] For traders from Germany and the U.K., the tendency to evaluate their home currency differently was less marked and not consistently positive. Why could this be? Different degrees of national identification of traders from various trading locations could be involved, as favoring national products is positively correlated with national identification.[66,67] The differences might also relate to traders' self-esteem[68–73] or to national political factors that influence traders' views of their home currency.

currencies to buy and which ones to sell. Foreign exchange traders then have different expectations not only because they interpret information differently,[xxv] but also because they hold different *attitudes* toward currencies.

Along with the semantic differential ratings of currencies, 288 traders ranked the likelihood of various scenarios of exchange-rate developments. Two relevant scenarios described the expectation of a Swiss franc appreciation and of a U.S. dollar appreciation. Of these two scenarios, 60.4% of traders rated the U.S. dollar appreciation as more likely, 29.2% rated the Swiss franc appreciation as more likely, and 10.4% assigned equal likelihood to the two future scenarios.

A comparison of expectations with traders' attitudes toward the dollar and the franc shows that expectations are systematically related to underlying attitudes. Traders who expect the Swiss franc appreciation to be more likely hold significantly more positive attitudes toward the Swiss franc in the *evaluation, potency*, and *activity* dimension than do other traders. Similarly, traders who expect the U.S. dollar appreciation scenario to be more likely hold significantly more positive attitudes toward the U.S. dollar in the *evaluation* dimension than do other traders. There is thus a marked relationship between market participants' *attitudes* toward currencies and their *expectations* of market developments. Positive attitudes toward a currency correlated significantly with expectations that the currency will appreciate; in other words, traders' *subjective* attitudes and evaluations have an effect on how traders forecast the market.[75] Moreover, evidence of home bias among foreign exchange traders shows that psychological processes influence the perceptions and attitudes, and that this influence persists on the level of large groups of market participants.

By no means are these results restricted to traders in Europe. In the North American survey, I asked traders to forecast a variety of actual exchange rates on various time horizons. Their answers underscore the extent to which exchange-rate expectations are influenced by subjective attitudes. For example, there is a strong correlation between traders' forecasts of the euro–dollar rate, and their attitudes toward the euro and the U.S. dollar: Traders who perceive the euro more favorably as compared to the U.S. dollar are also more likely to predict higher exchange rates of the euro, and vice versa. Moreover, the data from the North American survey confirm that such subjective factors as trading location influence attitudes toward and exchange-rate expectations of traders' home currencies. In comparison with traders in the U.S., the Canadian traders in the North American survey expect the Canadian

---

[xxv] See MacDonald and Marsh.[36]

dollar to appreciate against the U.S. dollar almost *twice* as much over the medium term and almost *three times* as much over the long term!

Psychology offers a convincing explanation why the influence of subjective attitudes on exchange rate expectations is so powerful. Attitudes are even more likely to influence decisions that are made under time pressure and when information is ambiguous.[76] As Chapter 2, "Psychology of Trading Decisions," has shown, currency trading takes place in an environment that is not only highly stressful but also extremely uncertain. Thus, the decisions of traders are influenced by psychological attitudes not in a peripheral way, but *decisively*.

SOCIAL DYNAMICS, META-EXPECTATIONS, AND THE FINANCIAL NEWS MEDIA

Asked how expectations about future exchange rates are actually formed, one trader replies that, "You talk to guys, you take their opinion, and you give your opinion. There is a selection of opinions in the market; of friends of yours, of other institutions and companies, and this helps you to form your [own] opinion." Another trader agrees, remarking, "People tend to talk to their colleagues, and they talk to people in the market at institutions that they know and have respected for a while." These answers tellingly illustrate that, like trading decisions, the expectations of foreign exchange traders are also not merely detached creations formed by isolated individuals. Instead, they result from the dynamic interplay among market participants who are influenced by *others*, and who influence others in return.

Accounts of market participants abound with examples of social dynamics in foreign exchange expectations. These examples demonstrate that social factors play an important role on a variety of levels. For instance, many traders observe that the opinions of colleagues influence expectations, and that these expectations are particularly affected by supposedly well-informed others. "People are very susceptible to a good idea from somebody who is considered to be in the know," one trader notes. Considerations about the social impact of others also determine which market news are selected for forming expectations. "If a piece of news written by somebody who has credence in the market or somebody who we know is followed by certain big funds ... we are interested to hear what he has got to say, because what he has got to say will influence certain people who will influence the market," another trader explains.

Another instance of the dynamics of expectations which is not simply information-based, but also social in nature, can be found in the division of work in how institutional market players develop market expectations and translate them into trading decisions. In-house economics departments and trading floor economists at banks regularly establish market scenarios and probable market developments. These projections allow traders to focus on comparisons of these pre-formulated expectations with the online news and to immediately act on any differences between expectations and market news. "You can mentally prepare yourself so you are much faster when the figure [i.e., economic release] actually comes out," one trader observes forthrightly. Thus, the theories of market economists have a decisive influence on the expectations of the traders and may force the traders to suddenly change their expectations. "Sometimes these economic forecasts will change during the course of the week ... before a big number like non-farm payrolls. And, all of a sudden, for some bizarre reason, some economist comes up with some quirky idea that everyone thinks is cute. Then the expectation of that non-farm payroll will climb or fall during the week. Then everyone else is scrambling to make sure they have positioned themselves to ensure that they are in the right way," a financial journalist remarks.[xxvi] However, the influence of economists on the expectations of traders varies and is subject to personal estimation. In the words of another trader, "There is a massive difference in quality between those guys. I mean I'm not an economist, but I could do at least as good a job as some of them ... Some banks have good economists and those economists are in demand. The bulk of them are nothing special very much, really!"

Thus, foreign exchange expectations result from a social dynamic rather than from a reflection of "objective" information about an outside world, which takes place separately from those forming expectations. One important consequence of the social nature of expectations is that they can be actively influenced and manipulated by market participants. Reflecting on just such a costly trading experience, one trader recounts, "A Swedish bank right in the forefront of Swedish krona trading called me up a couple of weeks ago. I want to know what these guys have got to say; I really want to know what they say, what their clients are doing. I am probably going to take a position based on the back of it. He called me up and gave me a whole story about why we should be doing such and such. And I said, 'Fine, OK, let's do it, I will do it.' And it then turned out, five minutes later, that he was doing exactly the opposite in the

---

[xxvi] These observations also underscore the importance of the anchoring and adjustment heuristic which is discussed in Chapter 2, "Psychology of Trading Decisions."

market. He was using everybody to get his position on, and the thing just collapsed. He made a fortune, we all lost money!"

Numerous traders observe that powerful market participants can drive the foreign exchange market, at least in the short term, by influencing the expectations of a large group of other market participants. This influence depends on how significant and credible a market player is perceived to be, the player's supposed own interests, and the player's closeness to important information sources. "I think for us it's quite easy to influence the market on a Thursday morning before the Bundesbank has a meeting, to tell the people what we think and what we expect, because the market anticipates that we as one of the big three German banks know a little bit more behind the scenes," one trader observes frankly. Leading banks are perceived of as more credible and informed than other banks and may move the market temporarily by merely inquiring about a currency. "We were number one in the world and we were killing people ... by frightening them. If the market is 28/30 and you feel it has to go up, and you call out [i.e., ask for a price on which you can deal] different banks, and they all make you 29/31 ... that means that they either think that you are a buyer or they ... want to get some from you. And if you pay those people at 31 or 32, they say 'Bloody hell, this guy is paying me [i.e., buying from me] above the market and it is paid everywhere [i.e., everyone else is buying as well].' Then they start to get frightened, then they don't know what's going on really, they anticipate again, 'What does this guy know?'" another trader says bluntly.

These observations demonstrate how the sellers and buyers of currencies play on each others' expectations. In a market known to be driven by expectations, to know the expectations of others is vital. Exchange-rate expectations are then directed not at an objective economic future, but at what others might know about the future (i.e., how others perceive and evaluate the future). Many traders observe in the interviews that their anticipations of what other market participants will think and how they will react are crucial to their own expectations and decisions. Such attempts to base one's own expectations on the presumed expectations of others are called *meta-expectations*; these expectations about other market participants' expectations occupy a considerable standing in today's market. "Nowadays, I think people are more focusing on the expectation of people's expectations," declares one trader.

Second-order and higher order expectations in financial markets are already addressed in Keynes' famous metaphor of the markets as a beauty contest. In this metaphor, investing is compared:

> to those newspaper competitions in which the competitors have to pick out the six prettiest faces from a hundred photographs, the prize

being awarded to the competitor whose choice most nearly corresponds to the average preferences of the competitors as a whole; so that each competitor has to pick, not those faces which he himself finds prettiest, but those which he thinks likeliest to catch the fancy of the other competitors, all of whom are looking at the problem from the same point of view. It is not a case of choosing those which, to the best of one's judgment, are really the prettiest, nor even those which average opinion genuinely thinks the prettiest. We have reached the third degree where we devote our intelligences to anticipating what average opinion expects the average opinion to be. And there are some, I believe, who practice the fourth, fifth and higher degrees.[77]

The analogy of the beauty contest suggests that what ends up happening in financial markets is the result of market participants' *beliefs* and *expectations* about other market participants' beliefs and expectations.[78,79] Some traders' observations that they need to decide according to how they feel the market would behave, rather than according to what they *personally* thought was right, fit in nicely with the story of the beauty contest. Other foreign exchange traders assert that, "It is important that more than half of the market participants think as you do." They assert that, as a trader, "You have to behave according to how you feel the market will behave mostly—not [to] what is right or wrong," and, "You have to think not only what is right, but also what the market thinks is right." These statements illustrate how the expectations of foreign exchange market participants attempt to anticipate future expectations and decisions of other participants. Such meta-expectations are psychological, rather than economic, in nature, as one trader observes, "Because we are all human beings working in [the foreign exchange] market, the psychology of the market participants plays a very, very big role!"

Good trading decisions, as voiced by a trader in the interviews, are then characterized as the ability to correctly anticipate the overall market reaction to news. However, when market participants collectively integrate their expectations of external market developments into current exchange-rate prices, to individual traders, the possibilities of profiting from integrating an identical expectation into their trades are reduced or may even be forfeited. This makes it necessary to develop entirely new kinds of profit strategies. As one trader observes, "[As] soon as everyone expects the same thing, it becomes null and void. Shall we say economic data in the U.S., if we were expecting good figures, then prior to the event the good figure is priced into the market already. You can't always trade on expectations because everyone is really expecting the same thing; you have to be a bit cleverer than that I think!" Many traders indicate that these more advanced strategies were based on a qualitatively different level of expectations. The focus of these expectations goes beyond external market events and instead is on *other market participants* (i.e., on the trading positions of participants and consequently on their likely behavior once the anticipated external event has taken place).

One trader expounds on how the foreign exchange market developed from focusing on economic information, to expectations about economic information, to expectations and meta-expectations about other market participants, saying, "We used to wait for economic data with anticipation. And the economic data came out, 'Oh, that's not very good!' or, 'That's good!' Then ... we were not anticipating if the economic data was actually good or bad in itself, it was then whether it was good or bad *against expectations*, so there is a shift already. Now the shift is, 'I don't care if the economy is good or bad. I don't care what the expectations were. [What I care about is] were people long or short because *they were expecting something*.'" Another trader provides an example for the last stage of this development, remarking, "The market now reacts to *how the market is positioned*, for example, if the vast majority of the players in the market had bought dollars on the expectation of a very good U.S. unemployment number. Friday was another classic example. We saw a fantastic U.S. number, rationally the market should fly, [however] it [only] went up 10 pips and then collapsed. Now that's an irrational thing, but it was simply because everybody had bought dollars on the expectation that it would move up so that they could [then] sell it. Now as soon as the market got the number, everybody started offering their dollars into the market. Suddenly there were no buyers because they already had bought, so everybody said, 'Well, I got to get out of this, this thing is just going to collapse,' and it did. That was sort of an irrational move to something that was a very bullish number. [The market] does move irrationally because it is now much more dependent on how the market is positioned rather than on a rational expectation or a rational reaction to a piece of economic news!"

For market expectations, traders describe that the media's role is twofold. First, the information provided by the media forms a backdrop for the formation of expectations among the trading participants. Second, news then either confirms or rejects these previously formed expectations. Consequently, a continuous expectation-formation and re-examination loop emerges in which the media plays the central role. In the apt words of one financial journalist, "Foreign exchange markets trade off financial, economic, and political developments which financial news media report to them. So they need the media—they [i.e., the media] are sort of the fuel in the engine!"

However, contradicting the naive assumption that the financial news media simply reflect the expectations of market participants, some traders observed in the interviews that the media plays an active role in shaping market expectations. For example, fierce competition between news providers influences their attempts to capture the attention of other market participants. The news media's own interest to reach as large a market audience as possible may lead them to focus on attention-grabbing news with word-of-mouth potential.[31] In the words of one trader, "They will filter their information according to their wishes. It cannot be absolutely wrong information, but it can be a sort of squeezing a little bit out of it, to draw more attention to a certain fact ... [For example,] with a final intention to move markets, they announce figures or numbers in a certain row. They first announce the bad news so everybody jumps on the bad news, and then come the good news. Or vice versa, first the good news—'Oh, fine!'—and then, 'wham!' the bad news. That is certainly a way to squeeze the markets."

The financial news media have *always* played a vital role in shaping the expectations of market participants; expectations are fuelled less by objective facts than by how these facts are presented. To give some examples, the financial news media affect market expectations by selecting, highlighting, repeating, and interpreting information and news. The order in which news is presented, the wording of a headline, the timing, and the format in which information is presented, can be decisive for market expectations.[80,xxvii] Also, the location in which news is presented and received may determine market expectations: "Facts where European markets remain calm can excite the East Asian market or the other way around," one trader observes. Moreover, the financial news media also influence the expectations of trading decision-makers in less obvious ways. One of the media's functions is to provide causal attributions for past market events and explain the reasons exchange rates have changed. When doing so, the press usually formulates its stories by explaining recent developments with good news and information after prices have gone up, and with bad news and information after prices have gone down.[82] Once such seemingly appropriate attributions are offered, market participants

---

[xxvii] For example, one study found that presentations by the *Washington Post* led to more accurate expectations of short-term future unemployment than news coverage by CBS television or the *Wall Street Journal*, which may be explained by the length and the ambiguity of the latter reports.[81]

become less likely to be regressive and more extrapolative in their predictions; in other words, they expect that recent changes remain in place or even carry on, and they do not suppose that the current trend may turn around.[1] Another psychological market dynamic, in which the news media play an important role, is rumors, as Chapter 5 illustrates.

ABBREVIATED REFERENCES

See the reference chapter at the end of the book for full details.

1. Katona, G. (1972)
2. Ito, T. (1990)
3. Anderson, M. A. and Goldsmith, A. H. (1994a)
4. Olsen, R. A. (1997)
5. Hogarth, R. (1981)
6. Kelly, G. A. (1955)
7. Frenkel, J. A. (1981)
8. Frankel, J. A. and Froot, K. A. (1990a)
9. Frankel, J. A. and Froot, K. A. (1986)
10. Oberlechner, T. (2001b)
11. Gotthelf, P. (2003)
12. Neely, C. J. (1997)
13. Pring, M. J. (1991)
14. Chang, P. H. K. and Osler, C. L. (1999)
15. Black, F. (1986)
16. Shleifer, A. and Summers, L. H. (1990)
17. Menkhoff, L. (1998)
18. Frankel, J. A. and Froot, K. A. (1990b)
19. Harvey, J. T. (1996)
20. MacDonald, R. and Taylor, M. P. (1992)
21. Levin, J. H. (1997)
22. Vigfusson, R. (1997)
23. Goodhart, C. (1988)
24. Allen, H. and Taylor, M. P. (1990)
25. Taylor, M. P. and Allen, H. (1992)
26. Lui, Y.-H. and Mole, D. (1998)
27. Menkhoff, L. (1997)
28. Merton, R. (1948)
29. Watzlawick, P. (1984)
30. Shiller, R. J. (1989)
31. Shiller, R. J. (2000)
32. Shiller, R. J. and Pound, J. (1989)
33. Soros, G. (1987)
34. Soros, G. (1994)
35. Cheung, Y. W. et al. (1999)

36 MacDonald, R. and Marsh, I. W. (1996)
37 Oberlechner, T. (2001a)
38 Bruner, J. S. and Goodman, C. C. (1947)
39 Vanden Abeele, P. (1988)
40 Buvinic, M. L. and Berkowitz, L. (1976)
41 Berkowitz, L. (1986)
42 Biek, M. et al. (1996)
43 Broemer, P. (1998)
44 Eagly, A. H. (1998)
45 Katona, G. (1975)
46 Fazio, R. H. (1986)
47 Fazio, R. H. and Towles-Schwen, T. (1999)
48 Bagozzi, R. P. (1978)
49 Breckler, S. J. (1984)
50 Ostrom, T. M. (1969)
51 Evans, J. S. B. T. (1987)
52 Osgood, C. E. (1952)
53 Osgood, C. E. et al. (1957)
54 Czernik, A. and Steinmeyer, E. (1974)
55 Hofstaetter, P. R. (1956)
56 Tajfel, H. and Turner, J. C. (1979)
57 Tajfel, H. (1974)
58 Tajfel, H. and Turner, J. C. (1986)
59 Turner, J. C. (1985)
60 Turner, J. C. (1982)
61 Hogg, M. A. and Abrams, D. (1988)
62 Hogg, M. A. et al. (1995)
63 Wagner, U. and Zick, A. (1990)
64 Brown, R. (2000)
65 Meier-Pesti, K. and Kirchler, E. (2003)
66 Feather, N. T. (1996)
67 Feather, N. T. (1994)
68 Abrams, D. and Hogg, M. A. (1988)
69 Blanz, M. et al. (1995)
70 Hogg, M. A. and Sunderland, J. (1991)
71 Hunter, J. A. et al. (1993)
72 Crocker, J. et al. (1987)
73 Long, K. M. et al. (1994)
74 Herkner, W. (1983)
75 Antonides, G. and van der Sar, N. L. (1990)
76 Liberman, A. et al. (1988)
77 Keynes, J. M. (1936)
78 Allen, F. et al. (2002)
79 Morris, S. and Shin, H. S. (1998)
80 Van Raaij, W. F. (1989)
81 Pruitt, S. W. et al. (1988)
82 Andreassen, P. B. (1987)

5
News and Rumors

> *We are now a business of information. Information is more important than money. Our job is to translate information to money.*
>
> Foreign exchange trader

The quote above suggests that, similar to medieval alchemists who attempted to create gold from other elements, foreign exchange traders attempt to use information to make money.[i] Indeed, every trading day, a vast network of sources provides market participants around the globe with a plethora of potentially relevant information. To note a prominent example, *Reuters*, one of the oldest and largest international information providers, daily publishes around 30 *thousand* news headlines and more than 8 *million* words of news in 19 languages across the world.[ii] An ever-broader spectrum of public news media ranges from the daily press (such as the British *Financial Times*, the U.S. *Wall Street Journal*, the Japanese *Nihon Keizai Shimbun*, the Swiss *Neue Zürcher Zeitung*, and the German *Handelsblatt*), to financial television channels, covering the markets 24 hours a day (like CNBC and Bloomberg Television), to online financial newswire services, such as Dow Jones Newswires, Reuters, Bloomberg, and Moneyline Telerate, which broadcast news to traders' desks, via their news and computer screens. In addition to publicly available news, traders receive vital information from private sources

---

[i] Parts of this chapter are reworked from material in *Journal of Economic Psychology*, **25**(3), pp. 407–424, T. Oberlechner and S. Hocking (2004), "Information, sources, news and rumors in financial markets: Insights into the foreign exchange market," 2004, with permission from Elsevier.

[ii] This information is taken from the Reuters homepage: http:/about.reuters.com/aboutus/overview/facts/index.asp

such as their bank's proprietary information system and their network of personal market contact.

The characteristics of news provided by these sources differ greatly. For example, while important market information may be predictably released (e.g., periodic official reports about inflation, employment, trade figures, and money supply), it may also arrive at unanticipated points of time (e.g., news about a political crisis or a large currency transaction of an international company). Relevant market information may range from the immediate, specific, and short-lived headline flashing up on a news monitor, to background analyses of long-term market developments, such as an article in the *Economist* magazine giving an overview of the Asian economy's progress.

All this news adds to a gigantic universe of information that is potentially relevant to exchange rates. "You have an enormous overflow of information," one trader remarks of the sheer amount of available market information. Consequently, as another trader aptly adds, "It is hard to filter out what is really important." Whereas traditional economic models simply assume that participants base their decisions on a full and unbiased analysis of *all* available information, no matter what its source and its characteristics are,[iii] psychologists and foreign exchange professionals alike emphasize that these models far from represent how information is *actually* perceived and processed. "It's a personal thing of what suits you," says one trader to explain his selection of financial analysts' reports, "Another person would throw away the one I read and would keep the one I throw away!" Another trader admits candidly, "I actually tend to dismiss 99% of the information that comes out, even if it's considered important!" *How* then do traders select on which information and news to base their decisions?

As this chapter demonstrates, in today's foreign exchange market, *speed* is decisive; the importance of speed surfaces both in traders' views of valuable information and in the type of information provider most relevant to the market (i.e., the wire news services). For speed, the wire news media are indispensable to market participants as they disseminate real-time news and information to those who trade and invest in currencies. Moreover, as the connection between the onset of speculative market bubbles (the Dutch tulip mania in the 1630s) to the introduction of newspapers shows,[2] the news media have played, and continue to play, a highly active role in the dynamics of trading—despite all their efforts to appear as impartial market observers. "All these media move the market by releasing information in one or

---

[iii] The efficient markets hypothesis postulates that market prices (e.g., exchange rates) fully reflect the available information, see Chapter 2, "Psychology of Trading Decisions."

another way," as one trader observes. "They are disseminating anything they know, and they *want* to move the market by telling us," another trader adds. Thus, one vital aspect of the market usually neglected by academic models is the *relationship between the trading participants and the financial news providers.* This chapter also shows that technological developments have changed not only the speed and the nature of reporting but also the very role of the financial news media in the foreign exchange market. These changes help explain the sustained importance of a vital type of market information: *rumors.*

CHARACTERISTICS OF IMPORTANT INFORMATION

I guess speed is everything in this market.

Foreign exchange trader

Good foreign exchange decisions are based on few facts and a good analysis, traders say, and the avalanche of trading information at the fingertips of market participants needs to somehow be reduced. "If you really want to absorb all this news, you can't deal, you have to read the whole day," one trader summarizes his experience of this dilemma in which more information does not necessarily mean better decisions. On the contrary: "The more news you get, the more you are uncertain of what to do ... and you might lose more than you get from it," another trader observes, while yet another wisely adds that, "If you read too much ... you end up confusing yourself and you don't take positions. And *that*'s the danger of over-reading."

As electronic real-time news providers send bits of disconnected information in the form of headlines and news flashes, market events have been covered faster and faster but with less and less simultaneous analysis. Today, traders are often trading more frequently than before, while at the same time having to sort through even more information,[iv] and they know more things more quickly but they do so also more superficially. "The market became quicker and quicker during past years," one trader observes. Similarly, another trader feels strongly that, "No dealer can work all these figures which are coming out ... you can't watch all these figures because sometimes you *have* to deal!"

While market participants thus need to *select and reduce* available information, there are no explicit guidelines on choosing information, and there is no

---

[iv] Mitchell and Mulherin found a steady increase in the average daily news announcements sent out by Dow Jones newswire from 1983 to 1990 and a direct relationship between the number of news announcements and trading activity in the stock market.[3]

Table 5.1 News characteristics important to foreign exchange traders ($n = 267$)

News item characteristic	Mean	Standard deviation
Available to me before it is to others	1.34	0.62
Will influence market participants	1.49	0.59
Unanticipated by the foreign exchange market	1.57	0.71
Contradicts an expectation of the foreign exchange market	1.63	0.71
Reported by a reliable source	1.75	0.70
Seems accurate to me	1.85	0.65
Confirms my feeling or intuition of a market trend	1.99	0.71
Appears in the midst of a volatile market	2.01	0.76
Unanticipated by me	2.03	0.73
Confirms my rational analysis of a market trend	2.11	0.70
Appears after a long period of stability in the market	2.17	0.80
Confirms an expectation of the foreign exchange market	2.26	0.76
Confirms an expert's analysis of the market	2.48	0.76

Scale: 1 = Very important; 2 = Important; 3 = Less important; 4 = Unimportant.

fixed system of how news needs to be filtered. Traders stress that ultimately every trader needs to develop a personal system of filtering news. "What is interesting and what is not interesting, what will affect a currency and what will not affect a currency, this is still a trader's decision," one trader explains. Thus, to find out more about the subjective criteria traders use to determine important news, the European survey asked traders to rate a number of information characteristics according to the importance for their trading decisions.

Table 5.1 shows that, above all, foreign exchange traders assess the importance of news according to a criterion of comparative *speed*. News that is personally available to traders before it is to other market participants is considered most important. "The first thing is, it has to be very fast," one trader explains in the interviews regarding the kind of information he considers. "Something of ten seconds ago is history and is of no relevance. It's quite good to know why something happened ... [but] to me there is no relevance. Because we have got to work out what is going to move next," another trader observes. Yet another trader adds of the time pressure that he is under, "I don't have time to listen to the explanations why GDP grew only blah, blah, blah. I don't have time!" Findings in the economic literature, showing that exchange rates adjust as fast as during the first minute of scheduled news releases (e.g., employment reports and releases of the consumer price index), corroborate the opinion of traders that speed decides the importance of foreign exchange news.[4]

However, it is not speed alone that determines the perceived importance of news; just about equally important is the expected *impact* on other market participants. The following account of a trader exemplifies the necessary interplay between speed and market impact in important news. "We had a rumor last week, I had [the financial newswire service] Knight Ridder on. Knight Ridder has the story—mine, mine, mine, mine, mine. [However], it [i.e., the exchange rate] is not moving. Why not? Because nobody else has Knight Ridder on, only us. What's that good for, if you are the only guy that has Knight Ridder on?" Thus, without market impact even the fastest news is irrelevant. "It's no point knowing that this jobs report is really strong or knowing this rumor if nobody else in the market knows and *they* are not moving!" a savvy financial journalist remarks, confirming this analysis.

The potential to surprise the market (i.e., news that is *unanticipated* and *contradicts* existing market expectations) is an important aspect of high-impact news; traders rate news that contradicts expectations as significantly more important than news that confirms them. "If the market expects completely something else, and then suddenly someone is coming up with certain information, it can cause dramatic movements," one trader notes.

Unanticipated news that contradicts shared expectations is important precisely because market participants discount existing expectations of the future in their present buying and selling decisions, as Chapter 4, "Expectations in the Foreign Exchange Market," has shown. Market participants thus create an anticipatory market reality that includes expectations about the future in the market's present time. Economic studies have shown, for example, that the news impact of a trade deficit figure depends on previous market expectations; an expected deficit may leave exchange rates completely unaffected.[5] Also, while interest-rate news may be relatively unimportant by itself, *revisions* of expectations about future exchange-rate levels are central to unexpected exchange-rate movements.[6] Similarly, reports of unanticipated rises in U.S. employment data strengthen the dollar.[7] This preemptive integration of future expectations explains why traders perceive news that contradicts, rather than confirms, market expectations as decisive.

Intriguingly, traders do not consider the truth and accuracy of news to be very important characteristics of news; the reliability of the news source and the perceived accuracy of news are far *less* important than information speed, expected market impact, and anticipated market surprise. Foreign exchange traders explain that market participants simply do not have the time to check the accuracy of news: "When a piece of news comes out and it is very bullish, we don't say, 'Wait a second—that may be wrong,' because meanwhile the rest of the world is buying it," explains one trader. Moreover, traders work on the assumption that other market participants will be equally affected by a given piece of news, regardless of its accuracy. Because the others are known to "just assume the news is correct," it is necessary to also decide personally as though a piece of news were correct, and not to question it. In the words of one foreign exchange trader, "It doesn't matter to me if it's really right or not. I have to take action on that because the market is doing [it], because the market knows that there is something going on, and everyone will prepare his position to be safe."

When traders' importance ratings of news characteristics were factor-analyzed, four main aspects which traders use to identify important news emerged: *timing, market influence,* and *surprise* require no further explanation. But how can *confirmation* determine the information selection of traders who, after all, rate information that *contradicts* market expectations as far more important than information that confirms these expectations? "It is the theory which determines what I perceive," Albert Einstein once remarked about physics. Likewise, participants in the foreign exchange market are not immune to the human tendency to integrate incoming news with existing personal attitudes and beliefs.[8,9] In fact, here the influence of subjective assumptions on interpreting market news may be especially strong: in the words of traders, one piece of foreign exchange news regularly "can be interpreted in more than one way," and therefore situations exist where "two contradictory pieces of news is actually good because at least it gives you an argument for one side, whichever you believe in!"

Subjective attitudes and beliefs thus serve as filters that distort the perception of new information in the direction of existing personal expectations. Consequently, news that contradicts existing attitudes and beliefs is considered *less* important and may more likely be disregarded and distorted. A trader typifies this kind of situation: "The major conflict arises between your view and the direction of the market. If you think interest rates are going lower, and the markets are actually going in there and messily borrowing, then that's a major conflict. So in your decision-making there are cases where you assume that it is just a volatility of the market and that—in a slightly longer period of time—it is going to go in your direction." This may even lead to the end result that news does not cause traders to change their perceptions and expectations, but conversely that existing perceptions and expectations determine the way information is perceived.[10] Such "confirmation bias" or "belief bias" may lead traders to rely on redundant information and to neglect contradictory data.[11,12] This is suggested by traders' comments on the importance of news that fits pre-held subjective expectations and beliefs: "If it fits to your position, or maybe to your expectations, then it's OK." In the case of conflicting news, traders then simply follow the news that is "best in their position" and filter out news that does not meet personal expectations.

FROM NEWS SOURCES TO INFORMATION LOOPS

> The appetite for information and the money they have is not matched anywhere else.
>
> Financial journalist

While the previous section has analyzed the characteristics of information important to traders, our understanding of how information and news are processed in the foreign exchange world would be incomplete without considering the actual information *sources*. Market participants have at their disposal numerous market information sources from global news services, to the economic reports of market analysts, to casual conversations with colleagues. Because of time and attention constraints, traders cannot make equal use of all these sources; instead, they weigh their importance and focus on some while disregarding others. "You are going to have so much information coming in you can't filter, so you become selective," one trader observes. Another trader adds bluntly: "You have a newspaper on the desk, you have a file of faxes, a pile of newsletters that have arrived from various institutions, the majority of it goes in the bin. One, you haven't got time to read it."

To find out more about participants' news and information-processing, the European survey asked foreign exchange traders and financial journalists for their most important information sources. While *traders* rated the importance of various information sources for their trading decisions, *journalists* rated the importance of information sources for their reporting.

Information sources of foreign exchange traders

Traders' importance ratings of various sources of market information are summarized in Table 5.2.

Table 5.2 shows that *online financial news services* are the most important information source to traders. These so-called wire services are the transmitters and intermediaries of current market information. They provide news via news screens that allow for real-time electronic news coverage with practically no delay between market events and news coverage. "I need to know what is

Table 5.2 Information sources of foreign exchange traders

Source of market information	Mean	Standard deviation	n
Wire services	1.48	0.66	153
Personal contacts: same bank	1.57	0.65	297
Personal contacts: other banks	1.59	0.69	295
Analysts: in-house	1.76	0.70	287
Analysts: external	1.91	0.71	276
Daily newspapers	2.17	0.90	86
Brokers	2.35	0.94	246
Magazines and journals	2.66	0.71	103
Financial television	2.76	0.71	102
Personal contacts: financial journalists	2.84	0.76	262

Scale: 1 = Very important; 2 = Important; 3 = Less important; 4 = Unimportant.

happening *right now* in the market," one trader says of the importance of the real-time news coverage by the wire services. Another trader agrees, saying that, "The wire services are the fastest, so you use the wire services." To ensure access to the fastest wire service, many trading floors provide their traders with several news screens. In the words of yet another trader, "The reason that I would want to have access to *all* of these news services is because I know at some time something is going to be reported on one before it is reported on another!" Thus the importance of online financial news services clearly underscores that speed is the decisive aspect of market information, as shown in the previous section "Characteristics of important information."

The real-time information from the wire services is particularly crucial when the half-life of trading positions is brief. North American spot traders estimated a median interval of 15 minutes from one of their trades to the next on a *quiet* trading day; the same figure for European traders was 10 minutes. During active markets, the time span between consecutive trades decreases further. On *busy* trading days, North American spot traders estimated a median interval of only 2 minutes between their trades; for European traders, this interval was no more than 1 minute. These estimates are given for the entire trading day; there are briefer periods in which the frequency of trading is considerably higher. Such trading intervals help explain why global news provider Reuters boasts financial data updates as frequent as several thousand times per second.[v] In the words of one foreign

---

[v] Information provided by the Reuters homepage: http:about.reuters.com/aboutus/overview/facts/index.asp

exchange trader, "If I take a short position, I have to look at interday news; I will have to follow the way the market develops." Rather than focusing on in-depth analyses, the perceived strength of wire services is their ability to answer the all-important "what" question immediately. "I don't have time to listen to the explanations why GDP grew; I don't have time. But if I know that the trade figure is *bad*, that is what I care about," explains another trader.

Personal contacts, both at their own bank and at other banks, are also especially important sources of market information to traders. "As many personal connections you have, you use. For me, personal connections are a *very* important information source," one trader comments. Unlike stock markets, the market is decentralized and thus provides traders with little information about the order flow of other participants.[13] "If we have a lot of sell orders somewhere around, then if I talk to other banks, and if they say they have some orders there and then, it's just information that you have to share with other banks or other friends ... Information sharing within the banks is most important to make any decisions," another trader remarks. Contact with other traders can thus provide traders with important information about current money flows (e.g., large currency transactions on behalf of corporate customers).

Unlike publicly available news sources, personal contacts are able to provide traders with privileged information. "You might have friends in the market who know people who might know of things, and you might find that somebody you know has been right for four out of five times, when he told you that something may be going on," one trader observes. "In the end you will probably call up somebody in the market in order to give you some more background information. Because, with due respect to the essence of Mr. Reuters and his colleagues, they do not have everything on the screen!" another trader adds. Thus, in contrast to even the fastest wire service, personal contacts provide information that cannot simply be purchased. As one trader observes regarding the information from wire services, "There is no time difference in receiving this information. Basically, whoever has the technical base, [also] has access to that information ... It is available to everyone for a fee."

"The newspaper is a very interesting amusement after the event," one foreign exchange trader declares dryly, and indeed the print media (daily newspapers, financial magazines, and journals) are significantly less important to most traders than real-time wire services. "Newspapers are not important anymore, that was once upon a time. Because when the newspaper is printed, it is not news anymore, it is historic," says another trader. Particularly for spot traders, newspapers become a second-level information source. In the words of a spot trader, "The newspapers are not fast enough. When newspapers print the news, it's already gone in the market perhaps 10 or 20 hours before, so it is not really useful to use newspapers for quick decisions." However, traders also testify to the fact that the newspapers' ability to add context and analysis to something that has happened a day before can be valuable. "If I understand what happened yesterday a little better by reading the *FT*, maybe I understand a little bit more about *today*'s dynamic," says one trader. Another trader echoes this sentiment, remarking frankly that, "Everybody has their own preference—*Economist*, *Euromoney*, *Sunday Times* ... Food over the weekend for new ideas for Monday morning!"

Paradoxically, the more information is sent in real-time to the traders, the more they need to ask for additional interpretations. Reports from financial market *analysts* are thus another important source of foreign exchange information; with in-house analysts being perceived as more important by traders than external ones. "You have your own economist and the minute the number comes out, he is on the box and is saying his own piece," one trader observes. With the help of analysts and economists, "You can prepare yourself in advance, if the figure comes out 0.2 it means [U.S.] dollar goes down, if the figure comes out 0.7, that means the dollar should go up because of that and that. You can mentally prepare yourself so you are much faster when the figure actually comes out," another trader declares of his approach. The information of financial analysts allows traders to group, reduce, and contextualize new information. Consequently, in the words of one trader, "The analysis helps you to decide what the market is thinking or which way the market is positioned."

Interestingly, *brokers* are seen as less important information sources today. In the past, their contact with a large number of market participants provided them with a clear picture of where the market was positioned and what traders were thinking. Therefore, conversations with brokers gave traders important insights about current market orders and money flows. However, as contemporary human brokers have been largely replaced by automatic broking systems, today's screen-based trading has led traders to place more weight on information seen over a computer monitor than on that heard over the telephone. Traders also report that electronic brokerage has made their trading more impersonal and that they have therefore had to adopt new strategies for dealing with their information sources. For example, while previously traders were often able to judge by a broker's voice if the broker was short or long on a currency, this sort of personal interaction made it easier to find explanations for exchange-rate movements. "You were calling your friends or some other bank and asking them for a price, and even from his *voice* you knew if he was long or short or if he was happy/unhappy," remarks one trader. Such contextual information is not contained in the detached numbers on the trading screens today.

Finally, *financial television* represents a relatively new supplier of foreign exchange information. To traders, seeing live press conferences and breaking news reports on CNN adds a new dimension to evaluating current events. "In the past, [you] got the information in short notes, in headlines, or the day after in more details. Now you can listen to Mr. Greenspan when he is testifying, and *how* he says it. And that in many cases is very important," one trader says. "It's much better to listen to [former Federal Reserve Board chairman Paul] Volcker than read about him on the Reuters screen. And look and go around dealing rooms today: Every screen, every desk now has the TV facility," another trader remarks observantly.

Watching live interviews, traders act as the interpreters of news themselves, whereas the role of the journalist is that of a broker, and not an interpreter, of information. "There comes a point in which you can't get the news much quicker," one trader notes regarding viewing the British Prime Minister, "We watched him in the garden of 10 Downing Street, announcing what he was going to do. So you don't have to wait for Reuters, Telerate, or Knight Ridder to report it, it's on the TV, and thus on *everybody*'s desk." The immediacy of unfiltered news reporting can visibly affect the market's reactions. "There is not much room for the financial journalist's point of view, to make a live interpretation on what has been said or what has been released. That means that the marketplace *itself* has to make an interpretation, and that is creating more volatility because not everybody is the same," one trader observes.

Information sources of financial journalists

Where does this other side of the market (i.e., the financial journalists and the news media they work for) *obtain* the information they report? Table 5.3 shows how financial journalists in the European survey ranked the importance of various information sources to their reporting of financial news.

To financial journalists, by far the most important source of foreign exchange market information is their contacts in the market (i.e., their *personal contacts* at banks). Thus, the astute observation of one foreign exchange trader, who remarks that he believes, "The media is dependent on the market, on the dealers, because they want to know the opinion of the dealers, they want to know what's going on," is echoed by a financial journalist: "I need the dealers, of course... You have to call a dealer and ask what he

Table 5.3 Information sources of financial journalists

Source of market information	Mean	Standard deviation	n
Personal contacts: commercial banks	1.25	0.58	57
Wire services	1.40	0.79	58
Brokers	1.53	0.76	57
Analysts/Reports: external	1.68	0.68	50
Personal contacts: central banks	1.72	0.98	54
Official central bank releases	1.74	0.93	58
Government releases: press conferences	2.05	1.00	58
Government releases: briefings	2.09	1.03	56
Daily newspapers: national	2.24	0.80	59
Daily newspapers: international	2.25	0.89	57
Personal contacts: same news organization	2.28	1.03	57
Economic databases	2.61	1.01	57
Analysts/Reports: in-house	2.71	1.18	48
Magazines and journals	2.86	0.81	58
Scientific/Academic journals	2.90	0.87	58
Financial television	2.97	0.92	58
Personal contacts: other news organizations	3.00	1.00	53
Internet	3.83	0.38	58

Scale: 1 = Very important; 2 = Important; 3 = Less important; 4 = Unimportant.

thinks about the [U.S.] dollar." Because traders are closest to the market, they are able to translate to the journalists the implications of current events and interpret exchange-rate reactions. For example, a journalist may call acquainted traders at banks to ask how a newly released unemployment figure will influence the market. As one journalist lucidly observes, "By and large, we get the prices, we know what happened. Everything else is explanation, and the explanation we get from talking to people *in the market*." Financial journalists state that only their personal market contacts will give them the in-depth information they need. If a central bank intervention is suspected, "You have to go into the market to find someone who will confirm they have actually seen it ... You must rely on your *relationships* because they must trust you and you must trust them," one trader states. "It all comes down to relationships," a wire journalist agrees, "To know your customers and know what they are like ... because there will be this two-way flow of information."

The vital importance of personal market contacts to financial journalists is corroborated by further survey answers. Asked whether "financial journalists rely on foreign exchange market participants to interpret the news," 63 European financial journalists responded as follows:

Strongly agree	11%
Agree	52%
Disagree	32%
Strongly disagree	5%

Acknowledging dependence on one's customers for performing one's work may not come easily for *any* professional, which puts even more emphasis on these findings: more than six of ten financial journalists agreed or even agreed strongly.

Alongside personal contacts at banks, the financial media itself is another important source of information to financial journalists. Whereas the group of *wire journalists* rate their personal contacts at banks as the most important information sources by far, *non-wire journalists* (i.e., journalists working for daily print media, magazines, journals, or financial television channels) rate wire services as most important and their personal contacts at banks as second-most important. "The Reuters screen is probably the main information just for watching the process move and for watching the news developments on an ongoing basis ... And I phone people a lot and talk to them," explains a journalist who works for a leading financial newspaper.

Implications for collective market information-processing

These importance ratings of market information sources to traders and financial journalists suggest an intriguing and far-reaching consequence for the collective information-processing dynamic in the foreign exchange market. Traders and financial journalists mutually rate each other as the most important information source; in other words, the most important information sources for wire journalists (i.e., their personal contacts at banks) are also the main customers of the financial wire services. "They are sources of information for us and we, in turn, are a source for them ... We're constantly in touch with banks, who are our subscribers as well, and that we're going after as market sources. And then they're reading what we are giving back," a financial journalist explains. As a result, a *cycle* of collective information-processing between the various professional groups in the foreign exchange market emerges: The market reports by the news services often consist of trading participants' perceptions and interpretations of the market, which are then fed back to the traders in the market.[vi]

[vi] The fact that, to non-wire journalists, the wire services are the most important sources of market information only further enhances this aspect of information gathering and disseminating.

It is fairly easy to consider the systemic[vii] consequences of circular information loops by visualizing a microphone that is positioned closely to a connected speaker. The resulting resonant circuit will reinforce *any* initial sound, and make it louder and louder. Similarly, when information is processed in circular loops in the social arena of the foreign exchange market, it tends to snowball and thus reinforce itself. Such self-reinforcing information loops not only distort the information flow among the involved market participants, but they also affect market outcomes (i.e., exchange rates).[14]

Knowing about the self-reinforcing nature of these loops allows participants to actively influence the dynamics of market news and information. As one trader knowledgeably explains, "Very often you can read your own words or quotes on the screen. This is a thing normally you don't tell [the news wire services] because otherwise they won't call you again ... That may influence the market if you say: The [U.S.] dollar, you just have to buy the dollar at that moment, and you see there is room for another one and a half [German] pfennig. But you say to yourself, [one] pfennig is more than enough, for half a pfennig you might cut the position."

Circular information loops are so consequential in the foreign exchange market because they reinforce "epidemics of opinion" phenomena and herding behavior.[15,16] Information loops also fuel *rumors*, as the final section in this chapter, "Market rumors," demonstrates. One wire journalist describes a private experiment in which an invented news item was put out on the wires. "We put into the markets a piece of information which wasn't true ... and we said, 'I have heard there is some really strong support at 1.44 [p.m.] and ... then we will see a rally.' And we got the same information back in the evening from other traders!" This journalist's "experiment" is a powerful demonstration of the circular information dynamics in the foreign exchange market. It shows how both traders and financial news services inform each other about what is happening in the market; each side of the market feeds back to the other possible causes for past movements, and each side relies on the other for the development of potential future market scenarios. "It's like an octopus feeding off itself all over the place," one financial journalist observes with striking imagery.

[vii] Systemic circulation is defined as "general circulation of the blood through the body, as opposed to the circulation of the blood from the heart to the lungs and back to the heart" (*The American Heritage Dictionary of the English Language*, 4th edn, 2000). Like blood in the human body, information in the foreign exchange market is also processed in circular and not in linear ways.

REPORTING TRENDS AND INTERDEPENDENCY

> [News] is changing on the screen so fast that you can hardly really pick up what is going on. As soon as you try to read it, it's gone and replaced by another sentence or another headline.
>
> Foreign exchange trader

> Banks depend on the news to make the markets. If there were no news, the markets would not move, and certainly if the markets don't move, there would be no news. So it is a very intimate relationship.
>
> Financial journalist

"Wanted. Young, skinny, wiry fellows. Not over 18. Must be expert riders. Willing to risk death daily. Orphans preferred," read a California newspaper advertisement recruiting riders for the famed *Pony Express*. In that year, 1860, it took riders longer than one week to deliver mail through what was then the fastest communication route between Missouri and California.[viii] While we may recall that less than a mere two centuries ago, news used to travel at the speed of a horse, train, or carrier pigeon, today the news revolution has arrived at the stage of global real-time information dissemination. In the course of this development, news has been redefined.

As this section shows, financial journalists' views provide a striking picture of change both in how financial news is disseminated and in the very role of the news media. The advances in information technology in the foreign exchange market have caused trading participants and news media to grow closer together and to engage in a highly interdependent relationship.

The European survey asked financial journalists about relevant and current trends in financial reporting. One survey question and the subsequent responses from 63 financial journalists were as follows: What is your opinion of the following statement on financial news and foreign exchange participants? "The speed of financial news reporting has increased".

Strongly agree	70%
Agree	28%
Disagree	0%
Strongly disagree	2%

[viii] This information has been retrieved from http://www.americanwest.com/trails/pages/ponyexp1.htm

There is an almost unanimous consensus among journalists that news reporting has become faster: altogether 98% agreed, most of them even agreed *strongly*. This increase in the speed of news has clearly affected *how* financial news is reported: 92% of the journalists agree or agree strongly that, "Recent technology has changed the style of financial news reporting." The responses of the financial journalists provided a clear signal about the direction of this change: Two-thirds of the financial journalists (67%) agree or agree strongly that, "Reporting of immediate events has become more important to the market than background analysis." This development is tellingly highlighted by a trader's comment: "When there is something going on, you have a headline, this headline is the thing. And [it is] very, very rarely that the story behind that headline moves the thing!"

As we can see, speed plays a dominant role, which is also reflected in the finding that more than half of the financial journalists (55%) agree or agree strongly that, "In financial news reporting, *speed* has become a more decisive factor than *contents*." As one wire journalist observes dryly: "If you could get a donkey to put a headline out, then the donkey would win if it was faster than yours, no matter how fast yours was written—if it was late, forget it, no one was interested!" When *what* is reported becomes less important than *how fast* it is reported, the danger of releasing wrong information increases: "If you make a mistake on an important piece of information and anyone who looks at your screen believes your information will make a wrong decision, which will prove very expensive for them ... And we would often speculate, if you really wanted to screw up the market for five minutes, how would you do it?" a wire journalist says. The danger of misreporting in the financial news does not only exist in theory but is concrete and larger than before; almost three out of five financial journalists (59%) agree or agree strongly that, "New media technology has increased the risk of reporting unverified news."

These changes in financial news reporting are significant, and the responses of the financial journalists show that they are no isolated phenomenon that only affects the financial news providers. On the contrary; in the contemporary foreign exchange market, these developments have greatly affected the *relationship* between the financial news media and the market participants who actively trade currencies. Both sides have developed an intimate relationship in which they have become more and more dependent on each other. Today, "everybody is a market participant, whether he trades or he provides information," one trader sagely observes.

This new relationship between financial news providers and trading institutions becomes particularly apparent in the blurred boundary between the two sides. One important reason for the close relationship between financial news agencies and trading participants is that the news organizations operating the wire services are financed primarily by the fees financial institutions pay for using their services, not by advertisers, as are other news organizations. Thus, in the words of a trader, the wire services, "Normally do what the one who buys the service wants ... And you can influence their behavior by telling them what you want to see, what you are willing to pay for, what kind of information." Moreover, banks are trying to increase their influence on the suppliers of financial news and have even begun to provide their own news. News pages on the screens supplied by electronic news services, for example, allow banks to feed the market with their own information. "On one side we are the customer, on the other side we are also the providers of information," another trader observes. On the other hand, news services have developed integrated electronic information and trading systems which allow market participants not only to collect market information, but also to actually trade with each other. The fact that the global news agencies provide trading possibilities through their news systems has made them assume the role of financial brokers themselves.[17,18] A recent development saw the news agency Reuters as an equal shareholder to JP Morgan Chase, Citigroup, and Deutsche Bank in a global, online trading marketplace that allowed banks to distribute their own research.[19]

Probably the main reason for the dramatic change in how the financial news journalists interact with the traditional market participants lies in the fact that modern equipment has created the technological possibility of delivering and receiving information in real-time. "Thanks to new technology, we're actually reporting on a real-time basis. So, the dollar moves sharply ... a minute or two after that has happened we have reported it and we have found a reason for why it has happened. Previously, it would've taken about six hours for that kind of information to filter out and filter back ... on to dealing desks. So it has sucked us in a lot more into the market, we have to talk to traders a lot more frequently," a financial journalist explains. In fact, according to another financial wire journalist, because of the technological advances, financial journalists are in fact almost doing the job of the traders, *without* actually trading: "If we weren't writing about it, we could be trading it easily because we are that close to the market," he says.

Survey responses of financial journalists in the European survey capture this overlap in the relationship between the once-separated consumers and providers of information. A question of the survey asked financial journalists: What is your opinion of the following statement on financial news and foreign exchange participants? "Financial news media and foreign exchange market participants have become more dependent on each other".

Strongly agree	11%
Agree	64%
Disagree	25%
Strongly disagree	0%

The resulting percentages in the responses show that full three-quarters of journalists agree that the mutual dependency between news media and market participants has *increased*. "The banks and the media are much closer. Both sides are ... in close contact, which they wouldn't have been before," says one wire journalist. A foreign exchange trader adds, "We thought one should not leave reports of the foreign exchange market only to people who just make headlines ... And, therefore, most of the bigger banks think in the direction of this interdependency." Further evidence for the interdependency is provided by the observant statement of another trader that, "Reuters even started with a TV station and with studios in trading rooms so that if something happens they can get an actual report from somebody in the market ... So the relationship becomes closer and closer."

More evidence for this permeable boundary between the financial news media and trading participants was provided by other survey questions. For example, almost nine of ten (87%) financial journalists agreed or agreed strongly that, "Foreign exchange market participants can *influence* news providers," and still four of ten financial journalists (44%) agreed or agreed strongly that "Foreign exchange market participants can *manipulate* the news providers." As a wire journalist cogently observes, "When you speak to a trader and say how is the [U.S.] dollar today, he might have a different view according to whether he has got a long position in dollars or a short position in dollars—you *never* know."

This striking trend toward interdependency and overlap between the financial news media and trading participants also emerges from the different perspectives of the traditional print media and the more recent wire media. As previously stated, wire news media are the most important information sources to trading participants; it thus comes as no surprise that wire journalists also perceive their reporting as more important for traders' decisions than do other journalists. Remarkably, it is the group of wire journalists who also perceive their own reporting as more dependent on their users' expectations, and the relationship between the financial news media and the trading participants as more dependent on each other, than do non-wire journalists. "It is a symbiotic relationship. We would not be here without them, and they would not be here without us. These two industries, the banks and news wires, have grown together," one wire journalist observes. More so than other journalists, wire journalists notice that in their interdependent relationship with trading participants they can be influenced and even manipulated. A wire journalist comments wryly, "There is one field in the whole economy and financial life where lying until the very last moment is permitted and necessary, and this is foreign exchange." Another trader echoes this sentiment, saying that, "The [wire] media, contrary to the popular belief, are the easiest thing to manipulate. The reporter wants a story. He doesn't have a clue about the subject. So as long as you can give him a story that looks credible, he's going to stick it down in a piece of clay!"

MARKET RUMORS

Rumors drive the market.

Foreign exchange trader

"A lie gets halfway around the world before the truth has a chance to get its pants on," Winston Churchill once observed. Similarly today, the candid remark of a contemporary trader echoes this sentiment: "It seems that rumors are even faster spread around than real news. All of a sudden, everyone knows them."

"Why is the ambulance parking in front of the White House if it's *not* the President? It can also be somebody else, but I would say the first thinking is [that] it's the President." Here one foreign exchange trader illustrates the likely start of a rumor. This example captures the essence of rumors: They are allegations that are passed along accompanied by *doubt* rather than by evidence.[20,21] Rumors bear a close resemblance to news since, like news, they provide explanations for meaningful events and are perceived as positive or negative by the receiver. As this section demonstrates, rumors are a *vital* kind of information in the social arena of the foreign exchange market. In fact, one trader even goes so far as to describe the thin demarcation line between market news and rumors by observing that *all* events reported "are first of all rumors."

Rumors play an essential role in newspaper reporting on the foreign exchange market. In fact, comparing daily press reports on U.S. central bank intervention with actual intervention data, a study found that interventions reported by the *Wall Street Journal* may actually have never occurred, no matter whether they were reported as facts or as mere rumors.[22] Accordingly, a central bank trader remarked in the interviews: "I have first-hand 100% access to intervention volume and so on, and I know what the press is writing. So I know about the big, big differences which they are assuming, and what the real figures are."

That rumors play a vital role in the dynamics of trading is markedly confirmed by many of the observations in the interviews. In the words of one trader, "Rumors sometimes are more effective than facts!" Particularly in the short run rumors can be powerful sources of currency fluctuation. For example, one trader observes about spot traders that "A rumor to them is very important because that's going to move something 20 [basis] points." However, as another trader notes, rumors can also have a more marked impact on exchange rates; as the assessment by one trader of the sudden depreciation of the South African rand in 1996 demonstrates, "It hadn't moved two years and then suddenly we had a 12% devaluation one morning. And that was all started by rumors that [South African president] Mandela had died." Accordingly, as another trader says dryly: "If there is a big rumor in the market, then nobody cares about the fundamentals."

Moreover, rumors have been able to flexibly adapt to changing market conditions, both in terms of their contents and in how they are dispersed. For one, rumor *content* has adapted to the times; because in the contemporary foreign exchange market, money flows initiated by large corporate and financial customers are important determinants of short-term exchange-rate changes, rumors about these transaction flows are blooming alongside more traditional contents of market rumors. Today, "There are not only rumors about political expectations or economic expectations, there are also rumors about big deals," one trader explains. Moreover, rumor *dissemination* has adapted to current market technologies. As the rumor or "idea" pages and columns provided by the financial newswire services show, electronic screens have joined, and often replaced, the traditional word-of-mouth spreading of rumors over the telephone. "Rumors spread over phone 10 years ago is now done through Reuters dealing. My guys, they sit there and write pages and pages what's going on. So they just do it over typing, not over talking," one leading trader observes.

Financial markets generally provide a fertile breeding ground for rumors. Here, all the social conditions for rumors are optimally met: Incidents of rumors generally increase with the degree of ambiguity present in the context and depend on a topic's importance.[20,23] For example, the situation surrounding the rumor of President Mandela's death was highly ambiguous. In the words of one trader, "Every half hour there was a difference in his [alleged] condition," to which another exclaims that, "The last thing that was seen, he was going into a health clinic!" This topic was extremely important to many market participants: "They bought South African rand, everybody was sitting on South African rand. So any news that was likely to hurt the South African rand meant that people were going to begin to worry about their position." Most importantly, the decision-makers in the foreign exchange market exist in a climate of personal *uncertainty* and *doubt* which surrounds them continuously. Rumors delight in these uncertain settings because they temporarily alleviate or at least provide some sense of focus to unpleasant feelings of doubt and ambivalence. "What I like about rumors," remarks one trader thoughtfully, "[Is that] when you hear the rumor, it makes you quickly think about it. You know, how do you evaluate it? Is it good, is it bad? Could it be true, could it be wrong?"

To decision-makers in such ambiguous environments as the foreign exchange market, rumors play an important *meaning-generating* function.[24] In the earnest words of one trader, "There usually is a lot of fantasy behind [a rumor]: What could that mean?" Even the most modern communications environment, where the newest technologies mediate the interaction of participants, leaves this function of rumors unchanged. Rumor-mongering is a problem-solving interaction, and thus the need for rumors is nurtured by the *uncertainty* and *anxiety* of market participants.[25] As foreign exchange traders observe, such time periods as the "twilight zones" between the closing of one trading region and the opening of the next, and certain market conditions, such as an extremely volatile or extremely thin market, provide especially conducive settings for market rumors. Not surprisingly, these are also the market circumstances in which traders experience particularly high degrees of uncertainty.

Rumors in the foreign exchange market tend to evolve and spread in stages.[21] During rumor *generation*, market participants develop a sensibility to rumors through a combination of uncertainty and anxiety. One trader lucidly explains, "If somebody spreads a rumor in the market, for example, 'the Bundesbank is intervening on the dollar,' then of course the market starts to become nervous. And everybody is uncertain and everybody will try and get the information, whether it is true or not *true*." For example, long periods of a quiet market give rise to such heightened sensibility to rumors. "If the market is very active the whole day and there is another rumor, the effect of the rumor will not be as big as if you have a very dull day and there is a rumor," another trader observes. In the following *evaluation* stage, participants assess the veracity of received information; they are more likely to spread rumors that they suppose to be true than rumors that they judge as false. In the words of one trader, "If somebody I know has very good contacts with the Bundesbank tells me that they want to lower the repo rate and I know that this guy is consistent, his contacts are good, and his information has always been good, I will tell probably another ten clients that I have information that that might happen." This statement also demonstrates that in order to judge the truth of news, traders use available knowledge and existing personal assumptions. If a piece of information fits available cognitions and confirms previously held views, it is more likely to be evaluated as true. The availability and salience of these cognitions and a concordant previous expectation reduce efforts to verify a rumor: in other words, the more likely a rumor will spread. As one trader states, "If it fits into your view, then you might go with it."

The circular nature of foreign exchange news-processing, a phenomenon discussed earlier in the section "From news sources to information loops," reinforces the weight of market rumors in the *dissemination* stage. Simply listening repeatedly to a story makes it appear *more* true;[21] repetitions that result from circular information loops make subjective belief in rumors even more likely. "The greater the number of people you know, the more sources from which you hear [the rumor] probably makes it influential," notes one trader. Moreover, rumor circulation not only results in repetitions, often it also leads to refinements that make rumors appear even more plausible. "You hear that your uncle has the flu and you tell your mother that your uncle has the flu and a fever. Your mother tells your father that your uncle has the flu, fever, and is in bed ... I would say it is the same in the financial markets," another trader explains.

Rumors thus play an important role in addressing the aspect of time technology has not been able to conquer: the *future*. "I can always read where a plane has been hijacked, but the newspaper will never tell me if there is a chance that the plane I intend to take this afternoon is going to be hijacked ... [Also] the Reuters system does not tell you the future, but it tells me the present," one foreign exchange trader explains regarding the different dimensions of time addressed by the financial wire services and by the traditional print media. Recent technological advances have dramatically increased the speed of market information and have made large parts of this information ubiquitously available. "It used to be that only a certain few were able to have access to that sort of information quickly, now it's available to everyone. It's a much more leveled playing field now," one trader observes. "Everybody now in Uzbekistan is going to get the news at the same second as we will here," a trader in Zurich adds. However, by shedding an instant light on the market present, real-time news services promptly turn the market present into an irrelevant past. "The information on the screen is history," one trader comments. Therefore, in their search for competitive advantage, market participants have shifted the focus of their attention away from the past and the present toward the *possible future* of the market. *Will* the afternoon plane in the scenario outlined by the trader at the beginning of this paragraph be hijacked? Hovering in the narrow band between market reality and possibility, rumors not only indicate how the future might look, they also promise to satisfy the psychological need of participants for orientation.

"By spreading a rumor, you can definitely influence the market *if* you are strong enough," a trader observes. Rumors suggest that collective processing of foreign exchange information is less about the actuality of economic facts than about how reality is subjectively perceived and about how reality is *actively shaped* by market participants. As one trader remarks shrewdly, "When banks have a position that is offside, that hurts them, and they don't really want to cut [that], and they think: 'Well, if we can manipulate the markets' ... So then they may spread a rumor!" Thus, the dynamics of rumors is yet another demonstration of the psychological and social nature of how foreign exchange information is processed.[26,27]

Modern technology and the ubiquitous availability of real-time news have done little to reduce the basic sense of ambiguity among foreign exchange decision-makers. On the contrary, vast amounts of complex information which are communicated to market participants by new information technologies often increase their uncertainties and result in the experience of information overload.[ix] In the words of one trader, "The more news you get, the more you are uncertain of what to do." Simultaneously, surplus information provided by new trading and information technologies leaves little time for thoughtful decision-making. "It is dangerous if you just put too much in front of people ... The most important component in my opinion is just being able to feel the market, and that's not done by sitting and watching the Reuters TV screen or reading analyses!" a head trader exclaims. Thus, while new information technologies succeed in swiftly putting large amounts of data at the disposal of market participants, they usually provide little help in interpreting this information and transforming it into decisions.[29] Instead, information technologies often help disseminate rumors, as is revealed in another trader's typical response when asked about his informants for the rumors he receives. "Normally, Reuters and Telerate, and then you have some direct lines

---

[ix] The concept of information overload, however, is not confined to the modern information age. For example, already between 1550 and 1750, Europe witnessed an explosion of information based on the dramatic increase in the production of scholarly books. Experiencing information overload may thus be based more on *how* knowledge is represented than by the amount of produced information. Possibly, "the very devices created to 'contain' information overload are the devices that 'create' it in the first place," historian Daniel Rosenberg speculates.[28]

to other brokers, and they are using other systems, maybe Bloomberg. And if there is an important rumor I have it in 20 seconds by telephone!" he remarks.

ABBREVIATED REFERENCES

See the reference chapter at the end of the book for full details.

1 Oberlechner, T. and Hocking, S. (2004)
2 Shiller, R. J. (2000)
3 Mitchell, M. L. and Harold, M. J. (1994)
4 Ederington, L. H. and Lee, J. H. (1993)
5 Frenkel, J. A. (1981)
6 Cavaglia, S. M. F. G. and Wolff, C. C. P. (1996)
7 Harris, E. S. and Zabka, N. M. (1995)
8 Eagly, A. H. and Chaiken, S. (1998)
9 Jonas, E. et al. (2001)
10 Van Raaij, W. F. (1989)
11 Evans, J. S. B. T. (1987)
12 Hogarth, R. and Makridakis, S. (1981)
13 Perraudin, W. and Vitale, P. (1994)
14 Kirman, A. (1995)
15 Kirman, A. (1991)
16 Lux, T. (1995)
17 Goodhart, C. et al. (1996)
18 Goodhart, C. and Demos, A. A. (2000)
19 Condon, T. (2000)
20 Allport, G. W. and Postman, L. J. (1947)
21 DiFonzo, N. et al. (1994)
22 Osterberg, W. P. and Wetmore Humes, R. (1993)
23 Rosnow, R. L. (1991)
24 DiFonzo, N. and Bordia, P. (1997)
25 Bordia, P. and Rosnow, R. L. (1998)
26 Scharfstein, D. S. and Stein, J. C. (1990)
27 Shiller, R. J. and Pound, J. (1989)
28 Rosenberg, D. (2003)
29 Slovic, P. (1986)

6
Personality Psychology of Traders

> *I do believe that there is a high correlation between trading success and personality.*
>
> Foreign exchange trader

In *The Money Bazaar: Inside the Trillion-dollar World of Currency Trading*,[1] foreign exchange trader Andrew Krieger describes his decision to sell a massive quantity of New Zealand dollars after hearing from other market traders who all confidently predicted that this currency should appreciate. Krieger's decision proved highly profitable. When shortly afterwards he stopped trading for Bankers Trust, he received a personal bonus of U.S.$3 million. Indeed, a large percentage of the more than U.S.$500 million in trading profits Bankers Trust reported for the same year may have been based on decisions made by Krieger.[2]

How can such extraordinary trading profits be explained? "It is the style of a person, rather than his or her academic qualifications, that shapes a good dealer. No amount of education can turn someone with the wrong personality into a good dealer," popular market books declare about successful foreign exchange traders.[3] Likewise, many practicing traders are convinced that success is based on such traits as the *personality characteristics* of the individual.[i] "There is something that is inherent in the very best traders that

---
[i] Traders' traits include cognitive abilities, skills, and personality characteristics. Personality characteristics are traders' styles of thinking, feeling, and acting which manifest themselves in a stable way across a variety of different situations.[4]

other people just don't have," the manager of a leading foreign exchange trading floor in New York declares. Another trader agrees, saying, "There is natural ability, and some have got *more* natural ability than others." Thus, according to market practitioners, good traders are rare and specific traits play a key role in their trading performance. "Everyone goes, 'Yeah! I'd like to be a foreign exchange trader!' But really only one in a hundred actually has got the abilities," the trader adds. "If you interview three hundred people and you hire six of them, I think one of them will turn out to be a great trader, two of them will be decent traders, and three of them you have to reassign to a different role," another trader concurs matter-of-factly.

Thus, the question arises if personality factors indeed exist which enable some traders to systematically outperform others? And, if so, what are the traits defining successful traders? These questions cannot be answered by market approaches that focus on collective market movements and by those approaches that prescribe trading rules and optimum investment strategies. Consequently, this chapter examines *empirically* the traits and personality characteristics of successful traders, based on findings from the European and from the North American surveys.[ii]

THE ROLE OF PERSONALITY IN TRADING

Academic market approaches usually do not consider trading a specific professional activity that requires a specific set of personal traits, skills, and abilities. The personality of those who trade plays no role in traditional economic models of the foreign exchange market: As Chapter 1, "From Rational Decision-Makers to a Psychology of the Foreign Exchange Market," has shown, these models propose that financial markets are efficient, that market prices fully reflect available information at all times, and that trading decisions are made by rational agents in unbiased ways.[6] Such assumptions certainly do not invite research into the personality of those who actually make market decisions. Even the more recent approach of behavioral finance has so far paid little attention to individual differences and characteristics of market participants. While this approach is largely driven by open-minded economists who include psychological knowledge about human cognition, insights from other fields of psychology (such as personality) are usually neglected.

[ii] Parts of this chapter are reworked from material in *Journal of Behavioral Finance*, **5**(1), pp. 23–31, T. Oberlechner (2004), "Perceptions of successful traders by foreign exchange professionals,"[5] with permission from Lawrence Erlbaum Associates Inc.

Moreover, some observers of financial markets suggest that from a statistical viewpoint, individual market performance and variations in trading success may be based on chance, not on personal abilities. A case in point is the mutual fund industry. Given the sheer amount of mutual funds (a number which in the U.S. alone goes well into the thousands),[iii] a random distribution of performance and returns alone explains why some fund managers outperform the market and why they may do so even for extended periods of time.[7] This too casts doubt on the value of examining individual and personal ingredients of trading performance: When performance is randomly distributed, the ability of some participants to outperform others is the result of luck and survivorship bias rather than of their skills and abilities. "We often have the mistaken impression that ... a trader [is] an excellent trader, only to realize that 99.9% of their past performance is attributable to chance, and chance alone," Taleb writes in a book tellingly titled *Fooled by Randomness*.[8]

In response to these arguments, trader and author, Viktor Niederhoffer, spiritedly replied that he had traded "Approximately 700 standard deviations away from randomness, a departure that would occur by chance alone about as frequently as the spare parts in an automotive salvage lot might spontaneously assemble themselves into a McDonald's restaurant."[9] The "hit and miss" approach to the performance of market participants is also contradicted by market practitioners who claim that it is possible to train people to become exceptionally successful traders.[10] Indeed, virtually all of the traders I talked to consider not only the traits of foreign exchange traders, but also the training of personality-related trading skills as *extremely* important. This is shown by the following advice, given by the head trader of a large trading floor. He counsels, "Work hard at knowing your own style. Work hard at knowing your own capabilities. Work hard at knowing your own limits. Work hard at analyzing why you might make money and why you lose money. Work hard at looking at your specific skill set." Indeed, the foreign exchange manager of another leading trading floor describes his role in similar fashion, saying, "You try to set some ground rules for [the traders] and encourage them to build the skill-set from their inherent personal abilities."

Unbeknown to market practitioners, the importance they attribute to the personality of traders is supported by new research from organizational and personnel psychology. Here, too, for many decades the connection between personality and work performance was questioned. Personality was

---

[iii] The Investment Company Institute provides statistical data on more than 8,000 U.S.-based mutual funds (information taken from the company's website at http://www.ici.org/stats/mf/).

assumed to have little influence on how well people perform in their jobs.[11,12] However, recent years have witnessed a striking change.[13] Assisted by adequate research strategies, modern studies show that personality helps explain and predict professional performance in a wide range of work settings.[iv] Such links between personality and work performance have been demonstrated for nurses, government security personnel, and air traffic controllers, among many other professions.[28–31]

Indeed, this research demonstrates that personality traits are linked not only to job performance but also to its prerequisite (i.e., job-related *learning*). In other words, personality also has an important effect on the speed and the extent to which professionals acquire professional knowledge and skills. This may also be true of foreign exchange trading, as the following observation of an experienced trader suggests: "I am a *natural* foreign exchange trader ... I picked it up and I became successful quickly in terms of my ability to make money for the organization I was working for."

However, while organizational and personality research has successfully linked personality and work performance *outside* the financial markets, traits and personality factors of professional traders have received little systematic attention.[v] To date only few studies suggesting that personality might indeed correlate with the quality and the outcomes of trading decisions exist. In a

---

[iv] One reason for this development is that many psychologists have agreed on one specific model of personality.[14,15] The model is commonly called the "Five Factor Model" (FFM) which dates back to the early 1960s.[16] As the name implies, it builds on five broad personality factors: Extraversion, Agreeableness, Conscientiousness, Neuroticism, and Openness to Experience. The FFM has helped to organize a variety of personality traits.[4,13,17,18] Its factors result in a high degree of consistency from analyses of ratings of people's traits in diverse groups and populations.[14,19,20]

Recent meta-analyses have established links between the FFM and work performance.[21,22] For example, *Conscientiousness* shows a consistent relationship to job performance across different occupations;[23] its overall predictive validity for job performance is as high as 0.31.[24] A recent summary of meta-analyses has found that *Emotional Stability*, the opposite of *Neuroticism*, also generally correlates positively with performance.[25] The other three traits of the FFM were found to predict performance only for some occupations. Today, the NEO Personality Inventory is the most widely used assessment instrument based on the FFM.[26,27] Its present form, the NEO-PI-R represents each factor of the FFM on six subscales which measure the factor's key aspects.

[v] Published accounts of personally successful foreign exchange trading are usually autobiographical (see the reports by Nancy Goldstone or Andrew Krieger)[32,1] or anecdotal (see Jack Schwager's interviews with well-known traders).[10,33] One reason for the scarcity of systematic research is the difficulty to gain access to real-life market participants; traders work in a highly competitive and stressful field[34] and the institutions they work for keep their trading activities confidential.

simulated market experiment, one such study related various psychological traits and cognitive biases of students to their trading performance. The study found that impulsive students (as defined by their tendency to act rapidly and without forethought) placed more, but not more unprofitable, trading orders, while overconfident[vi] students showed a greater tendency to place loss-making orders.[35] In another study, traders with an especially pronounced illusion of control[vii] were found to *underperform* as compared with other traders.[36] Thus, my own research attempts to systematically describe and analyze the characteristics important for traders in the real-life setting of the foreign exchange market.

WHAT MAKES SUCCESSFUL TRADERS?

What do the best traders share, other than being cynical?

Foreign exchange trader

The European survey suggests some answers to the question of what best traders share. For the survey, an initial list of potentially important characteristics for successful trading was established, assisted by the informal feedback of foreign exchange traders. This led to a catalog of 25 personality traits as well as other items which expressed personal skills and cognitive abilities. Hundreds of traders then rated the importance of these characteristics and were asked to add any additional characteristics that they also considered important. Table 6.1 ranks the characteristics according to their importance as perceived by the 291 traders who submitted ratings for all of the items. This table shows that, while traders rated quick reaction time as the most important characteristic for a successful foreign exchange trader, discipline, experience, concentration, and stress resistance were also rated as highly important. None of the characteristics was rated as actually unimportant; however, social skills, computer literacy, and organization skills were least important.

A subsequent statistical factor analysis revealed that traders' ratings were based on eight comprehensive personality-related factors. These underlying factors, on which foreign exchange traders base their perceptions of successful

---

[vi] Overconfidence is discussed in Chapter 2, "Psychology of Trading Decisions."
[vii] In this study, traders' degrees of illusion of control were measured by their self-perceived ability to influence the movement of a dot on a screen. The role played by illusions of control in the foreign exchange market is discussed in Chapter 8, "The Foreign Exchange Market—A Psychological Construct."

Table 6.1 Importance ratings of successful trader characteristics (*n* = 291)

Item	Mean	Standard deviation
Quick reaction time	3.71	0.50
Discipline	3.65	0.55
Experience	3.62	0.52
Concentration	3.62	0.53
Stress resistance	3.54	0.57
Willingness to take risks	3.43	0.61
Intuition	3.42	0.56
Emotional stability	3.38	0.68
Ability to teamwork	3.33	0.72
Simultaneous information-processing	3.31	0.67
Judgment of information sources	3.21	0.61
Learning ability	3.19	0.60
Communication skills	3.14	0.72
Integrity	3.13	0.79
Independence	3.05	0.75
Analytical thinking	3.03	0.73
Aggressiveness	2.97	0.80
Optimistic attitude	2.90	0.79
Mathematical ability	2.82	0.82
Curiosity	2.67	0.76
Organization skills	2.56	0.73
Computer literacy	2.54	0.78
Social skills	2.52	0.74

Scale: 1 = Unimportant; 2 = Less important; 3 = Important; 4 = Very important.

traders, are listed in Table 6.2, which ranks the factors according to their importance and lists the specific characteristics that contribute to each factor.[viii]

Traders' observations of successful traders in the interviews provide a striking confirmation of the importance of these factors. Note that, when discussing their trading experience in the interviews, traders were not aware of the factors that had resulted from the systematic survey data.

Disciplined cooperation

"I would say discipline is the biggest thing," declares one trader confidently of the personality factors important to successful trading. In an unpredictable

---

[viii] Importance ratings of the eight factors were determined as statistical means of the single characteristics that contribute to the factor.

Personality Psychology of Traders 155

Table 6.2 Personal success factors in foreign exchange trading ($n = 291$)

Factor	Included items	Mean	Standard deviation
Disciplined cooperation	Discipline, ability to work in a team	3.49	0.51
Tackling decisions	Aggressiveness, stress resistance, willingness to take risks, concentration, quick reaction time	3.45	0.39
Market meaning-making	Judgment of info sources, intuition, experience	3.42	0.38
Emotional stability	Emotional stability	3.38	0.68
Information-processing	Analytical thinking, learning ability, simultaneous processing of various information	3.18	0.47
Interested integrity	Curiosity, integrity	2.90	0.63
Autonomous organization	Independence, organization skills, optimistic attitude	2.84	0.54
Information handling	Computer literacy, mathematical ability, social skills, communication skills	2.76	0.53

Scale: 1 = Unimportant; 2 = Less important; 3 = Important; 4 = Very important.

environment, where sudden market swings may turn gains into losses within moments, trading discipline may be the *only* factor that can actually be controlled. This comprehensive factor has at least three important aspects relevant to trading performance.

The first aspect of disciplined cooperation expresses a strong motivational component. "Successful traders often don't really care about impressing other people. They are focused on *making money*," in the words of one foreign exchange trader. This focused ambition, directed at the market, is likewise reflected in another trader's observation that, "[Successful traders] are driven by one particular thing ... very successful traders do have absolute passion for the marketplace and almost a little bit of obsession." A further trader defines the most successful traders as those, "who live and breathe the market for 24 hours a day, whose goal in life is to be a *master* of the markets." The motivational component of disciplined cooperation reinforces other success factors. For instance, regarding the third factor, market meaning–making, this is clearly expressed by a trader who observes that, "You have to take the time to focus on a lot of factors that go into the market, and unless you're *driven*, you can't possibly push yourself to understand, read, and be informed on all the factors."

The second aspect of disciplined cooperation stresses the discipline involved in adhering to stop-loss limits[ix] and counteracting such risk-taking biases as overconfidence and the illusion of control.[37] Disciplined cooperation thus also involves a trader's readiness to cut losses early and to hold on to profit-generating positions instead of realizing gains prematurely. "By discipline I mean having a very clear idea of what your risk/reward is and sticking with it. It is also known as stopping yourself out if you're wrong, not letting your losses run ... One thing that a lot of successful traders have is that discipline in being able to take profits and cut their losses, over time, with a good risk/reward ratio," one trader explains. This second aspect of discipline cooperation helps explain why in the experimental market study by Biais et al. highly self-monitoring participants placed less frequently unprofitable orders than did others.[35]

The third aspect of disciplined cooperation is directed at traders' cooperation in the trading team and trading institution. For instance, only traders who are disciplined in their reporting of trading losses receive the timely support of colleagues or supervisors. As we have seen in the examples of Nick Leeson and John Rusnak,[x] the spectacular losses caused by rogue trading exemplify the consequences of what happens when this third aspect of disciplined cooperation is missing. Then, traders allow bad trading situations to escalate by concealing their losses while pursuing a spiral of higher and higher risks.

Tackling decisions

This factor addresses traders' readiness for assertive and proactive decision-making in a risky environment. As we saw in Chapter 5, "News and Rumors," long after the far-flung era when Nathan Rothschild capitalized on Napoleon's defeat in the Battle of Waterloo hours after the battle,[38] in today's foreign exchange market, traders need to act and react within seconds.[39] Electronic dealing and matching systems allow traders to buy and sell hundreds of millions of dollars in mere seconds.[40] "A lot of it is quick thinking on their feet; I think a big part of it is not being afraid to be wrong," one trader declares, aptly capturing this tackling attitude in trading decision-making. Another trader adds sagely that, "You don't want somebody who doesn't have the ability to turn on and quickly react to some news that has come out. You don't want someone to always *think* because [then] it might be too late." The importance of a tackling attitude in trading decisions also finds support in the experimental market study conducted by Biais et al.[35] In this

---

[ix] Stop-loss limits are discussed in Chapter 3, "Risk-Taking in Trading Decisions."
[x] See Chapter 3, "Risk-Taking in Trading Decisions."

study, "impulsive" students who act more rapidly and with less forethought did not have a greater tendency to place unprofitable trades.

One of the key aspects of a tackling approach toward trading decision-making is the willingness to forge ahead by taking a risk. "You need somebody who wants to take risk ... To be successful, you need the personality that is comfortable with their position and is actively interested in taking on risk and making money," comments one trader. This personality aspect is even mentioned as a hiring prerequisite by the manager of a large trading floor. In the manager's words, there needs to be, "Evidence in [applicants'] background [that] they are comfortable with risk, whether it is in their personal life or their financial life." Moreover, because trading a hectic market environment requires high degrees of concentration for extended periods of time, the ability to cope with stress and remain focused is another important aspect of tackling decisions.[34,41]

Market meaning-making

"Do they actually have views that they want to express in the market?" one trader addresses the difference between top foreign exchange traders and those who are average. While trading decisions can never be made with certainty, in the long run they can be made with some degree of accuracy, based on understanding complex market processes. "Successful traders need to understand the dynamics in various markets," one trader explains. Another trader agrees, observing that, "The challenge comes in because there's so many things at play. Understanding the correlations between events, really understanding a macro picture in the world, and trying to correlate that into trades that make money." The factor market meaning-making expresses the ability of quickly formulating a view of the market by using personal judgment. This factor requires, "*Experience* because the market is changing. It takes some time to be a successful trader," in the words of a trader. Market meaning-making involves intuition, thus allowing traders to rapidly anticipate possible market developments. In the words of one trader, "That's why they are the best—and that's where it becomes *intuitive* and not the discipline thing—that they know when they should be adding to a position because they have the market on the run. And if you look at the *best* traders, that's the trait that they show. They maximize the opportunity that they have when they have it!"

Emotional stability

Emotional stability is also considered crucial for successful trading. In the frank words of one trader, "Just not lose your cool, just not snap at it. Be a professional on the trading floor. Every time you go ballistic, you lose your concentration ... Sometimes things happen, but you just have to deal with it ... [When] it's gone, then move on. Some people just can't get over it!" Another trader concurs, saying that: "The kinds of traits I like to see in a trader: someone who has a well-tempered personality and sees trading as a business." Emotional stability allows traders to focus on their strategy and to *stay focused* when the going gets tough. As one trader explains, "You definitely need a lot of [emotional] control because you need to stay in positions when things seem like they are going the wrong way, focusing on the big picture!" Controlling their emotions helps traders cope with the ever-present tension between their trading strategy and changing market information. As another trader wisely observes, "There is a fine balance between changing your view because you're always processing data, and at the same time maintaining some sort of discipline with what your original position was, why you had it, and when is that view wrong."

Moreover, emotional stability allows traders to cope with losses. "The one skill that I really can't teach is how you handle losing money," observes one trader, adding that, "The best ability top foreign traders have is how to handle *losing* money." After trading losses, emotional stability (together with disciplined cooperation) counteracts the tendency to take asymmetric risk, discussed in Chapter 3, "Risk-Taking in Trading Decisions." Emotional stability, the trader continues to explain, allows decision-makers to handle losing, "In exactly the same way as they handle winning ... If you are making £100 [thousand], if you are losing £100 [thousand], that can't cloud your judgment. The loss must not cloud what you think is right or wrong."

How exactly does emotional stability contribute to this ability? Most importantly, it allows traders to experience themselves and to evaluate their trading abilities *independently* of the inconsistent outcomes of erratic market movements. "Successful traders ... are detached, i.e., the value of them as persons is not really attached to the P&L they would use for the firm," one foreign exchange trader explains. This aspect of emotional stability adds an important perspective to the discussion of overconfidence in Chapter 2, "Psychology of Trading Decisions." In the words of one trading floor manager, traders, "*Need* a strong confidence in themselves. Even though the market goes against them, they have their own strong belief in their own scenarios or strategies." Another trader even states that the degree to which successful traders are "feeling competent [is] very high, I would say in fact extremely high, and it's of high importance!" Yet another trader agrees, observing that, "There's an aura about [successful traders]. It's about how they handle things. It's a confidence ... a certain amount of ego." However, this trader also points to the dangers of overly inflated self-confidence, remarking that, "There is a very thin dividing line between being self-confident and having the right amount of ego, and cockiness. To manage risk, you need the *confidence*, but you will be the worst trader in the world if you are *cocky*."

Information-processing
The first aspect of information-processing is the ability to quickly and simultaneously process various information. "A lot of it is quick thinking on their feet," one trader observes of successful traders, while another trader states that, "They are focusing not only on the fundamentals, but also on market sentiment, orders, and situations in various markets, and they are eager to [collect] such kind of information."

The second aspect of information-processing is analytical thinking. The importance of the ability to process market information analytically may have even increased over recent years. In the words of one trader, "A lot of the newer traders that are more successful tend to be more analytical [and] quantitative. [They are] looking at more fundamentals, trying to tie together information from various sources. And they make informed decisions, factoring in a lot of data as opposed to, 'I like this currency and that's why I want to buy it.'"

Interested integrity
While traders perceive none of the eight personality-related factors as unimportant for a successful trader, interested integrity and the following two factors are perceived as comparatively less important. Interested integrity has high loadings in the characteristics curiosity and integrity. This factor is probably best captured by one trader's description of a successful trader as one, "who sees trading as a real business and who approaches it with a high business ethics." Another trader concurs, saying, "I think you do have to be straightforward, it's of high importance."

Autonomous organization
Autonomous organization characterizes traders' ability of, and positive attitude toward, independently organizing the work process of their trading. One trader addresses this factor by observing that it is the sign of successful trading if, "someone keeps a record of what he does that can show me his track record; has written a paper about his trading strategy; has ideas about position sizing [and] money management strategies; and has thought those processes through, and made the effort to bring them onto a sheet of paper."

Information handling

Information handling is perceived by foreign exchange traders as the least important of the success factors. This factor relates to how information is collected, handled, and passed on to others, including the processing of information by mathematical means or with the help of computers. One trader addresses this factor, for example, by observing of successful traders that, "A lot of the skills are their ability to communicate [and their] mental mathematics."

Detailed analyses of traders' ratings revealed a considerable consensus on the importance of these eight factors. Numerous aspects of traders had no affect on how important the factors were perceived. For example, the traders' family status, age, gender, the type of the trading institution, the number of coworkers in the trading department, the level of trading seniority, and the size of the trading limit did not influence how important the success factors were perceived. Moreover, nearly all of the answers traders provided on the open question about additional characteristics important for a successful trader were clearly related to one of the eight factors. The exceptions were "being able to play blackjack," "flexibility," and "luck"; thus, no new systematic factor involved in successful trading had to be added, which also supports the validity of the factors described.

However, a breakdown of traders according to three trading aspects led to different importances of the eight factors. There were *significant* differences (1) between traders in various work locations (e.g., between traders in Continental Europe and traders in the U.K); (2) between traders using various foreign exchange instruments (i.e., between spot, forward, money market, and derivatives traders); and (3) between traders in different trading roles (i.e., interbank traders, customer traders, and salespeople). These findings suggest that there are geographically different job requirements and that various areas of foreign exchange trading require different personality characteristics.[xi]

Thus, rather than materializing as an isolated phenomenon, the personalities of traders interact with their specific trading environment. For successful trading, not only personality but also the *fit* between personality and trading environment has to be considered. Particularly important aspects of this fit may be the interplay between traders and their trading group, and traders and their trading institution. Foreign exchange traders work in groups in which they

---

[xi] Accordingly, Carew and Slatyer compare spot traders to short-distance sprinters who concentrate on short-term judgments, and forward traders to long-distance runners with longer term perspectives who design more complex strategies.[3]

complement, support, and compete with each other; trading floors of various banks have divergent approaches and philosophies of trading. That interactive phenomena between individuals, groups, and organizations[42,43] play a decisive role in the performance of individuals is suggested, for example, by research on financial analysts: To the disappointment of many, star analysts often do not continue to perform on a top level after being hired by a new financial institution.[44] Thus, only when trader personality, skills, and abilities are related to the specific demands of the environment can optimal personality–environment matches, which ultimately determine personal trading success, be formed.

Since, thus far, my discussion of personality-related characteristics involved in foreign exchange trading has been based on the views of practicing traders, readers may object that these views are *subjective*—that they do not show a connection to *actual* trading performance and profits.[xii] In other words, to really determine the link between personality traits and trading success, *objective* data about traders' personality characteristics and trading performance is required.

The North American survey accomplished precisely this, thereby refining my analysis of personality in trading performance in two substantial ways. First, to assess trading-relevant personality aspects of foreign exchange traders, I developed a comprehensive personality scale. This scale consisted of dozens of items that were formulated on the basis of the personality-related factors just discussed. Hundreds of foreign exchange traders completed the scale. Second, independently from traders' ratings on the personality scale, I obtained external data on their trading performance. Dozens of head traders assessed their traders' profits, trading potential, and overall contributions to the trading floor. As Figure 6.1 shows, these three aspects capture trading performance from various angles.[xiii]

[xii] However, a study by Robertson and Kinder demonstrates greater validity coefficients for the relationship between performance and those personality aspects rated to be predictive by practitioners.[45]

[xiii] While the meaning of *trading profit* is self-evident, *trading potential* was defined as the degree to which traders were perceived to have the making of a successful trader in their specific trading role. This aspect of trading performance was assessed because it is possible that trading profits do not directly reflect trading potential (e.g., it is possible that young traders have not yet realized their full trading potential). *Overall organizational contributions* include, but are not limited to, trading profits: the performance of traders also lies in "contextual" contributions, such as supporting other traders or sharing relevant information, allowing the collective trading floor to be more successful.[46]

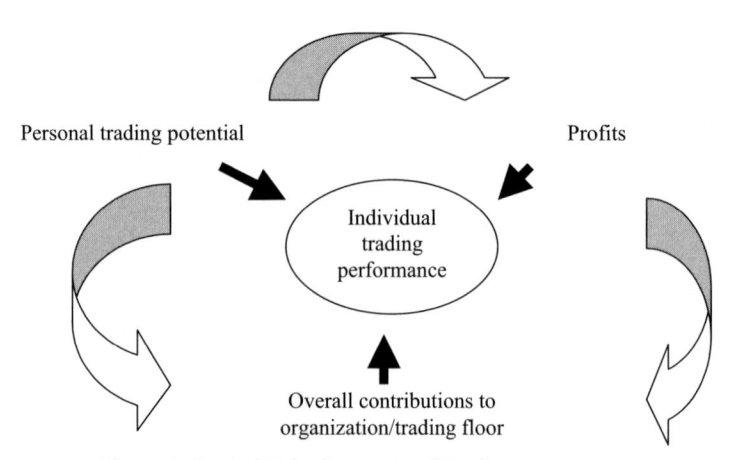

Figure 6.1 Individual aspects of trading success.

Linking traders' personality ratings to the external data about their trading performance yields an objective assessment of personality in trading performance. The analyses of the data are still in progress. However, all preliminary findings clearly confirm that personality indeed plays an important role in trading performance.[47]

These findings demonstrate that the personality of traders explains and predicts a *substantial* part of their trading performance. While some traits are generally involved in trading performance, others are more specific to certain trading roles. For instance, the performance of foreign exchange professionals in interbank, proprietary, and customer/sales trading is best explained by various models that include different traits. Traders' observations that different trading roles involve different decision-making demands support these findings. In the words of one trader, "For an interbank trader it is not their choice whether or not they want to trade. If someone asks you for a price, you are obliged to quote ... Either way, if you like it or you don't like it, you have to decide, 'Will I keep it or will I get rid of it, and if I do get rid of it, what's the liquidity like?' Which on propriety side, you don't."

Moreover, the new findings indicate that characteristics of the trading institution indeed influence what kinds of traders are successful. This is unmistakably reflected in the words of a trading floor manager who declared that, "Each floor is unique in terms of the dynamics, the risk appetite in the institution, the strategic focus. I put a high value on cultural fit within the organization." Hence, with regard to individual trading performance, the manager explained that, "A lot of it depends on the culture of the place and of the rest of the team ... We had a number of people who came here from big shops that were not successful."

MARKET APPLICATIONS

Foreign exchange dealers did not need to be particularly skilled during the Bretton Woods period of fixed exchange rates, when currencies were bought and sold at official rates. At that time, the activity of traders consisted in executing foreign exchange trades at set prices. However, personal trading skills, investment styles, and trading strategies became important when floating exchange rates were introduced.[2] Today, the personality of traders opens the proverbial door to a new and better understanding of foreign exchange trading.

Opening this door and exploring the personality traits and individual differences between market participants represents a radical departure from the traditional economic understanding of the foreign exchange market. However, as this chapter has shown, this approach is influential in the practice of market participants, and its implications for trading may be enormous. Thus, considering "trading personality" deepens our understanding of *actual* participants in the market, and it may do so in a highly profitable way.

A systematic understanding of the role of personality brings numerous advantages. It encourages self-reflection and learning among market decision-makers, supports the training of traders, and may lead to more valid hiring mechanisms.[xiv] Indeed, trading institutions could *greatly* benefit from a better understanding of the personality-related characteristics involved in trading performance. An increase of prediction accuracy in the selection of candidates, even by a small degree, could substantially increase trading profits.[50] At reported individual trading profits of $100,000 per trading day or of $2.5 million per trading year,[10,51] an expected increase of 9% in output would no doubt substantially raise absolute profits.[24]

Finally, a personality psychology of traders goes a long way in explaining different trading styles. Personality may determine how market participants invest and trade *indirectly* via establishing preferences for certain

---

[xiv] It is important to keep in mind the dangers and disadvantages in the unqualified use of personality instruments in trader selection. Mostly for good reasons, job applicants often do not react favorably to personality inventories.[48] Thus, in contrast to many self-help assessment tools, valid psychological instruments for selecting traders need to be carefully developed and applied.[49] They must build on a thorough analysis of work aspects and need to be carefully matched to specific job criteria.[4]

decision-making styles.[xv] A particularly striking possibility of doing so is by influencing traders' implicit market conceptualizations, and by thus shaping their subjective theories on how to best interact with the market. As we will see in Chapter 7, such implicit market understandings are expressed by *metaphors*.

ABBREVIATED REFERENCES

See the reference chapter at the end of the book for full details.

1 Krieger, A. J. and Claflin, E. (1992)
2 Millman, G. J. (1995)
3 Carew, E. and Slatyer, W. (1989)
4 Costa, P. T. (1996)
5 Oberlechner, T. (2004b)
6 Fama, E. F. (1970)
7 Bazerman, M. H. (2002)
8 Taleb, N. N. (2001)
9 Niederhoffer, V. (1997)
10 Schwager, J. D. (1992)
11 Ghiselli, E. E. (1973)
12 Guion, R. M. and Gottier, R. F. (1965)
13 Tokar, D. M. et al. (1998)
14 Digman, J. M. (1990)
15 Wiggins, J. S. and Trapnell, P. D. (1997)
16 Tupes, E. C. and Christal, R. E. (1961)
17 Goodstein, L. D. and Lanyon, R. I. (1999)
18 Neuman, G. A. et al. (1999)
19 Goldberg, L. R. (1992)
20 Goldberg, L. R. (1993)
21 Salgado, J. F. (1997)
22 Tett, R. P. et al. (1991)
23 Barrick, M. R. and Mount, M. K. (1991)
24 Schmidt, F. L. and Hunter, J. E. (1998)
25 Barrick, M. R. et al. (2001)
26 Costa, P. T. and McCrae, R.R. (1985)
27 Costa, P. T. and McCrae, R. R. (1992)
28 McCloskey, J. C. and McCain, B. (1988)
29 Riggio, R. E. and Taylor, S. J. (2000)

[xv] To give an example for the intervening role of trading styles in the link between gender and trading performance of private investors, women have been shown to hold more successful investment accounts than men by virtue of their more passive, and less overconfident, investment style, which avoids the transaction costs of more active portfolios.[52]

30 Inwald, R. E. and Brockwell, A. L. (1991)
31 Oakes, D. W. et al. (2001)
32 Goldstone, N. B. (1988)
33 Schwager, J. D. (1989)
34 Kahn, H. and Cooper, C. L. (1993)
35 Biais, B. et al. (2001)
36 Fenton O'Creevy, M. et al. (1998)
37 Goldberg, J. and Nitzsch, R. V. (2001)
38 Cohen, D. (2001)
39 Cheung, Y.-W. and Chinn, M. D. (2001)
40 Luca, C. (2000)
41 Kahn, H. and Cooper, C. L. (1996)
42 Kichuk, S. L. and Wiesner, W. H. (1998)
43 Kristof, A. L. (1996)
44 Groysberg, B. (2001)
45 Robertson, I. T. and Kinder, A. (1993)
46 Borman, W. C. and Motowidlo, S. J. (1997)
47 Oberlechner, T. (2004a)
48 Rosse, J. G. et al. (1994)
49 Hogan, R. et al. (1996)
50 Earles, J. A. et al. (1996)
51 Lyons, R. K. (1998)
52 Barber, B. M. and Odean, T. (2001)

7
Surfing the Market on Metaphors

But the greatest thing, by far, is to be a master of metaphor.

Aristotle, *Poetics*

Any attempt to understand the foreign exchange market starts out with a question. What precisely is the nature of this market? How do participants form expectations and trade currencies? Certainly, one can research these questions by consulting one of a plethora of economic books currently available on financial markets and thus learn how financial theory explains exchange rates. But another worthwhile possibility is to directly address and learn from the actual decision-makers who participate daily in the market by actively trading currencies and reporting market events. Considering their immediate market experience and paying attention to the descriptions and images they use when talking about the market can prove extremely valuable, as this chapter shows.[i] This chapter shows that this approach is not only unusual but also extremely fruitful.[ii]

---

[i] This chapter is reworked from material in the *British Journal of Social Psychology*, **43**(1), pp. 133–156, T. Oberlechner et al. (2004), "Surfing the money tides: Understanding the foreign exchange market through metaphors",[1] with permission from The British Psychological Society. The quotations used throughout the chapter are verbatim segments of interviews with traders and financial journalists both from the European and the U.S. studies.

[ii] Market metaphors are striking psychological expressions of how market participants "frame" the foreign exchange market and their own trading decisions, see Chapter 3, "Risk-Taking in Trading Decisions".

However, it must be duly noted that examining the foreign exchange market on the experiential level of participants' descriptions differs *radically* from modeling the market as an objective and determined phenomenon. This novel approach digs deeper than simply considering such visible and easily measurable market results as exchange rates on a collective and averaged level.[2] Instead, it considers all market outcomes, and the economic decisions and the behavior of market participants which precede them, not as givens but as, "a function of how people perceive the world," in the words of economic Nobel prize-winner Douglass North.[3] Therefore, to understand the foreign exchange market as a psychological and social institution rather than merely as a predetermined physical phenomenon, the inclusion of the views of its participants is essential. Accordingly, this approach of the foreign exchange market focuses on how participants *themselves* implicitly and explicitly conceptualize the market.[iii]

MAIN MARKET METAPHORS

In the course of the European and the North American surveys, dozens of foreign exchange experts at leading banks and financial news providers shared their experience of the market in comprehensive interviews. One striking observation in these interviews was that their accounts of the market abounded with *metaphors*.[iv] Technically speaking, such metaphors are non-literal linguistic expressions that connect elements of one domain of human experience to another.[10] For example, take the following account of a foreign exchange trader who was in charge of trading currencies for a leading bank: "We were ... number one in the world and we were killing people. We were really killing people by frightening them." While the trader refers to the size of his bank's trading operations and their impact on other traders, the conceptualization of currency trading implicit to his account appears to be a matter of life and death; involving the menace of and lethal attack on others. A similar basic understanding of trading is found in the account of another trader who

---

[iii] The theoretical framework of this approach is based in social representations (i.e., collective elaborations of social objects and phenomena in order to structure communication about and behavior toward these objects and phenomena).[4] Such social representations are not communicated intentionally but are circulated in everyday discourse through behavior, images, and, perhaps most importantly, metaphors.

[iv] The general importance of metaphors to human understanding has been stressed by Ricoeur.[5] Although the importance of metaphors for economics has been documented in principle, metaphor analysis has only recently begun to create a better understanding of financial markets.[1,6–9]

simultaneously takes care to differentiate it from gambling: "No gambling, you go for a kill. Gambling to me is entertainment, to the point where it becomes obsessive. But that [kind of gambling] is sick, you need a doctor; it is not like war, you don't go out for a kill [when gambling]. [Trading] is more brutal, this is more abusive than gambling. People get abusive on trading floors." Clearly, the metaphorical conception in the quotations of both traders equates the foreign exchange market with a warlike setting and connects currency-trading with the dangers and brutality of fighting in war; thus the metaphor of war is used here to conceptualize the nature of the foreign exchange market and what it means to trade in this market. This characterization of the foreign exchange market in warlike terms, however, is only the tip of the figurative iceberg in terms of the use of metaphors to describe the foreign exchange market.

When metaphor analysis, a method based on cognitive linguistics,[v] is systematically applied to the experience of market participants, it shows that the metaphors that participants use when talking about the market are not chosen accidentally or randomly. Instead, these market metaphors are shared among market participants and revolve around certain common images. Seven main metaphors can be distinguished in participants' accounts of the foreign exchange market: The market as a *bazaar*, as a *machine*, as a *living being*, as *gambling*, as sports, as *war*, and as an *ocean*. Examples of verbatim statements for these market metaphors are presented in Table 7.1.

These images convey fundamentally different understandings of the foreign exchange market. Each of these images emphasizes particular aspects of this market while downplaying others; in the words of metaphor analysis, metaphors not only *highlight*, but also *hide*.[13] While the hiding function of market metaphors is easily overlooked, it is also vital; as Arthur Conan Doyle had Sherlock Holmes famously remark in *Silver Blaze* about a dog that did *not* bark on the night of the murder: "*That* was the curious incident!" Moreover,

---

[v] Psychologically, metaphors can be approached from cognitive and discourse perspectives. The *cognitive approach* to metaphors emphasizes that metaphors are powerful organizing principles of thinking and experiencing. Cognitive linguistics assumes that metaphors are not linguistic decoration but they express shared realities and natural ways of thinking in social groups.[11-14] For example, expressions such as "a battle between sellers and buyers" or to be "bombarded with information" indicate that market participants' thinking is structured by the war metaphor. This metaphor then organizes their experiences of the market and helps them to understand market events. In contrast, *discourse theory* focuses on the context within which market participants use metaphors and on how they actively mobilize metaphors within particular conversations in order to manage their social goals in the linguistic interaction.[15-17]

Table 7.1 Main metaphors of the foreign exchange market

Bazaar
Like a supermarket, you can buy or sell currencies ... as you can, say, sell and buy bread and butter
Very similar to people buying and selling vegetables
You buy apples cheap and you sell for a higher price, buy low, sell high ... it might be petrol; it might be wheat, anything. For me it is a product, the dollar
A supermarket ... second-hand car dealing
What they are doing is buying and selling clumps of money

Machine
The mechanics of dealing
I should have got more mileage out of this machine
It's going well; let's make sure we leverage up on it
Spreading a rumor to engineer a move
Like this gearbox or transmission mechanism of developments in the real economy

Living being—beast
It's a beast ... you can either stroke it and it will sit down for you, or it'll bite
An animal nobody should ever get himself into
The market always moves in the direction in which it will hurt the most people
It is like an octopus, feeding off itself all over the place
I don't get an image, I get a word, rapacious
Knowing where foreign exchange rates will go is to understand the beast ... understand what moves it, and why it moves

Living being—lover
A great trader feels and hurts and touches what he is doing ... I feel and touch and caress the subject
You have to be emotionally ready to do something. To be triggered, to be stimulated
This emotional involvement can get much too deep. And, we say, you get sort of married to a position; you just can's let go of it
It can give you a lot of satisfaction, a lot of great feelings

Gambling
Trying desperately to make that money back; it becomes like a compulsive gambler's syndrome
If I had a really bad day, I would like to explain the job as to be in a casino and play roulette
Casino describes a lot of the environment that takes place. That people get carried away ...
I'm putting on red because I think it's going to land in red
Once you have a cushion, and the little chips on your table you can use, then it doesn't matter if you lose three or four chips and put them on your first bet

Sports
Trading is like sports. It's about winning. It's a competitive game that starts every morning at 7 o'clock
Like a keeper at a penalty kick ... he jumps in one direction and hopes the shot goes there

You have to be good as a single individual, but you have to be a team player as well
You live in a world of competition ... you want to be better, quicker ... so you have to watch your competitors
Not scoring the goals anymore, you are off the track
[If] someone phones you up, you have to judge whether he sounds like he is playing in the first division

War
A real battle between Singapore and Tokyo
If you do nothing, you are killed
That customer may be able to bury you or totally kill you
As long as you can justify your actions and you are successful, you will survive
No prisoner taking out there, they don't take prisoners. If you take prisoners, you don't make it

Ocean
A beach ... global on this side and very local on the other
An ocean ... because it is so deep and so liquid ... it can flow; it has tides, and it is all one; it is all connected ... When it all flows out this way that means the level rises there
A tide ... washing in and out, things washing up on shore
I visualize the foreign exchange market as a big wave that is rolling in and one of these days it is going to hit that beach so hard
We are part of the water; we are part of the liquid I guess, or we could also be the moon that is pulling the tides one way or the other, or whatever it is that makes the ocean move or makes waves

each of these market metaphors carries specific implications for the very nature of the foreign exchange market; for example, what goals the market serves, what kinds of rules are valid in the market, what is the role of market participants, and whether and how it is possible to predict the market's future.

The foreign exchange market as a bazaar

While the understanding of the foreign exchange market as a bazaar seems obvious at first sight, the bazaar metaphor represents a distinctive market conceptualization. This metaphor translates the highly abstract and intangible concept of the foreign exchange market into a concrete and spatial location where physical goods change human hands. In viewing the foreign exchange market as a bazaar, foreign exchange trading simply means a certain form of market (i.e., a "place where people are buying and selling money"). The currencies traded in this market can be compared with any other kind of merchandise such as fruits or used cars. One foreign exchange trader underscores this similarity, observing that in, "Buying and selling of one commodity for another ... the foreign exchange markets are no different." Another trader expressed his agreement with this assertion, saying wryly that, "Currency is a commodity, as you can sell chairs, refrigerators ... If you could move refrigerators through a Reuters screen, you would probably be selling them by now."

As with all the metaphors of the foreign exchange market, the bazaar metaphor implies a certain basic setting and specific human behaviors which are rational and consistent with such a setting. In a bazaar, people encounter other people since bazaars are locations "where buyers and sellers meet." The prices of goods in a bazaar are not objectively determined by external mathematical algorithms but rather result from the social interaction between buyer and seller. "There are no rules, and there is no right price; the right price is the price you've done the deal," one trader explains. Moreover, in a bazaar, buyers and sellers do not form detached prices in isolation, but in interaction with and in dependency from other traders. Before buying, customers in a bazaar may first window-shop and put other sellers to the test: "Customers who access the market go to a couple of shops ... they compare prices and then after seeing a couple of prices from a couple of stores, they then just go to one," says another trader. Sellers in a bazaar, in turn, have to adjust their prices to the market price and take into account information and the behavior of other sellers. "He realizes that the other guy is selling plates for two dollars, so he drops his price to one dollar ninety and all his customers come back," a foreign exchange trader declares. Sellers who fail to adjust their prices and to find a buyer may find the value of their goods quickly evaporate. "If you don't find a bid somewhere, then you sit on your apples and oranges, then you can eat it or make marmalade," another trader concludes. Hence, the usage of the bazaar metaphor of the foreign exchange market stresses human interaction and also conveys the need for a strong awareness of the social market environment.

The foreign exchange market as a machine

In stark contrast to the market as a bazaar, the foreign exchange market when understood as a machine is characterized as a system governed by set rules and firm mechanisms. "These movements can be calculated in probability terms. And [thus] this is a purely mathematical process," explains a trader. This metaphor of the foreign exchange market highlights a market mechanism that usually works with perfection and reliability: "I don't think there is any irrationality at all in the foreign exchange markets. I think it's per definition perfect," another trader confidently declares. Like every machine, the foreign exchange market according to the machine metaphor requires a defined input, provides a defined output, and regulates a defined built-in process that transforms inputs into outputs. This input–output orientation of the foreign exchange market is illustrated in a financial journalist's comparison of the financial news with, "The fuel for the market's engine." Although the inner mechanisms of a machine are usually hidden, the operator of a machine is able to gain knowledge and expertise about the machine (e.g., through observation and experience). "If you drive a car for 20 years, and the car makes a noise, you can pretty much tell where this noise is emanating from," quips one foreign exchange trader.

Because a machine has no emotions, dealing with a machine usually does not involve emotions: "Any trading decision is a totally emotion-free thing," according to one trader. To market participants, understanding the foreign exchange market as a machine implies a logical, analytic, and detached decision-making rationality. "You have to make decisions on certain probabilities on the basis of your past experiences but not on the basis of your personal emotions," sums up another trader. Thus in the machine metaphor, the foreign exchange market emerges as a mathematical, reliable, perfect, rational entity, where emotion and departure from rules, norms, and tested precision play no part.

The foreign exchange market as a living being

The foreign exchange market as a living being is a comprehensive metaphorical conceptualization that assigns characteristics that are usually associated with living beings to the market. In contrast to the static and rational machine metaphor, the market is perceived here as an animated and emotional organism following its own rules.[vi] As a living being, the market is "crazy," "too fast," and "has no time to think," according to traders. Likewise, as a living being, the market reacts emotionally to environmental stimuli; for example, when "news items panic the market" or when "factors came along that made the market nervous," in the words of a trader and a financial journalist. The foreign exchange market as a living being is also able to anticipate and interpret events independently; hence, "the market then draws its conclusions" or "thinks this way," as stated by one trader.

"They view the market as almost a living being that they are interacting with, and [that they are] trying to anticipate and outsmart," one trader remarks on his colleagues on the trading floor. For market participants, intuition and empathy are important when reading the market's mind in order to predict its behavior, even when the market mind seems irrational or

---

[vi] This metaphor expresses the notion of independent agency and has also been labelled "animal" by others.[12]

unintelligent. "What market participants often seem to be doing is not trading on what they think the significance of information is, but what they think the market will *interpret* the significance of information to be. I tend to think of markets just like this big brain but of a very stupid person," observes another trader. Because the behavior of the foreign exchange market as a living being is not always intelligible in logical terms, it may be "extremely difficult to find out why the foreign exchange markets do what they do." A living being does not function according to established rules but according to its shifting mood, thoughts, and intentions: "Market behavior changes from one day to the other," in the words of one trader. The foreign exchange market as a living being shows different reactions depending on whom it deals with. "If the health minister says he thinks the dollar is overvalued, then probably markets don't worry. [But] if the Treasury secretary says so, then they listen," says another trader. Because it thinks, feels, and reacts, market participants may socially interact with the market as a living being and thus try to influence it in an active manner. Participants then "let the market know what [their] intentions are or may keep the market guessing."

Viewing the foreign exchange market as a living being serves as the basis for two more specific metaphorical elaborations: the market as a beast and the market as a lover. The foreign exchange market as a beast—"a great big creature"—is huge and always hungry: "It's so large and the appetite for information is so strong." Traders, like heroes, must fight and tame this dangerous animal or at least cope with it in some other way. "[As] a wild animal, I think the challenge is to master it ... and there are days you are doing well, and there are days you are going to be bitten by it," says one trader. The existential danger represented by the foreign exchange market as beast also indicates an overlap with the war metaphor, "Because if we don't govern it, we are destroyed," in the words of one trader.

In contrast to this, the relationship with the foreign exchange market as a lover is characterized by the experience of strong feelings of attraction and fascination. "All dealers who are really dealers, they have an erotic relationship to the market," remarks a foreign exchange trader. This intense relationship may cause passionate emotional swings among market participants. For example, the market as lover may be the source of pleasurable feelings of excitement and being high: "It can give you a lot of satisfaction, a lot of great feelings," according to another trader. Yet it may also lead to the danger of emotional dependency to a wrong and harmful lover in a painful relationship. "I've lost a lot of money, because I felt, I got emotional on a position. Getting married to a position ... getting emotionally attached to it," one trader describes the potential danger of developing too strong feelings for the market as lover. These statements clearly show that participants' interaction with the market as a living being is not characterized by detached and rational decision-making, but by personally and emotionally involving *relationships*. "The market reflects myself, and I will be sometimes brought up [and raised] by it. It is indispensable in my life ... I like it. [It is] so closely related to myself," one trader states.

The foreign exchange market as gambling

Another commonly used metaphor for the foreign exchange market, that of gambling, expresses a market "rationality" based primarily on coincidence and luck. "[It] is sometimes like a casino where you are betting on rouge or black or zero," one trader remarks. But while operating a machine can be learned and requires knowledge of its inherent mechanisms, it is generally acknowledged that the decisive factor in gambling is *luck*.

The gambling metaphor of the foreign exchange market stresses both the risk-taking and emotional involvement of market participants. As gamblers, foreign exchange traders may become unreasonable, "Get carried away ... lose their sense of sensibility, and lose all sense of why they put that position on," as one trader observes. Moreover, the gambling metaphor diminishes and externalizes market participants' responsibility and influence over outcomes of the gamble: "Some of the best returns from fund managers are [from] people who are incredibly lucky," another trader notes. As in the machine metaphor of the foreign exchange market, other market participants are usually less important since they do not influence the algorithm of the gamble.

"It is something like chess. You sit there, you see how the market develops, how the chess game develops. You have to guess what the opponent might be able to do or what you are going to do when the opponent does something. And the market place is, I think, a leveraged dimension chess game where you play many, many opponents at the same time," one trader explains. Closely related to the gambling metaphor of the foreign exchange market are metaphorical market conceptions that involve a more strategic kind of game-playing, such as "a game like chess" or "professional poker," in which the combination of chance and strategic thinking becomes manifest. "Trading is a mental game," one trader observes. These kinds of games involve interaction with other participants; besides luck, they highlight elements of discipline, skilfulness, and expertise. Thus, they may be seen as a link between the metaphorical fields of gambling and sports.

The foreign exchange market as sports

"If you are going out to play an important game of soccer and tennis, you feel that knot in your stomach before you go out. It is good tension, a good anxiety. And I think if you sit in a trading room, just before an unemployment number comes out ... it's same thing," one trader explains. Thus, in the sports metaphor, the foreign exchange market is perceived in terms of a competition or race. The ultimate goal is to win against the others; in the words of another trader: "To have the competitive spirit, to be the best, the ambition to beat others, to be a little quicker, a little more excited, maybe a little sharper." In the sports metaphor of the foreign exchange market, "Everybody becomes Mr Iron Man", as yet another trader observes. This goal of winning is usually pursued in the highly competitive interaction with other market participants.

The sports metaphor gives the foreign exchange market a generally more foreseeable and less dangerous undertone than the war metaphor, which will be discussed later. Sport competitions are always conducted within a defined framework that has an agreed-on beginning and end; they take place on a particular "playground" and follow a certain set of accepted rules. However, there are also additional characteristics that distinguish sports from war: Competitors in sports are also not destroyed completely, since they are needed to start the competition anew. Sports thus often imply a noble air of fair play and sportsmanship, which help to hide the market's existential and potentially harmful consequences to the social and political world outside. The focus in the foreign exchange market when characterized by the sports metaphor is on the action and players in the arena, not on the spectators or bystanders. Despite their ambition to win, sportspeople in the arena may lose, and the market can be cruel to, and fail to remember, sports heroes who have passed their prime: "Like in horse races or in a soccer team, individual competitors only have maybe five or six years when [they] are the best runner or the best scorer, if they are not scoring the goals anymore, [they] are off the track ... and will never come back again," says one foreign exchange trader of the market. Additionally, closely related to the sports metaphor of the foreign exchange market are a group of images of hunting and chasing which maximize the evocation of dynamic movement, speed, and inciting. In these pursuits, the market participant's own motivation to run and to compete against others, which is also present in a sports competition, turns into a necessity to run after a target or away from some threat which is forced on the participant by the environment. The description of, "Rabbits running around ... being chased by a fox," as articulated by one trader, for example, evokes imagery less of winning a race than of fundamental survival and fighting for self-preservation in the face of danger. Consequently, the foreign exchange sports arena and its participants become less contained in these settings that link the market metaphor of sports to the metaphor of war.

The foreign exchange market as war
War as a metaphor appears frequently in participants' experience of the foreign exchange market: Currencies may come "under attack," market participants have to "defend positions," and they follow certain "strategies" or actively "intervene" when they are "powerful and strong enough," and so forth. As is the case with sports, when the foreign exchange market is a war, there are opposing individuals or parties which face competition. However, in contrast to taking part in sports, waging and winning a war is a matter of survival, not ambition. "If you're weak, you have no chance to survive there ... you're even going to be hit by your own colleagues sitting next to you," in the words of one trader. In war, opponents are not only defeated in the way sport competitors are in a contest, they become enemies who must be "hurt" or even "killed." "Make them run, if you want to move the market. You have to hurt people. If you hurt people, they run; if they run, the market moves. And you have to be very aggressive in that," says another trader. The market as war is a setting characterized by a continuous and vividly realized threat in which trading is a matter of life and death. "There are always people who are quick enough to get out. The best. The quickest. And they make money on it. And then you have the stampede, and they [who get caught up in it] die. They get run over," observes a trader. In this omnipresent fight for survival and victory, market participants think in terms of self-defence, the survival of the fittest, and martial law. Moral rules that are valid in everyday life may be abrogated in the continuous state of emergency constituted by the foreign exchange market as war because "this is a dirty industry."

In the foreign exchange market as war, market participants can be expected to use every one of the weapons at their disposal and whatever tactics seem promising. Describing the best timing for a speculative "attack" against a currency, one trader declares: "Ice cold, regularly, when you'll be on the loo, that's when I take and will throw my hand grenades into your shelter. That's the way to do it ... why do you think soldiers always attack at four in the morning?" Operating in such a grave and constantly perilous environment implies an extremely intensive personal involvement on behalf of individual market participants who at any given moment have to fight for their lives. Personal characteristics such as being strong, brave, and fearless are considered decisive in this setting. "It is a tough world. It's neat for people who can take punches. If you don't like to hand it out, if you can't fight, don't get into it," one trader sums it up. Consequently, viewing the market as war represents the experience of an all-encompassing, existential threat.

The foreign exchange market as an ocean

"People say beware of the sea, because underneath the nice calm sea the waves will pick you up. And this is why people die; they die in rivers and [elsewhere in the sea]. It's exactly the same in foreign exchange," one trader explains the perils of the market. The metaphor of the foreign exchange market as an ocean is found in a number of liquidity-related expressions throughout the interviews, including many references to "channels," "flows," "currents," and "streams" which exist in the market. The working of the market as an ocean can be compared with liquids in a hydraulic system: "The market tends to move things to an equilibrium level where the market feels its fair value," according to one trader. Fluidity is an important precondition of the smooth working of this hydraulic system. "In a market where there is no liquidity, markets jump. A guy could just come in with ten [million] dollars and move the market massively. When liquidity comes in, instantly it will be realigned back," another trader observes. The interviews also show that ocean-related expressions are used not only to describe the foreign exchange market as a whole, but also its components: Currencies can "fluctuate" or "float," market information is a "source" or gets "absorbed," and a certain country may come to stand for a "bottleneck [for] big Western money trying to get into the East."

Depicted as an ocean, the nature of the foreign exchange market appears less predictable and less deterministic than as a machine, and remains constantly affected by its environment. For example, the foreign exchange market as an ocean, "Is open to nearly every influence that influences people's lives in terms of technology, politics, economics and geography," in the words of a trader. Such external factors do not directly affect the workings of a machine. Moreover, while variations in the system's functioning, such as "economic cycles," are inherent in the nature of an ocean, they would be signs of malfunctioning in a machine. Thus, the market as an ocean knows of both quiet and of stormy times. There are, "Times when everything is calm and you have normal market conditions ... when the currency markets are flat in the water," in the words of one financial journalist. However, as various examples from other traders and financial journalists show, invisible "underlying flows," such as "trade flows or portfolio flows," may "knock the dam over." Then,

"Currency markets fluctuate," "money sloshing around ... sloshing like water." In such times of crisis, it happened that, "The lira plunged and [German chancellor] Kohl had to go onto Italian television with [Italian minister of the treasury] Dini to try to smooth the waters." Then, just as the sea after a storm, currencies can also "calm down" again.

Another important characteristic of the ocean metaphor of the foreign exchange market is that it implies neither the complete inanimateness of the machine metaphor nor the intentionality of the living being metaphor. In an ocean, people interact with the organic rhythm of the "ebbing and flowing" of tides, in the words of a journalist. Observing this rhythm, "People are very obsessed with levels," and "Certain levels ... will at times initiate extensive price movements," in the words of traders, because, "Shock waves created within one country very, very quickly go around the globe," according to one financial journalist. In the foreign exchange market as an ocean, market participants' influence and responsibility are insignificant. Because an ocean does not need human attendance to function, market participants often find themselves primarily in the role of observers and bystanders. Market participants may, however, also be adventurous seafarers who, "Take some cover on board," and, "Put in the auto-pilot and cruise," in the words of two traders. Alternatively, they may instead be surfers, "riding the crest of a wave," according to a financial journalist. Although the foreign exchange market as ocean is not intentionally harmful in the way enemies are to one another while at war, at times the ocean may become a dangerous and hostile environment, wiser to avoid in lieu of the safety and security of firm ground. "You are riding a wave; at some point it comes to an end and you want to get off before it hits the shore. That is what makes the difference between the winners and the losers in any financial market: You have to know when to get in and, more importantly, when to get off," remarks a financial journalist of this conundrum.

The powerful dynamics of the foreign exchange market as an ocean, expressed in its constant "going up and down" (financial journalist), emphasizes its self-contained existence, independent from the participants, and plays down human-made and fragile market aspects. The ocean metaphor also allows market participants to forget that there simply are participants who lose at the expense of others. The supposed self-sustaining powers of the ocean, its endless and effortless "ebbing and flowing" (financial journalist) give rise to the façade that all participants can equally profit from its unlimited, ever-renewed energy: The vastness and limitlessness inherent in the concept of an ocean suggest that all market participants may have their share, and this without affecting the ocean and without harming others.

METAPHORS SHAPE MARKET PERSPECTIVES

The market as a bazaar, as a machine, as a living being, as gambling, as sports, as war, and as an ocean—each of these main market metaphors is a filter that sheds light on the foreign exchange market and on trading decisions from a specific perspective.[18] Metaphor theory suggests that the differences between these perspectives are extremely consequential because so-called metaphorical "entailments" impart characteristics of underlying metaphorical images onto the target domain of the foreign exchange market. Take, for example, the metaphor of the foreign exchange market as war. This metaphor suggests that the market possesses a number of characteristics that are specific to war; in other words, the implicit logic of war gives rise to a whole series of entailments on what the foreign exchange market is actually about.

What exactly are these entailments? Commonplace cultural knowledge helps to grasp the entailments carried by a certain metaphor.[14] A war, for example, is a brutal and dangerous environment in which attacks and counterattacks take place. In a war, others are either allies or enemies. Danger and death are constantly present, and failing to defeat one's opponent's means running the risk of being defeated or even destroyed oneself. War may bring along civilian casualties, innocent victims who are labelled as collateral damage and who are sacrificed in order to win the war. Such metaphorical entailments are extremely important to understanding not only the foreign exchange market but also trading decisions: They not only suggest the nature of the foreign exchange market, but they also advocate which rules are valid in the market, and they provide guidelines on how to act and decide in it.

Figure 7.1 provides a comprehensive look at the main metaphors of the foreign exchange market. Permeable borders and overlaps between the metaphors in the figure indicate that metaphorical expressions may relate to more than only one of the main market metaphors. For example, strategic games such as poker contain elements both of the gambling and the sports metaphor. Moreover, the figure reveals that all market metaphors address two consequential dimensions of metaphorical entailment. Each metaphor provides different answers to two *key* questions to market practitioners and theoreticians alike: (1) Who (or what) are the participants in the foreign exchange market interacting with? (2) To what degree—and how—is the market predictable?

Market metaphors are about the psychological "other"

The first reason the metaphors used to describe the foreign exchange market are important is that they let us know *who (or what) market participants*

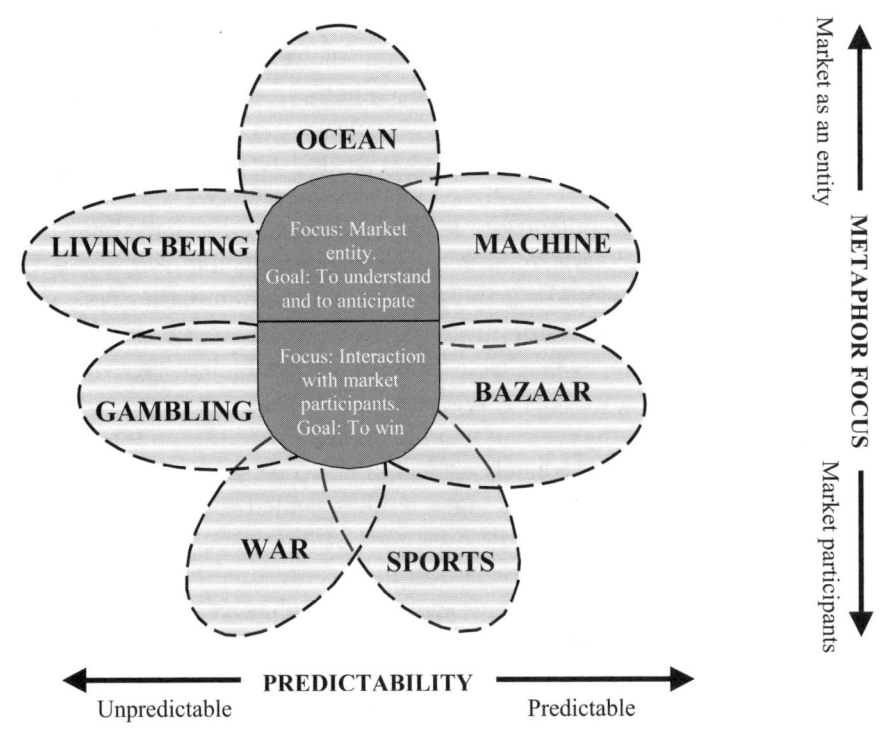

Figure 7.1 Main metaphors of the foreign exchange market.

psychologically deal with on a daily basis. As shown in Figure 7.1, there are two kinds of market metaphors regarding this fundamental question of the psychological "other" in the market.

One group of market metaphors (which includes the foreign exchange market as a bazaar, as sports, and as war) ultimately expresses primarily how market participants relate to each other. These *interaction-oriented metaphors* express possible ways to interact with others in the foreign exchange market (i.e., trading goods with them at a bazaar, competing with them at sports, or fighting them at war). Assumptions about the nature of the foreign exchange market itself are implied here by defining the background setting for participants' interaction (i.e., a marketplace, a sports arena, or a battlefield). Interaction-oriented metaphors are goal-oriented in that they refer to a final goal of winning through interaction or competition with other market participants. Winning can be achieved in different ways: through trading, sportive competing, or belligerent fighting. The interaction expressed by these metaphors is entertaining, thrilling, and even dangerous;

it involves different degrees of risk-taking and demands various degrees of personal involvement of the individual, from the relatively casual bargaining and exchanging at a bazaar to the fight-or-flight extremes in a war. Interaction-oriented metaphors frame the outcome of one's own market behavior relative to other market participants, and this behavior may result either in winning or in losing.

The metaphorical entailments of the various interaction-oriented metaphors vary significantly. For example, both sports competitors and warriors have to demonstrate such superior skills and traits—strength and fearlessness among them. However, achieving victory in sports is less crucial to the individual than it is in belligerent fighting, where winning is a matter of human survival. Buying and selling such everyday goods as vegetables in the bazaar metaphor also refers to winning (namely, in the sense of making money by skilful trading). Winning in this situation is less immediately critical and involves less rivalry with one's opponents. In contrast to the other interaction-oriented metaphors, the bazaar image thus plays down the competitive and thrilling aspects of trading, and obscures the high stakes involved in decisions concerning potentially sizeable gains or losses. Instead, the bazaar metaphor emphasizes social interactions between traders and customers.

The remainder of the metaphors (i.e., the foreign exchange market as a machine, as gambling, as living being, and as ocean) describe the experience of market participants who are mainly oriented toward the entity of the market which exists more or less independently of other human actors. These metaphors can be called *ontological metaphors*[vii] as they focus on the character of this market entity (i.e., the controlled functioning of a machine, the unpredictability of a random generator, the flowing of an ocean, and the will of a living being). In these metaphors, the interaction of a participant is directed less at other participants than at the foreign exchange market entity, for example, by managing a relationship with the market in the case of the living being metaphor, by observing and surfing the market in the case of the ocean metaphor, by trying one's chances with the market in the case of the gambling metaphor, and by operating and regulating the market in the case of the machine metaphor.

Ontological metaphors construct the foreign exchange market as an entity. Each of these metaphors implies a certain understanding of the market and a distinct way of relating to it. Unlike action-oriented metaphors, ontological metaphors do not construct the foreign exchange market as a human-made creation that evolves in the social interactions of participants, but instead as an

---

[vii] In metaphysics, ontology is the study of being and existence.

outside reality with which market participants are confronted. This conception of the market as a separate object indeed has a crucial effect on the perceived controllability of market events. The market as an ocean or as a machine follows its own rules, largely uninfluenced by market participants. The market as random generator is ignorant of any rules and is immune to any external influence or control. The market as a living being may be affected by and react to social interaction, but will decide to do so only by its own will. Furthermore, ontological metaphors allow not only foreign exchange market participants but also those who write about the market to conceal what psychologists call the "agent": This group of market metaphors ultimately tends to attribute market events and developments to an anonymous outside force rather than to the actions of market participants.

To summarize, all metaphors define the experienced counterpart of market participants. Going beyond the abstract concept of the market, they tell us who participants psychologically interact with when they trade and how they do so (e.g., by attacking, surfing, throwing dice, and falling in love in a market as varied as war, an ocean, or a lover).

Market metaphors are about market predictability

A second essential function of the main market metaphors is that they all contain implicit messages about *market predictability* (i.e., whether it is possible to predict the market and future exchange rates, and how to do so). It comes as little surprise that predictability plays a central role in these metaphors: Like all financial decision-makers, foreign exchange market participants spend much of their time anticipating future market movements and attempting to figure out successful ways of doing so.

Indeed, there are systematic connections between the main market metaphors and market participants' notions of predictability. To analyze the relationship between traders' use of market metaphors and assumptions about market predictability, a statistical analysis was conducted.[viii] As Figure 7.2 shows, results clearly show that different foreign exchange market metaphors are meaningfully related to various degrees of market predictability.[ix]

The figure illustrates the similarity of different metaphors with regard to assumed "rules" about market predictability; the closer metaphors are

---

[viii] The method used was correspondence analysis, a statistical method to visualize the associations between the levels of a two-way contingency table.
[ix] For the analysis, trader interviews were analyzed by independent raters for usage of market metaphors and traders' views of market predictability.

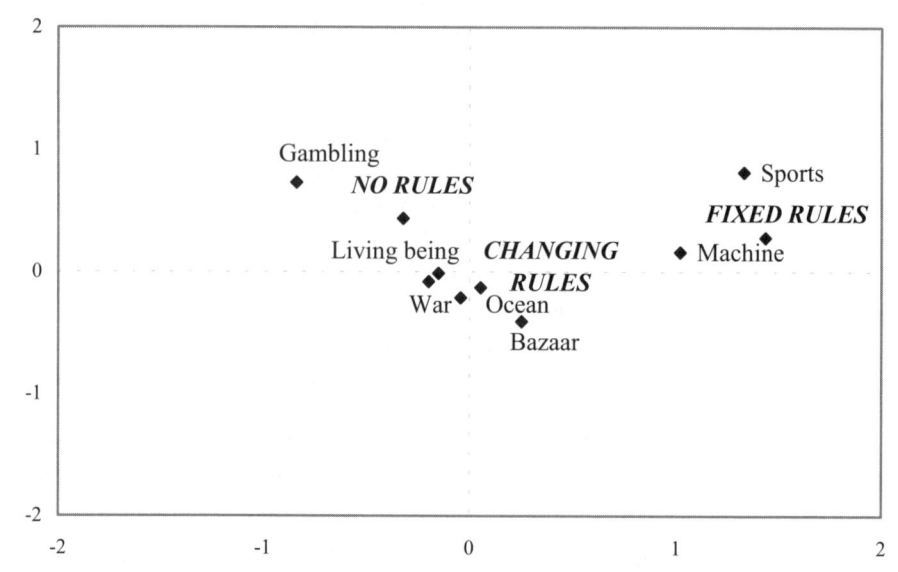

Figure 7.2 Market metaphors and subjective predictability assumptions.

located within the graph, the more similar they are with regard to the associated understanding of these rules. The figure demonstrates that in comparison with other metaphors of the foreign exchange market, the machine and the sports metaphors are more strongly associated with the notion of fixed rules about determinants of exchange rates and with how the market can be predicted, while the bazaar and the ocean metaphors tend to be associated with the notion of partial and changing rules about market predictability. The living being and the war metaphors of the foreign exchange market are associated with the notion of partial and changing rules and with the assumption of missing rules comparatively more often than the other market metaphors, suggesting that these two market metaphors allude to a conception of a foreign exchange market which may follow variable rules but which also includes possible unexpected reactions. Finally, the gambling metaphor of the foreign exchange market is most strongly associated with the notion that there are no rules about market predictability.

These links between usage of foreign exchange market metaphors and assumptions about market predictability are based on participants' *subjective and psychological perceptions* of the market, and they can easily be explained if these perceptions are considered. For example, if the foreign exchange market is perceived as a machine, then predicting and forecasting the market follows the logic of an input–output prognosis. Specific events produce specific reactions in the market which can subsequently be computed by algorithms and mathematical probabilities. In contrast to this, the ocean and the living being metaphors express a fundamentally different sense of anticipation, where predictions and forecasts can be called less logical than organic and where the market's future behavior not only depends on external events, but also on pre-existing internal market conditions. For example, in the ocean metaphor the market's reaction will depend on the degree of "liquidity" available, on existing "flows," and on simultaneous "influences" which determine the relative importance of an event. In the living being metaphor, anticipation implies empathy and even mind-reading as the reaction of the market depends on the market's subjective moods and interpretations. The random generator in the foreign exchange market metaphor of gambling can either not be predicted at all or only by means of luck.

Interaction-oriented metaphors also imply different degrees of market predictability. For example, in the foreign exchange market metaphor of war, other participants are enemies who are likely to behave in a way that is difficult to predict and can be expected to break rules. However, in the market conceptualized as sports, the behavior of the other players will follow more clearly defined rules in a more predictable framework and setting. Thus, these results confirm the importance of metaphors to participants' thinking about the market, and they show that there are psychologically meaningful connections between metaphors and participants' assumptions about whether and *how* the foreign exchange market is predictable.

EXPLICIT AND IMPLICIT METAPHORS OF THE FOREIGN EXCHANGE MARKET

When people use metaphors, they sometimes do so consciously by deliberately expanding (e.g., on the comparison of life with a journey) and contemplating the aspects of life which indeed resemble a journey. However, on the whole, metaphors are used unintentionally, as many examples of metaphors in the language and the market descriptions of traders have shown. This is yet another vital aspect of foreign exchange metaphors: the difference between "explicit" metaphors (i.e., metaphors that are consciously and deliberately produced) and "implicit" metaphors (i.e., metaphors that surface unintentionally and that spontaneously express participants' market experience).

"Please find a metaphor or an analogy for the foreign exchange market," foreign exchange traders and financial journalists were asked during the interviews to deliberately produce a personal market metaphor. To this specific question, basically the same seven main market metaphors emerged that also permeated participants' general explanations and descriptions of the market. However, the relative frequencies of these consciously produced metaphors are significantly *different* when compared with the metaphors in participants' ordinary talk about the foreign exchange market. In other words, while the kinds of metaphors which were (1) generated explicitly and deliberately in order to symbolize the foreign exchange market and (2) used implicitly and unconsciously in spontaneous discussions of the foreign exchange market are identical, their relative frequency and importance is clearly different.

For example, Figure 7.3 shows that while on the explicit and deliberate level the sports metaphor appears more often than the war metaphor, on the implicit and unconscious level the foreign exchange market is more often

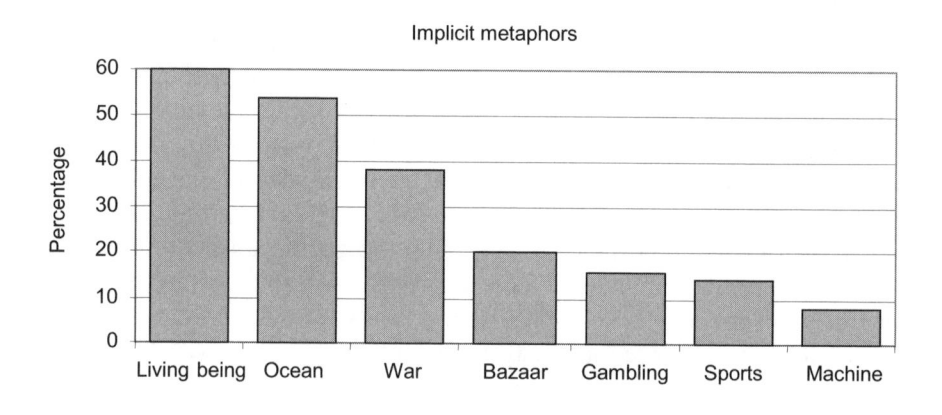

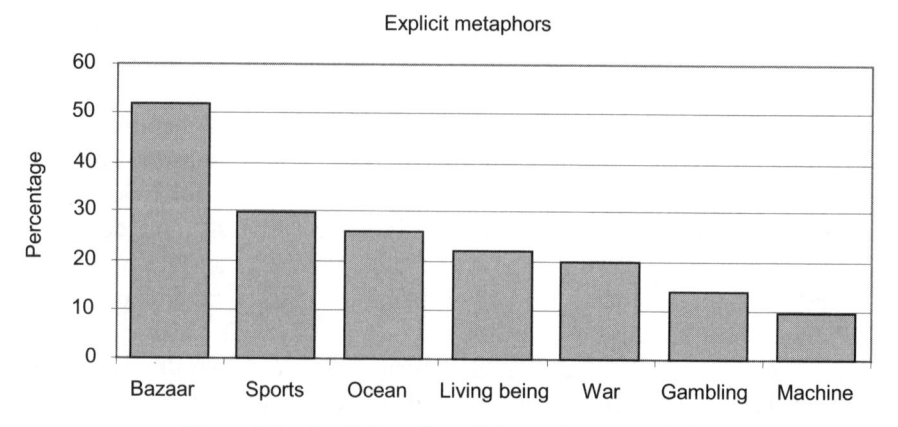

Figure 7.3 Implicit and explicit market metaphors.

conceptualized as war than as sports. Further, the bazaar metaphor appears most often in deliberate productions, while it plays a far less important role in implicit metaphorical conceptualizations of the foreign exchange market. Moreover, the "organic" metaphors of the market as ocean and living being are the most frequently used implicit metaphors, while they appear with only medium frequency in explicit characterizations of the foreign exchange market. To summarize, the living being, the ocean, and the war metaphors are used more often *implicitly* than explicitly, and the bazaar and the sports metaphors are produced more often *explicitly* than implicitly. In contrast, the gambling and the machine metaphor rarely appear on both the explicit and the implicit level.

These differences between explicit and implicit metaphorical conceptualizations of the foreign exchange market are significant as they address the distinction between "in principle" and "in fact" views and interpretations:[19] While *explicit* metaphors tell us what market participants think are relevant metaphors in principle, *implicit* metaphors tell us about the participants' understandings of the foreign exchange market in practice. Thus, the difference between explicit and implicit metaphors indicates how market participants think they *should* think and talk about the market, and how they actually think and talk about it. For example, the dominant explicit use of the bazaar metaphor conceptualizes the foreign exchange market in a way which is not only close to common economic discourse but which also represents a socially acceptable and harmless explicit characterization of the market. The same interpretation follows from the finding that the foreign exchange market is conceptualized deliberately more often as sports (which is organized and fair) than as war (which is volatile and destructive). Strikingly, as Figure 7.3 shows, these importances of the sports and the war metaphors are reversed for implicit conceptualizations of the market.

The fact that the machine metaphor occurs the least frequently in metaphorical conceptions of the foreign exchange market contradicts traditional academic models of financial markets and orthodox economics, which are both governed by mechanistic metaphors.[9,20] In these models, specific and clearly definable events lead to specific and clearly definable reactions, and the relationship between market events and reactions can be expressed by mathematical equations. In contrast to these models, however, not the machine metaphor but organic and interactive metaphors dominate market participants' subjective experience of the foreign exchange market:[x] The dominant

---

[x] These findings support the proposal that biology might be an alternative more suitable metaphor for economics.[9]

metaphors in their spontaneous and intuitive discourse of the foreign exchange market are the market as a living being, as an ocean, and as war. Moreover, the next section shows that these metaphors are not isolated and static but instead interact dynamically in the experience of market participants.

MARKET METAPHORS IN ACTION

More than a hundred years ago, Sigmund Freud published his landmark book *Interpretation of Dreams*.[21] To Freud, dreams were a "royal road" to interpreting the unconscious, which allowed analysts to explore their patients' thoughts, wishes, and actions. What dreams meant to the analysis of his patients, metaphors may be for a better understanding of foreign exchange market participants today. Thus, this section puts two traders on the proverbial couch and examines in depth the metaphorical notions in their interviews. The analysis demonstrates that various market metaphors support and complement each other. Moreover, a comparison of the traders (one of them trades for a central bank, the other for a commercial bank) suggests that different market roles and trading goals are associated with different metaphorical conceptualizations, both in the basic choice and in specific elaborations of foreign exchange metaphors.[xi]

The central bank trader showed a predominantly statistical and mathematical understanding of the market. For example, referring to exchange rates, he observed that, "These movements can be calculated in probability terms. And this is a purely mathematical process." This logical and scientific understanding of the market resurfaces in various parts of the interview, such as in the description of a good trader as one who, "Has no emotions ... Intuition is really nothing else but experience unquantified, and experience is such a rational thing."

As the experience of the central bank trader shows, secondary metaphors may be used in order to support other metaphors (e.g., by enhancing or strengthening certain aspects of a primary metaphor). For instance, the trader used a living being metaphor when discussing the selection of information sources: "You are in a similar situation a doctor is in, when he is confronted with a patient who says I have pains, you are the doctor and you will tell me what my [disease] is." Here, the metaphor of the market as a living

---

[xi] Statements are taken verbatim from two interviews selected from the European study. Commercial and central banks are among the most important institutional "players" in the foreign exchange market. The different roles and goals of these two kinds of market participants are explained in Chapter 9, "The Basics."

being in the form of a patient provides the trader with the identity of a physician, allowing him to diagnose information quickly and react appropriately. The metaphorical co-activation of the two domains of trading and of medicine evokes the image of advising and helping in a medical assessment, with the trader–physician functioning as a benevolent authority and knowing expert. However, although a living being metaphor was used, the trader's otherwise analytic approach of the market remained dominant. The supportive metaphor of the physician was used here to stress the importance and the value of one's personal actions in the market, on which the healthy functioning of the market depends.

Elsewhere in the interview, in the discussion of trading expertise, the central bank trader again evoked the image of a physician, this time in order to emphasize the role of personal experience in trading. "Let us assume that you go to a surgeon ... If you had a malignant [tumor] in your lower intestines, perhaps you would shrink back from the proposal that a young doctor who is doing his first operation should try it on you ... [Thus,] it is also a question of experience. And with experience, in time, the foreign exchange trader will be more apt or more successful in handling the instruments that are at his disposal." It is evident that the physician's task in the metaphor is not to establish a personal relationship with a sick patient but to perform an "operation" in an experienced way, skilfully using the "instruments" at hand. Thus, the living being metaphor here aims not at a market as a person, or patient, who is endowed with feelings and individual will, for example, but aims at a body functioning according to set rules and at the role of personal expertise in the surgical treatment of a dysfunction in this body.

These examples demonstrate how participants use metaphors not only to illustrate important aspects of the foreign exchange market, but also to define their own trading actions and to conceptualize their involvement in the market. The metaphors of the central bank trader portray the market as largely calculable and his own position as one of being in control. This aspect of personal control and being in charge was also reflected in his observation that, "The authorities have to watch continuously what reports on those smaller markets get published and, if they feel that the picture is incomplete, make the necessary completion." It is evident that as somebody acting on behalf of a central bank, this trader referred to himself when defining the role of the authorities. The subject of personal control and the image of the operator in the machine metaphor of the market resurfaced in this trader's description of dealing with financial news media. Here, he called attention to the central bank's responsibility to, "Do [their] best to satisfy the information media ... so that the whole system works."

In contrast to the central bank trader, the commercial bank trader conceptualized the market as behaving like a living being–animal, which can be expected to show simple stimulus-reaction responses. "If the market has reacted, people assume that the market is going to react again; it's almost like a Pavlovian type of response." These simple connections between market reactions and the causes that trigger them, however, cannot be relied on for an extended period of time, for when, "The whistle rings a couple of times and no food comes, people forget about the whistle." Thus, the commercial bank trader's understandings of learning and expertise in the foreign exchange market differed from the notion of the expert physician described by the central banker above. While he conceded that learning about the connections between causes and effects in the market *may* take place, he saw these connections as *unstable* and *changing*.

To the commercial bank trader, acting in the market involved a constant second-to-second search for orientation: "Almost like being in a dark room and groping around trying to find your way. [When] you touch something and it doesn't feel right [then] you turn a little bit and you know what that thing is." Acting in this dark room requires both trial-and-error and intuition: "You are listening to what people are telling you; you are listening to the price action; you are looking at the news as it comes up; you are hearing what you know a friend has to tell you about which way they think that the market is going. And all of a sudden, within that environment something happens [and] you just say 'right.'" Individual rationality in this conception of the market is defined purely by the results of one's actions (i.e., winning or losing money). "Every time I take a position I know that there is the possibility that I'm wrong and I'm going to lose money, and there is always the possibility that I'm the irrational one and everybody else is rational." This description of the commercial bank trader contrasts the physician's expertise in the metaphors of the central bank trader, which at most included residual risk or incidental medical malpractice; it involves an even more omnipresent risk with uncertainty as a constant. In a market understood this way, behavior can often only be interpreted by its consequences: "There's no right or wrong ... if you take a position and then you make money on it, that's right. Wrong is if you take a position and you lose money ... only time will tell whether it was right or wrong." Accordingly, the commercial bank trader used the gambling metaphor when explaining his most successful trading: "Sometimes your best decision might be maybe your luckiest thing. Because there is an element of luck in these markets, there is good luck and there is bad luck."

Furthermore, the commercial bank trader invoked the war metaphor in order to describe the danger and unpredictability of the market. "There can be times when you just can get it right between the eyes ... What you don't expect can and will happen!" In the account of the commercial bank trader, the war metaphor expressed not only the danger of trading in the market but also the need to immediately change a losing strategy when the next step can mean certain death. "There are landmines everywhere, and you just don't know. And you just have to be quick enough to be able to admit defeat on something."

While the market metaphors of the central bank trader stressed the role of experience and accountability, those of the commercial bank trader did not express personal responsibility for the efficient working of the market. Individual decision-making and acting here were perceived without political implications, as mere reactions to what was perceived out there, limited in their consequences to either being right and winning money or being wrong and losing money, and limited in their aspirations to being right. "I just want to be able to see the future; in particular to be on the right side of it." The portrayal of a market "so big and so deep" which cannot be influenced in a goal-directed way by "all these little guys in the [trading] room" justifies not carrying personal responsibility for the market collective. Consequently, the interaction with the market takes place almost apart from the real world and outside consequences, as became evident in the commercial bank trader's description of rumors. "The American shooting down of the Chinese jet ... put dollar–mark up a penny, and of course when it was denied, [the exchange rate] came back down a bit. (...) Somebody comes out and says Clinton has been shot, [there is] war, a nuclear bomb has been exploded somewhere, something like that." The belittlement of the connection between the market and the real world becomes particularly evident in the contrast of the terrors of war, murder, and a nuclear catastrophe to the notion that the dollar–mark exchange rate "came back down a bit."

In summary, both interviews demonstrate a dynamic interplay of market metaphors which express and manage how the traders understand the market, how they interact with the market, and how they define their own role. The same market metaphors (e.g., the market as war) may be elaborated in different ways (e.g., when traders assign themselves different places and roles in the battlefield of the market as war). Thus the meaning and the implications of the main market metaphors should not be generalized in a simplistic manner, for each metaphor allows for distinct elaborations with unique psychological entailments.

WHAT WE CAN LEARN FROM MARKET METAPHORS

Two related questions stood at the onset of this chapter: What is the nature of the foreign exchange market? How do participants form expectations and trade currencies? Metaphors lead to an in-depth understanding of the foreign exchange market (i.e., what the market represents psychologically and how participants act). Understanding the market through the metaphors of participants portrays market decisions not as economic givens but as psychological constructions. Trading behavior is different in the market understood as war than in the market as bazaar. In the words of one trader, "If you don't like a certain counterparty, for example, you end up like you try to fight against him, with sometimes taking silly positions which under normal circumstances you would not. And this normally causes a lot of losses!"

Because metaphors express psychological and experiential understandings, they communicate individual and collective "realities" of the foreign exchange market. Through metaphorical entailment, core market aspects (e.g., the nature of the market, the way market participants interact with each other, and the goals of trading) are integrated into an experiential whole. Metaphors allow participants to grasp the abstract notion of the market, make coherent sense of complex market events, and manage their own trading decisions.

Unlike the traditional economic notion of universal rationality, market metaphors show that the foreign exchange market is experienced and understood differently by various participants. Thus, while some market observers respond to the complexity of the market only with continued efforts to measure and calculate, such efforts may do little more than increase this complexity.[22] In contrast, exploring market metaphors' meanings and consequences leads to a qualitatively better understanding of the market and of trading decisions.[xii,xiii]

[xii] Moreover, analyzing market metaphors may lead to a more differentiated grasp of how subgroups of market participants experience and shape the market. For instance, there are many more male than female foreign exchange traders, and the leading role played by war metaphors may be generally expressive of a predominantly male culture and reflect male rather than female foreign exchange market experience. Moreover, the gendered nature of market language may support male dominance in the markets and even represent a means of excluding women from this professional arena: Metaphors not only have the power to name, but also the potential to exclude.[23]

[xiii] A better understanding of foreign exchange metaphors may also lead to insights into market developments (e.g., the prevalence of market metaphors may be a function of time). Economic research shows that the macroeconomic indicators market participants pay attention to change over time.[24] Also the dominant market metaphors may undergo change and indicate a change in how the market is collectively conceptualized.

Understanding the foreign exchange market through metaphors unlocks a window into the psychological world in which participants live and act. Once this window is opened, it becomes evident that "rationality" in trading decisions may not depend as much on expected utility and mathematical probabilities as it is rooted in a psychological and metaphorical understanding of the market. As one trader wisely observes in the interviews, "I don't think you can really say rational–irrational. It depends on how you approach the market and what is your thinking of it." This aspect of market metaphors suggests that participants' approaches and understandings of the foreign exchange market are psychological constructions. Some striking implications of the constructed nature of the market are presented in the next chapter.

ABBREVIATED REFERENCES

See the reference chapter at the end of the book for full details.

1   Oberlechner, T. et al. (2004)
2   Maital, S. (1982)
3   Bennett, A. (1994)
4   Farr, R. M. and Moscovici, S. (1984)
5   Ricoeur, P. (1975)
6   Kubon-Gilke, G. (1996)
7   McGoun, E. G. (1996)
8   McCloskey, D. N. (1990)
9   Hodgson, G. M. (1993)
10 Schmitt, R. (1995)
11 Johnson, M. (1987)
12 Lakoff, G. (1987)
13 Lakoff, G. and Johnson, M. (1980)
14 Lakoff, G. and Johnson, M. (1999)
15 Edwards, D. (1991)
16 Edwards, D. (1997)
17 Weatherall, A. and Walton, M. (1999)
18 Black, M. (1977)
19 Ichheiser, G. (1949)
20 McCloskey, D. N. (1995)
21 Freud, S. (1900)
22 Gray, J. (1997)
23 Altman, M. (1990)
24 Frankel, J. A. and Froot, K. A. (1990b)

8
The Foreign Exchange Market—A Psychological Construct

> *Economic actors do not perceive an objective reality, but rather generate their own notion of reality, which then conditions their behavior.*[1]

The first-hand evidence from market participants presented in this book—for example, about the subjective characteristics of selecting and processing market information, the asymmetries in risk-taking, the social aspects of forming expectations, the influence of herding mechanisms, and market rumors—demonstrates that the dynamics of the market is driven by participants who decide and act *psychologically* rather than rationally. "People bring a good deal more to financial markets besides money and information. They bring themselves," in the words of economist Shlomo Maital.[2] Market models need to reflect these psychological dynamics; without doing so, they are merely mechanistic and thus incomplete.

Not only is the very heart of trading in the market *psychological*, but psychology also influences the theories about the market on a meta-level that is rarely addressed. Every day, every minute, and even every second, currencies are traded in the foreign exchange market. There is little doubt that instability is a defining characteristic of today's market; even to experts the movements of exchange rates are essentially unpredictable. For example, a number of systematic econometric studies have shown that spot rates (say, today's euro–dollar rate) are far better predictors of future exchange rates (say, the euro–dollar rate in one month from today) than economic models.[3]

In such ambiguous environments, psychology predicts that people form *subjective theories* about the events that they observe, the causes behind these events, and likely future developments. Once they are formed, these theories resist change because the assumptions on which they rest are typically self-bolstering.[i] Consider the case of superstitious roulette gamblers who hold the theory that praying ensures winning money. If they win at the casino, they will see their theory confirmed. If their lucky numbers fail to materialize, instead of doubting their theory, they may tell themselves, "We did not pray hard enough!"[5] In foreign exchange, the tenacious nature of subjective market theories is suggested by the observation of traders that early trading experience has a lasting effect on traders' approaches to the market and on their trading strategies.

The consequences of precisely what may happen when people form and interact based on subjective theories were shown in a notable experiment by social psychologist Alexander Bavelas. In this experiment, pairs of medical non-expert participants were separated and shown pictures of cells for which they had to decide whether they were healthy or sick cells. For each pair of participants, person A received accurate feedback about her choices ("true" or "false"), which allowed her to learn about the two types of cells and ultimately discriminate between them at the end of the series of pictures with a fairly high accuracy of 80%. Simultaneously, however, without knowing it, person B received feedback that was independent of her own diagnoses; instead it reflected the correctness of *the other* person's choices. Thus, person B received no appropriate information on which to base her learning about the two types of cells. Nevertheless, person B also formed subjective assumptions about what discriminates sick from healthy cells. In addition, something most intriguing occurred when both participants were brought together to explain their hypotheses about the difference between healthy and sick cells. While person A's assumptions were simple, concrete, and fairly correct, person B developed a highly detailed and complex theory, though an incorrect one, as it was based on contradictory information. When discussing their respective theories, person A was very impressed by person B's detailed and complicated theory; the more absurd this theory was, the more convincing it appeared to person A. Most pairs of participants decided that person B's elaborate theory was far superior to person A's "simplistic" (but actually correct) theory.[5]

---

[i] Human decision-makers often "fall prey to biases which severely restrict their imagination of the ways in which hypotheses may be tested. In consequence, subjects may consistently fail to eliminate false hypotheses and instead become convinced of their truth. Once this has occurred subjects may then become strongly fixated on their belief and resistant to subsequent demonstrations of its falsity."[4]

The virtual unpredictability of foreign exchange rates may lead to an even *more* fervent search for explanatory and predictive market models. In nearly random environments such as foreign exchange, explanatory models not only promise an *understanding* of the environment, but they also suggest *guidelines* for how to act. However, more often than not, they are explanatory fictions and "illusions of control" (i.e., personal convictions that some events are causal for others when actually they are not). In addition to their explanatory function, these theories provide a sense of control over erratic events. Psychological studies indicate that people interpret unsystematic sequences as actually structured and that they perceive patterns in purely random series of events.[6] For example, basketball fans often believe in the so-called hot-hand phenomena (i.e., that a player's chance of scoring is greater when the current attempt to score follows a hit than when it follows a miss on the previous attempt). However, analyses of professional basketball teams, such as the Boston Celtics, demonstrate that there is no correlation between the outcomes of consecutive shots.[ii]

Likewise, theories about trading and about the market may be based on misperceived reality and erroneous subjective theories. As one trader explains, "You find sometimes that someone who has just come into the market, has never really lost money—because they've been long, they have had a couple of good hits—they have come in and have tried something, it works, they have come in, they have tried something, it works, maybe the third time it works again. All of a sudden, the guy thinks he is invincible. I've seen this happen so many times, and they're just set up for a massive fall because they believed that they really do know, and that they really do understand, *as if they had some control* over the outcome of events. But I think if you do it for a long enough period, you realize you don't."

Similarly, weather forecasts are important to people even when weather conditions are completely unpredictable; at least they mitigate some of the doubts that unpredictable environments produce and lend a sense of comfort to an unknowable future.[8] Thus, although their objective "truth" is limited, theories about the market at least produce the comforting feeling of traders' having a modicum of control over the environment. Currency forecasts and models of the foreign exchange market fulfill a comparable function; they often serve as reassuring mechanisms in a highly unpredictable

---

[ii] The erroneous belief in such "hot hand" phenomena might express a misconception of chance which is based on the representative heuristics (see Chapter 2, "Psychology of Trading Decisions"). People assume that short random sequences are representative of the underlying process that produces these sequences.[7]

trading environment. Accordingly, one trader remarks frankly of the use of computer models to predict the market that he is "Not sure if the true reason behind that is to gain a higher hit ratio when it comes to predicting, to make it predictable, or whether it is human nature's general desire to control everything that ever happens!"

While the resort to illusions of control when the environment cannot be managed by means of objective information and empirical knowledge alone is certainly not "rational" in the economic sense, it can be understood *psychologically*. Further, as the difference between various groups of fishermen of the Trobriand Archipelago (south-east of New Guinea) demonstrates, superstitions help reduce anxiety in situations where outcomes are uncertain.[9] In the sheltered inner lagoon of the Archipelago, a life's work of catching fish is simple and safe. The fishermen in these protected habitats thus have developed no superstitions and magical rites about fishing. In stark relief to this non-threatening environment, one may examine those fishermen exposed daily to the harsh elements and treacherous conditions of the open ocean, where deadly perils may arise at a moment's notice and where the catch is uncertain at best. This group of fishermen holds many superstitious beliefs about fishing and cultivates elaborate rituals to increase their chances of catching fish. Participants and observers of the foreign exchange market experience the same unstable climate as the open sea fishers of the Trobriand Archipelago.[8] The following exploration of the implications of this "open sea" nature of the market demonstrates that the market and the explanations of exchange-rate movements are human constructions in a state of flux.

THE MARKET AS A CONSTRUCT AND ILLUSION

While information plays the central role in the foreign exchange market, the chapters of this book have clearly shown that exchange-rate movements cannot simply be deduced from detached facts of the "objective" market environment and from the mechanical workings of economic givens. It is not the information itself but the perceptions, interpretations, and expectations by participants that drive trading decisions and the resulting dynamics of the market. "What data would move the market—that depends on what's in fashion," one trader maintains. "It is the perception of the data's importance that changes frequently," a financial journalist adds.

How strongly do unemployment rates influence a currency? What is the effect of a lowered interest rate? What weight is given to trade balance figures? The answers to these questions are not simply predetermined by an economic reality. Instead, traders observe that there are no fixed rules about which kind of economic or political information determines exchange rates and in what way.[iii] For instance, foreign exchange traders do not see purchasing power parity theory, *the* standard economic textbook explanation for exchange rates, as helpful in predicting exchange rates.[11] Today, the purchasing power parity theory in the words of one trader is "Irrelevant, a dead dodo."

Thus the foreign exchange market is not about the actuality of facts, but is about how facts are *perceived* and *interpreted* by the participants and about how the participants *interact* regarding their perceptions.[iv] Market participants do not merely passively and impartially receive information about the market; instead, they process this information psychologically, and they actively influence and shape it. Because the market is devised and interpreted by humans, the principles that govern market movements do not function apart from its participants.

Thus, akin to the market, market models also do not represent an objective reality that is independent of the participants who believe in it and who enact it. Instead, all approaches to understanding and predicting the market are formed by *people*, and they should not be viewed as functioning separately from those who hold and espouse them. They are often *illusions*[v] that turn into collective market reality when they are fuelled by shared perceptions and beliefs. Thus, the revised picture that emerges of the foreign exchange market shows it to be both a psychological and social *construct*. Instead of economic givens, this construct forms the basis of changing market realities, as is shown in the next section.

[iii] This observation opposes the traditional economic view that sees exchange rates mechanically regulated by predetermined economic fundamentals. "It seems that the fundamentals' place in neoclassical research is so deeply entrenched that years of accumulated evidence of its incompatibility with the real-world exchange market have led economists not to change the theory, but to simply focus on those circumstances in which it is least inappropriate," according to economist John Harvey.[10]

[iv] For example, the importance attached to specific kinds of news varies with what market participants perceive as important at any given point in time. Interest rates, employment rates, and money supply figures may all carry a different importance at different points in time.

[v] The *American Heritage Dictionary of the American Language* defines "illusions" as erroneous perceptions of reality and as beliefs which can deceive people.

MARKET CONSTRUCTS CHANGE

In today's foreign exchange market, "Strong economic figures are sometimes interpreted as leading to a stronger currency and at other times as leading to a weaker one," one trader lucidly observed in the interviews. Identical objective market information may hence lead to entirely different market reactions depending on such situational factors as the current trading positions of market participants. "If everybody is long, more good news make people sell," in the words of another trader.

This lack of firm and established rules about *what* moves the market and *how* it is moved is perceived by traders more clearly today than in the past; indeed, many traders remark that the market has become increasingly unpredictable and volatile.[vi] One trader even reflects that, "There are no firm rules anymore in the market." Another concurs, claiming further that, "There are no predictive rules whatsoever—neither mathematical ones nor ones derived from artificial intelligence." Thus, the only remaining rule seems to be that, "There are no certainties," in the blunt words of another trader.

Traders do however agree that the kind of information that influences the buying and selling behavior of market participants is subject to a systematic process of change. Thus, rather than firm and established, traders see rules that have governed foreign exchange movements as "definitely changing," and they perceive this change on a variety of levels. For instance, traders observe influential macroeconomic figures as changing among market participants. One trader remarks that, "From time to time they are looking only at the interest side of the market. Then they are looking only at the unemployment figures ... You always have to change what you are really looking for."

Traders quote many examples for this changing relationship between economic exchange-rate determinants and the reaction of the market over recent years: The market has alternately focused on money supply, employment rates, trade numbers, etc. In the 1970s, trade balances are reported to have been particularly important, while in the 1980s money supply was dominant. Today, the movements in supply and demand created by

---

[vi] This observation is confirmed by systematic research. In 1995, Harris and Zabka found that the U.S. employment report had grown notably over the last years and that usually unexpected increases in employment numbers strengthened the U.S. dollar value.[12] These authors quote earlier research which indicates that at other times different numbers and variables were most influential. For example, of the variables considered by Hakkio and Pearce and by Hardouvelis in the 1980s, only money supply news exerts a consistently significant effect on the value of the U.S. dollar.[13,14]

commercial and financial market participants are seen as most important. One trader illustrates how today's market reacts differently from some time ago with an example, remarking that, "Figures came out in the U.S., and they were completely bad. The dollar went down about thirty points, and then dropped down one big figure—and then it recovered. It's amazing! Four or five years ago, if such a figure would come out, the dollar would explode." Moreover, traders observe that, while market expectations have *gained* in importance, actual information has *decreased* in importance. Likewise, while new information had previously a prolonged effect on the market, today market adjustments happen almost as instantaneously as the news.

In addition to these changes over time, traders describe the market as interpreting events differently in different parts of the world, an observation suggesting that the "rules" about what determines the market also vary geographically. "Facts ... where European markets remain calm can excite the East Asian market or the other way round," one trader asserts. Another trader cogently remarks that "The market gets itself not only into different modes of interpreting different events, but it also interprets identical events in entirely different ways." These observations are confirmed by a systematic comparison of results from the European and the North American surveys. Hundreds of foreign exchange traders rated the information important to their trading decisions. One question asked: What kind of information do you consider more influential for your foreign exchange decisions: Quantitative information (numbers and quotes) or qualitative information (words)?

Possible answers ranged from 1 = Only quantitative information to 7 = Only qualitative information; traders who answered 4 considered quantitative and qualitative information equally important. With an average of 3.9, the answers of 718 traders are close to this midpoint. However, separating traders into various trading locations revealed significant differences. While 407 traders in the U.S. and in Canada considered *quantitative* information more important (average rating 3.6), 311 traders in Europe rated *qualitative* information more important to their trading decisions (average rating 4.4).

What could be the reasons for these differences? We can only speculate that in U.S. society numbers and statistics may generally be more important as can be seen in the meaning of batting averages to sports spectators or of the grade point average scores to students. In any case, these numbers clearly show a difference in how "the market" perceives information, a finding that was also confirmed by traders' answers to another question: What kind of information do you consider more influential for your foreign exchange decisions: Private information (not available to everybody) or public information (potentially available to everybody)?

Again, differences materialized as to what information was perceived as important. On a scale from 1 = Only private information to 7 = Only public information, there was a stronger tendency among European traders to consider private information as more important (average 3.4) than among North American traders (average 3.9).

This evidence for changes over time and variations in place clearly brings to light the fluid nature of what determines exchange rates. In other words, traders notice that there is no objectively correct price for exchange rates. Thus, while one trader explains the observation that the market possesses no, "Real, fundamental values underlying the currencies," by the nature of foreign exchange as a second-order market that (unlike the stock market) is about the price of money itself, another trader remarks dryly that, "*the market dictates the price.*"

Such statements suggest an understanding of the foreign exchange market in which participants *actively construct* the market. At any given point of time, rather than being independent givens, the determinants of exchange rates are only valid if market participants explicitly or implicitly *agree* that they are valid, if they *act* accordingly, and if they *interact* with each other in ways that support their constructions. In the apt words of one trader, "There are no rules but the ones carried by consensus." Hence, it has been convincingly argued by economist Alan Kirman that, "The relationship between fundamentals and exchange rates is not well understood and seems to vary considerably over time. Furthermore, exchange-rate movements depend on what market participants believe that relationship to be, and this also adds weight to the importance of the role of communication between agents in the market."[15] Only those determinants that are communicated strongly enough in the market are followed, because participants *know* they are also followed by other market participants.

Since market rules are fluid, trading in the foreign exchange market is about understanding what is important at any given time. As a consequence of the ever-changing nature of market rules, the ability to adjust flexibly one's own strategies to these changing rules is indispensable. "The basis for decision-making is going to change because the market will change ... You have to adjust yourself," in the words of one trader. Successful foreign exchange participants consequently are characterized by a constant openness to new constructions of the market and by the ability to form new theories about the market as rules change.

These transformations in the rules regarding which determinants drive the foreign exchange market lead one to ask further questions about their genesis: Who forms these rules, and who is able to change them? Traders observe that these rules are generally constructed by market players themselves, and that more powerful market participants are also more influential in generating and changing them, as in the observation of one trader that governments are influential because they are able to *create new perceptions* in the market.

However, what constitutes a powerful market participant has changed over the last decades. Some of the most important reasons for this change may be found in the fundamental regime change from fixed to floating exchange rates, and in the development of new information and trading technologies. Possibly the most dramatic effect of these technologies is the ubiquitous availability of real-time information, which has minimized many of the previous information differentials between market participants. Because market participants receive news simultaneously, trading advantages that were once based on prior access to news have largely disappeared. This, one trader observes, has significantly, "Changed the parameters of the game." As the speed of ubiquitous information dissemination approaches a limit, the introduction of new parameters which define market advantage is needed.

A case in point, because the new information technologies have made corporations more knowledgeable, banks have lost some of their information advantage over their corporate customers. As traders point out, banks cannot manipulate foreign exchange rates in their customer business as easily as they used to because the customers themselves now see current market rates on their own screens. Some traders believe that this has greatly contributed to the development of complex foreign exchange products; such products represent efforts by the banks to reinstall a differential of knowledge and expertise *vis-à-vis* their customers.

Moreover, decreased spreads in their customer business force banks into taking larger trading positions for achieving similar gains; this may be one reason for the increase of market volume. "In former times, you were able to make the same amount of money on five million dollars. Nowadays, you have to do five hundred [million dollars]," one trader notes of the changes. Thus, because trading volumes increasingly determine the markets, traders also observe that the power of large funds has dramatically increased.

A final intriguing consequence of real-time information technologies is the market's focus on participants' expectations, beyond information about objective market events. Today, "What will move [the market] is something that changes expectations," in the words of one trader. In today's market of omnipresent real-time information, "Everyone's got the same information at the same time, [therefore] you need to find a different way of finding an edge over your competitor," another trader observes. Therefore, to be ahead of other participants, anticipating expectations and changes in the expectations of other participants is crucial. As one financial journalist candidly notes, "The guy who used to win was the guy who had the edge on the news. These days it is hard to have an edge on the news, so maybe what you try to get is an edge on expectations."

The key to the new edge over other participants may be market size, as one trader reasons convincingly in the interviews: "If the media starts giving information that everybody knows, or [if] all information starts to be released instantly and every market participant is active on exactly the same information, it will be other variables that are going to have an effect on the foreign exchange market. Because then all of a sudden everybody is acting on exactly the same information, which would mean nobody has the advantage. So where is the advantage going to come from? Maybe it is going to come [from the] pure size of the market player." This observation correlates with the recent tendency toward market concentration in fewer and fewer hands: The number of banks responsible for the biggest part of foreign exchange turnover has clearly decreased since the mid-1990s. Whereas in 1995, 75% of turnover in the U.K. was conducted by 20 banks, by 2001 this number had fallen to 17 banks. In the U.S., the number even dropped from 20 to 13 banks.[16]

Thus the constructed nature of the foreign exchange market ultimately forces its participants to continuously evolve and adjust to new market constructions. Moreover, not only do market participants have to adjust to the new rules governing foreign exchange, but in addition they *themselves* attempt to influence these rules in order to control and to shape the market in their own individual ways. As Chapter 7, "Surfing the Market on Metaphors" has shown, market participants name, shape, and create realities through using metaphors. Once again, *psychology* may be the key to understanding the future of the foreign exchange market.

ABBREVIATED REFERENCES

See the reference chapter at the end of the book for full details.

1 Anderson, M. A. and Goldsmith, A. H. (1994b)
2 Maital, S. (1982)
3 Meese, R. A. and Rogoff, K. (1983)
4 Evans, J. S. B. T. (1987)
5 Watzlawick , P. (1976)
6 Hake, H. W. and Hyman, R. (1953)
7 Gilovich, T. et al. (1985)
8 Gimpl, M. L. and Dakin, S. R. (1984)

9   Malinowski, B. (1925)
10 Harvey, J. T. (1996)
11 Cheung, Y.-W. and Chinn, M. D. (2001)
12 Harris, E. S. and Zabka, N. M. (1995)
13 Hakkio, C. S. and Pearce, D. K. (1985)
14 Hardouvelis, G. A. (1988)
15 Kirman, A. (1995)
16 Bank for International Settlements (2002)

9
The Basics

> *[The foreign exchange market] is the purest market around ... And it is open to nearly every [factor] that influences people's lives in terms of technology, politics, economics, and geography.*
>
> Foreign exchange trader

FUNCTION AND SCOPE OF THE MARKET

Non-economists are often surprised to learn that the foreign exchange market is by far the largest financial market worldwide. Every day, currencies worth 1.2 trillion U.S. dollars change hands in the foreign exchange market.[1,i] No other market comes close to this amount in trading volume.

The foreign exchange market functions like any market: Buyers and sellers of a commodity meet and trade. In the foreign exchange market, as in any market, a currency whose demand exceeds supply will see its value go up, and vice versa.

The nature of the commodity involved in the foreign exchange is however one difference between foreign exchange and other markets. In most markets, goods or services are exchanged for money. Prices are quoted as units of the transactions medium (money) per unit of the commodity. In foreign exchange, however, one type of money is exchanged for another (e.g., British pounds for U.S. dollars). Even so, it is possible to draw an exact analogy between currency

---

[i] $1.2 trillion is equivalent to 1,200 times $1 billion or $1,200,000,000,000. About three days of trading volume translate in a stack of one dollar bills reaching from the earth to the moon.

markets and others. In each currency market, one currency is treated as the commodity, and the other currency is treated as the transactions medium. For example, in the dollar–yen market, dollars are the commodity, and yen are the transactions medium; therefore, prices are quoted as yen per dollar.

The U.S. dollar is involved in the vast majority (90%) of currency transactions as either the transactions medium or the commodity currency. The euro is involved in 38% of transactions, the Japanese yen in 23%. In a third tier of importance, the pound sterling is involved in 13% of transactions, the Swiss franc in 6%, and the Canadian and Australian dollars in about 4% each.[1,ii]

The dollar is traded so frequently because it is the market's vehicle currency, which means that it is involved in almost any exchange from one non-dollar currency into another. To accomplish such an exchange one must first acquire dollars in exchange for the first currency, and then sell dollars in exchange for the second. Most notably, this is the case with currencies from transition economies, such as the Russian rouble, and from emerging markets, such as the Thai bhat, which are referred to as "exotics." Exchange rates that do not involve the dollar are called "cross rates." Only a few cross rates are actively quoted by dealers, and these involve only major currencies.

Historically, the oldest function of the foreign exchange market has been the facilitation of international trade. Since countries have different currencies, the foreign exchange market must exist for us to trade with international partners or travel abroad. A second central function of the foreign exchange market is speculation. When exchange rates are not pegged by governments, people can try to profit by buying a currency when its price is low and selling it when its price is high. "With the liberalization of capital flows, you have more people and individuals who have access to money, who handle money, who are rich. And consequently they go cross-border; they go from one currency into another currency. And then they get a part of that pure speculation, the motivation behind which is purely speculative," explains one foreign exchange trader.

"Speculation" comes in many forms. Sometimes it is as simple as a commercial customer deciding to purchase currency tomorrow instead of today, hoping that the currency will move favorably. More substantially, since an international investor's realized return depends on exchange-rate levels, individuals have implicitly speculated on currency movements for as long as capital has flowed across borders. To estimate their anticipated return, investors must necessarily forecast exchange-rate changes and assume exchange-rate risk. When the focus of international investment is a foreign

---

[ii] Because each foreign exchange transaction involves two currencies, the percentage sum of all currencies totals 200%.

stock, foreign bond, or perhaps an entire firm located abroad, the associated speculation on currencies can be called "derived" speculation. Sometimes, however, the focus of speculation is the foreign currency itself; investors then treat "currencies as an asset class," a phenomenon that has dramatically intensified in recent decades.

"We have spent a lot of time trying to investigate how much of the daily [market] turnover is truly speculative by nature and how much is not ... You can only answer are that question if you are the guy that originates the flow. And you have virtually to interview every single market participant and find what their answers are to *why* they move," a trader reports of the difficulties of precisely determining the extent of speculation in the foreign exchange market. Indeed, foreign exchange turnover is dozens of times as large as the value of world exports of goods and services, which suggests that the role of speculation is *substantial*. In the words of one trader, "I think it's only one percent of the daily turnover which is commercial. So there's an awful lot left over which is speculation, and if markets are simply dealing with speculation, it can always be that a currency loses its value completely. It's just a question of how big is the seller or how big is the buyer." Another trader says of the considerable consequences of increased currency speculation: "People are more aware, there is much more speculation which obviously caused some currencies to devalue and revalue. As the rules change, the economies of the countries have changed."

The foreign exchange market also differs from regular markets in that it *cannot* be identified with any single place. Your supermarket has a specific address, as does the New York Stock Exchange. By contrast, the foreign exchange market is a decentralized worldwide network of parties connected electronically. Trades can be instantaneously arranged between counterparties as mutually distant as a U.S. commercial bank and a Brazilian manufacturers' exporter, a European investment bank and an Australian investment fund, or a Japanese commercial bank and a Hungarian central bank.

Though foreign exchange trading takes place around the world, and there is no single physical location where all traders meet, trading does tend to concentrate in certain cities.[1] London is the capital of foreign exchange trading, with 31% of global turnover in 2001. New York (16%) and Tokyo (9%) are the next most important. A third tier of trading centers includes Frankfurt (5%), Singapore (6%), Zurich (4%), and Hong Kong (4%).

Foreign exchange trading literally moves with the sun: The trading day begins in Sydney; trading gets heavier as the Tokyo market opens along with the other Asian centers. Towards the end of the Asian trading day, London opens, as do other trading centers in Europe, bringing the heaviest trading of the day. Around midday in Europe, trading opens in New York. Trading in New York tapers off when London traders leave for home and is fairly light during the New York afternoon. Trading is lightest late in the New York afternoon, since only a few scattered traders are active anywhere. During the New York evening, morning arrives in Sydney, and trading accelerates once again.

Moreover, the foreign exchange market differs from regular markets in the absence of any visible physical manifestation of the thing that is traded. While you carry bread home from the supermarket and your hair looks different after a haircut, in the foreign exchange market, the exchange of one currency for another is manifested only by a new set of numbers in various computers around the world. This may surprise those for whom "foreign exchange trading" means stepping off the airplane in Paris and simply changing U.S. dollars into euros. However, to foreign exchange professionals "the market" refers exclusively to the wholesale market for currencies, in which transactions typically exceed $1 million and in which participation requires a line of credit for each potential counterparty.[iii]

Comparing the foreign exchange market with stock markets, which are generally more familiar to private investors, reveals a final important difference. When the shares of a given firm rise relative to the market, one can automatically infer that there is good news about the firm. However, when the currency of one country appreciates relative to the currency of another, one cannot automatically infer anything about either country. "In foreign exchange, you always have two currencies ... and therefore you have two whole sets of data that need to be processed to arrive at sort of the right direction. Whereas you look at the bond market or you look at equities and you are focused on a single stock," one trader explains. Thus, trading in the foreign exchange market requires a grasp on the interplay between various economies. "As a currency trader, you are naturally exposed to other economies ... The client base you talk to, competitors you face, colleagues you work with are from different areas around the globe. So you have to be global-minded," remarks another trader.

[iii] Credit lines are arrangements in which participants grant a specific amount of unsecured credit to a specific counterparty. They entail the risk that a counterparty fails to deliver its currency.

INSTRUMENTS

As in most markets, also in the global foreign exchange market a variety of items are traded. There are over 100 currencies available for exchange. One key dimension of trading these currencies is the settlement date (i.e., the date on which the currencies are actually exchanged). In spot transactions, settlement occurs typically two business days after the trade date. Forward transactions are those for which the settlement date is farther away than two business days. For example, two market participants agree to exchange $10 million into euro in six months from today, at an exchange rate that they determine already today. Each day an average of $387 *billion* is traded in the spot markets and $131 *billion* is traded in the forward market.[1,iv]

Forward contracts help market participants protect themselves from adverse exchange-rate developments. Consider, for example, an exporter of Japanese cars to Europe that expects to be paid in euro two months hence. The company is exposing itself to a currency risk: If the yen appreciates against the euro, the future euro payment will be worth fewer yen than it is today. To eliminate the currency risk, the company may prefer to sell the euros in the forward market, thereby locking in a certain euro–yen exchange rate.

Spot and forward contracts are traded "over the counter," which means that, simply by agreeing on a price, the two parties involved make a binding contract with each other. Because parties trade with each other directly and in a decentralized way, not on a formal exchange, they must have substantial credit lines with each other. Futures contracts are superficially similar to forward contracts, in that they involve an agreement to trade specific amounts of currencies at a future date. There, however, the similarity ends.

Futures contracts are structured to facilitate short-term speculation by relatively small market players. Futures are traded on formal exchanges, such as the Chicago Mercantile Exchange and the London International Financial Futures and Options Exchange, in standard currency amounts and with standard maturity dates. Though a price is agreed with another futures market participant, the exchange's "clearing house" immediately steps in to serve as each trader's counterparty. If one undertakes a reverse trade before

---

[iv] Another $656 billion of market turnover is reported for daily trading in a third foreign exchange instrument, foreign exchange swaps.[1] Swaps involve the synchronized sale and purchase of a certain amount of currency against another currency at two different dates. They are usually a combination of a spot trade and a later opposite exchange of the involved currencies. Swaps are for market participants who want to move out of one and into another currency for a certain period of time

the contract's maturity date, the net gain or loss relative to the clearing house is immediately calculated and settled, and no further action is required.

The last important foreign exchange instrument to consider is the currency option. A standard "call" option allows the holder to choose whether to buy a specific amount of currency A in exchange for a specific price amount of currency B by a certain date. A "put" option is similar but the holder can choose to sell currency rather than buy it. Since the holder will only exercise the option (i.e., undertake the transaction) if it is profitable to do so, the holder must pay upfront for options. Currency options may be traded over the counter like spot transactions or on formal exchanges like futures. While they were originally designed to reduce currency risk, they may also be used to leverage the gains (and losses) of traders and thus dramatically increase risk.[v]

TRADING

The majority of foreign exchange trading is conducted between foreign exchange traders at banks. Every day, $689 billion are traded between banks, as compared with approximately $329 billion between banks and other financial institutions, and $156 billion of trading between banks and non-financial customers.[1]

Market-making banks stand ready to buy or sell from other market participants. They post the prices at which they will trade on the screens of electronic dealing systems and provide quotes when contacted by other market participants. The market moves extremely rapidly—in a given day there are tens of thousands of transactions. Prices can change every second. For efficiency, quotes are given simply as a pair of two-digit numbers, one signifying the rate at which the trader is willing to sell, and the other signifying the rate at which the trader is willing to buy. If these two exchange rates are 1.4630 Swiss francs per euro and 1.4635 per euro, the trader will say "30–35."

---

[v] The history of insurance shows that, from the beginning, the *reduction* of risk was closely connected to gambling (i.e., something that *increases* risk). In the coffee houses of 18th-century England, gambles could be placed on such future events as the outcome of war or the lives of relatives. While wagers on life represented an early type of life insurance, they could hardly be differentiated from other forms of betting. Moreover, because of incorrect calculations, these early insurance contracts truly resulted in a game of chance: while widows "fortunate" enough to see their husbands die early received benefits, for latecomers there was no money left.[2]

The Basics

The initial portion of the exchange rate, 1.46, known as the "big figure," is assumed.

The distance between bid and offer price is called the "spread." Spreads are one of the major sources of foreign exchange profits for market-makers. In the most frequently traded currency pairs, such as U.S. dollar–euro, the spreads quoted by a market-maker are typically less than 5 pips and may be as low as 2 pips (a "pip" is the last decimal place of an exchange rate, the smallest amount by which an exchange rate can move). Spreads can be substantially wider for less frequently traded currency pairs, in "thin" markets where there is not much trading (e.g., New York on Friday afternoon) and in volatile markets. Widening the spread may also be a defensive strategy for traders who do not want to deal, because it makes the transaction unattractive to the counter-party; however, quoting spreads that are too wide may impair trading relationships, inducing potential counterparties to take their business elsewhere.

In the interbank market, a typical spot trade is for about $10 million. When other market participants contact a market-maker, participants typically state the amount of their desired trade (in terms of the commodity currency), but do not reveal whether they are interested in buying or in selling. The market-maker then quotes the two-way price. Finally, the caller declares whether she will buy, sell, or pass.

DEALING ROOM STRUCTURE

There are three types of foreign exchange professionals: interbank traders, salespeople, and proprietary traders.

Interbank traders, as their title implies, deal almost exclusively with other market-makers. Usually, different traders are in charge of spot and forward transactions.[3] Spot traders at major banks either focus on just one of the major currency pairs, such as euro–U.S. dollar, or they trade several of the less liquid pairs. In addition to providing liquidity, interbank traders try to speculate based on short-term market opportunities produced by large customer transactions.[4] These positions are typically closed by the end of the trading day. By contrast, forward traders take a longer term view of the market than spot traders and pay specific attention to interest-rate differentials.

In contrast to the interbank traders who conduct trading among large banks, foreign exchange salespeople manage the banks' relationships with their customers. Their first responsibility is to provide quotes to existing customers. The customers call them directly, requesting a quote for a particular amount in a given currency pair, without indicating direction. The salesperson asks the relevant interbank trader for an indicative quote to this customer, which she may pass on directly or spread wider. The salesperson's responsibilities also include establishing relationships with corporate and financial customers and providing information to customers about important foreign exchange market developments. "As a salesperson, you have to be very strong on a relationship side," declares one trader.

Banks compete fiercely for the foreign exchange business of corporate and financial customers, as they benefit from these customers in many ways. First, they benefit by typically quoting wider spreads to their customers than they themselves find in the interbank market.[vi] In addition, they benefit as information about their customers' trading activities is vital to the trading room. As one trader explains, "There are particular customers who, for one reason or another, are very indicative of where a currency is going to go. For instance, a big U.S. hedge fund may sell something to you, and if he's a seller, he's going to wait a while, and then sell some more, and then he's going to wait a while ... and then sell some more. Some of these funds are so big and so leveraged that in order for them to make any dent at all on their returns, they must have massive positions. Each individual bank can't give that hedge fund a big enough [credit] line for ... all of its transaction ... So, if he hits me for $200 [million], I know that he's going to give me some time to get out of my position. But in five, ten minutes, [an] hour's time, he's going to be selling another $200 [million]."

Because large customer orders for currencies have the potential to move market prices temporarily, traders who execute large trades for customers may generate profits by "front-running"; this means that traders execute parallel orders on behalf of the bank before executing the customer's order. When the traders reverse the bank's trade as soon as the customer's trade has moved market prices, they can make safe profits. While front-running is illegal in most well-regulated financial markets, like the NYSE, currency markets are essentially unregulated. Countries recognize that they would see currency trading go elsewhere if they tried to restrict trading within their boundaries.

With the banks, the divergent goals of the sales/corporate desks and the interbank dealing desks may lead to conflicts between sales and interbank traders. One sales trader poses a fundamental question on the minds of many in this position: "Was it a good price that the trader gave, [or] a bad

---

[vi] As customers themselves have started to gain direct access to interbank market information through wire news terminals, this practice has become more difficult for the banks. In the words of one trader, "Spreads are now narrow, margins are decreasing, it's generally tougher for people to make money."

The Basics

price?" The comments of another salesperson are equally telling: "As a salesperson, I am dealing with the client, right? So our objective is to try and get the best price from the trading side or interbank market. So, the conflict is, if I'm trying to get a price for my client right, and my client is looking to buy currency from me—where does my interbank trader cover it? Does he truly give me a market-making price? ... You have to have an element of trust with the trading side, [to know] that they are providing you with a good clearing price, the price that would be equivalent to what I would get if I went directly to the interbank [market]. That does not happen all the time, so there is some conflict."

The third major type of foreign exchange market professional is the proprietary trader. Proprietary traders undertake speculative trades with a medium to long horizon in a variety of financial markets. Their positions are typically larger than those of interbank traders and last much longer.

The spot traders, salespeople, and proprietary traders of a dealing room are supported by middle- and back-office support staff. For example, economists, market analysts, and currency specialists in the middle office help traders analyze and forecast the markets. "We have of course also our own research team, they are picking up information from the research people: What is the expectation, what are the fundamentals?" explains one trader. The middle office also monitors the traders' profits and losses. The back office handles clearing and settlement of trades.

Foreign exchange dealing is supervised by treasurers, who carry overall responsibility, and by chief dealers, who are responsible for teams of traders. As one trader explains, "Each trader plays his role, and you have quite a hierarchy of the trading room. You have the trading room manager, you have a department head, you have a chief trader, you have a deputy chief trader, you have a senior trader, and you have a junior trader. And each person has his own [position] limit,[vii] has his own responsibility, and plays his own role. The department head runs perhaps the proprietary trading or the manager position or whatever you call it. The chief trader takes care that the whole group is within the limits of the group, and is taking most probably the biggest positions. The senior trader conducts the normal business. The junior trader is going to try and deliver, as much as possible, quotes to the team."

[vii] Position limits are institutional measures to restrict traders' exposure to risk, see Chapter 3, "Risk-Taking in Trading Decisions."

MARKET PLAYERS

The contemporary global foreign exchange market is dominated by large international banks. Other important players in the market include brokers, central banks, pension and investment funds, hedge funds, individuals, and the financial news media.

Commercial and investment banks

Every year, magazines such as *Euromoney*, *FX Week*, and *Global Investor Magazine* publish rankings of the top foreign exchange banks in such dimensions as market share, trading revenues, or customers' ratings of trading quality. For example, UBS, Deutsche Bank, Citigroup, JP Morgan Chase, HSBC, Goldman Sachs, Barclays Capital, Credit Suisse First Boston, Royal Bank of Scotland, and Merrill Lynch are the banks with the largest market shares of foreign exchange business listed by *Euromoney* in 2004. These are just some of the largest dealing banks handling the extremely large flows of institutional and corporate business, the deals that influence exchange rates. Smaller banks trade smaller amounts and are usually more customer-driven.

Bank customers have traditionally traded by telephone, but today their foreign exchange business is increasingly conducted through electronic systems that automatically connect them to single dealers (such as Goldman Sachs's WebET). Alongside such single-dealer systems, multi-dealer systems have developed that connect groups of leading commercial and financial customers to groups of dealing banks. Multi-dealer systems have included Atriax, FX Connect (which connects over 25 banks to hundreds of asset managers), Currenex, and FXall.[viii] In the words of one trader, "Nowadays, customer business also becomes electronic ... Each bank is trying to develop their own website; they are trying to suck customers into their own web system."

When bank traders deal with each other directly, they typically use a computerized dealing system, such as Reuters Dealing 3000 Direct. This system and others like it link banks to each other on a one-to-one basis similar to the more traditional telephone, while allowing traders to conduct

---

[viii] Atriax was formed by Citibank, Deutsche Bank, JP Morgan Chase and news provider Reuters; while it once included more than 50 banks, it has now stopped its operations. FX Connect was originally State Street Bank's proprietary trading platform. For a general discussion of single-dealer and multi-dealer foreign exchange trading systems, see Liebenberg.[6]

many more "conversations" with other banks. Such systems also reduce possible misunderstandings and permit automatic record-keeping for executed trades.

Central banks

Central banks, such as the U.S. Federal Reserve, the European Central Bank, the Bank of Japan, and the Bank of England issue their respective national currencies and control the currencies' supply and demand. Usually regarded as the staunch guardians of their national currency, central banks generally do not speculate in the foreign exchange market (the most notable exception being Malaysia's Bank Negara in the mid-1990s).[ix] Central banks focus primarily on relatively long-term issues, such as inflation, unemployment rates, and economic growth. By controlling interest rates, most central banks indirectly affect exchange rates, whether or not they intend to do so. A higher domestic interest rate tends to attract more foreign investors in domestic bonds; when foreign investors buy the domestic currency in order to purchase those bonds, the value of the currency tends to rise. Central banks also sometimes intentionally intervene in foreign exchange markets. By buying or selling foreign currencies against the domestic currency, they can directly affect their currency's value, either to target a particular level or to "calm disorderly markets." Interventions can provide liquidity at times of crisis.

Central banks can also influence exchange rates through their role as market opinion leaders. For example, central banks can decide to intervene in concert, rather than separately, thereby communicating their determination. In the words of one trader, "If a central bank comes to a commercial bank, for an intervention, and they sell 50 million dollars—50 million dollars is nothing in the market ... But don't forget that all these interventions are concentrated actions. So all the central banks are intervening, and if the Bank of Japan *and* Bundesbank *and* Fed intervene, then a certain market volume comes together."

Opinions have varied across central banks and over time regarding the appropriate extent of foreign exchange intervention. Under the Bretton Woods Agreement, in force from 1945 through the early 1970s, central banks actively managed fixed parity rates; in the late 1970s and much of the

---

[ix] Bank Negara started to aggressively trade in the foreign exchange market after the Plaza Agreement in 1985 led to a significant loss of the value of its large U.S. dollar holdings. Bank Negara was criticized for exploiting the competitive advantages of central banks in its unusual trading-for-profit operations, such as access to confidential information and to vast amounts of currency. However, other banks also strove to take advantage of their trading relationships with Bank Negara, using their knowledge about Negara's trades in order to place parallel trades on their own behalf.[7]

1980s exchange rates were supposed to float freely without central bank involvement, but intervention was not uncommon. Since the late 1980s, many of the leading currency nations have turned to infrequent interventions that are often coordinated among different central banks. Others, however, have continued to intervene frequently.

Most traders agree that the influence of central banks on exchange rates is diminishing. As one trader aptly puts it, "The currency markets grew up and got quite expert, and so they had a lot more power to move currencies where they wanted rather than where the central banks or governments wanted them."

Brokers

Bank dealers can also trade with each other through brokers. Foreign exchange brokers do not take active trading positions; instead, they find the best available rates, and link matching requests for currency purchases and sales among dealers. To ensure fair trading, brokers protect the anonymity of the involved parties until just before a trade is executed. For their services, brokers get a commission paid in equal parts by both parties to a transaction.

Traditionally, the role of broker was performed by individual "voice brokers," who would continuously shout the best available bid and offer rates over open telephone lines to dealers at many banks. Today, the role and the profits of traditional voice brokers are greatly diminished by electronic brokerage systems, such as the EBS Spot Dealing System and Reuters Dealing 3000. "In 1995, 14 of us in dollar–mark averaged $140,000 bank brokerage [every day]. In the year 2003, 16 or 18 guys are probably averaging $17,000 to 20,000 a day," one trader remarks. Reuters links more than 1,000 banks to each other. EBS, launched in 1990 by several market-makers as a competitor to Reuters, today links more than 750 banks with each other; every day, more than $90 billion are traded on its approximately 2,000 workstations.[x] Electronic broking systems are cheaper, more transparent, and more efficient in the trade execution and record-keeping of traders.[6] "A huge amount of business is now done electronically rather than verbally. But most of what people have done via the electronic media is really to try and replicate the voice trading, so the actual mechanics of dealing and the process in the transactions are much easier, more streamlined, and cheaper, obviously. If you look at the actual mechanics, *how* it works, it's not that different," a

---

[x] These numbers are taken from producers' websites at the following URLs: http://www.ebs.com/products/spot/docs/spot_sheet.pdf and http://about.reuters.com/productinfo/treasury.asp?seg=1

trader explains. In particular, smaller banks have benefited through easier access to the market.

To traders, the shift from voice brokers to electronic broking systems has likewise been a shift from more *auditory* to more *visual* perceptions and representations of the foreign exchange market. While previously traders could hear other traders call out quotes, today quotes are seen on the computer screen. "Price discovery was something that would actually take a little bit of time, so you would call other banks as part of the process, either to clear business which you could do in a better way because they were not aware of quite where the price should be, or just to find out where the price should be. So there was lots of interbank calling that used to go on, nowadays the machine tells you exactly where it is," a trader says of the changes. One trader observes that this has led to a less emotional way of trading. While previously, "Nobody knew where the market was. Some guy called 90–95, some guy called 80–85, and some guy called 10–15, so everything depended on the traders' mind," today, "We can see all the bids and offers there, so people don't feel much fear in the market." However, other traders disagree. In the words of another trader, "The fact that everything is on one screen ... makes it even more of a psychological game."

Investment companies, pension funds, and hedge funds

Every year, a variety of *investment companies*, such as Fidelity and Vanguard in the U.S., make billions for their clients (and themselves) by managing and investing the pooled funds of investors. For a fee, their funds offer investors the advantages of easy diversification and low transaction costs of traded investments. Depending on the investment goals and philosophy of the investment fund, fund managers may invest in domestic or in international securities or bonds. As the purchase and sale of international assets requires foreign exchange transactions, investment companies are important players in the foreign exchange market.

Pension funds manage and invest money from pension plans, often at a very low risk. Such pension plans may be individually sponsored or set up by corporations, labor unions, or governments and aim to ensure that employees have money for retirement. Some of the largest pension funds are ABP, Europe's largest pension fund, and California Public Employees Retirement System, the largest pension fund in the U.S.; each with over $100 billion in assets. Many pension fund managers enter foreign exchange transactions, using global diversification to ensure a specific return for their fund.

Hedge funds are essentially partnerships of a limited number of wealthy investors. According to U.S. securities law, hedge funds are exempt from registration and can trade a large variety of different financial products. Hedge funds tend to be highly leveraged, and they may employ aggressive trading strategies off limits to investment companies operating mutual funds. Similar to investors in mutual funds, investors in hedge funds pay a management fee; however, hedge funds also collect a percentage of the total profits. The impact of hedge funds became highly visible when George Soros's Quantum Fund made over $1 billion by selling British pounds in September 1992, helping to force the pound out of the European Exchange Rate Mechanism.

Corporations and multinational companies

Corporations and multinational companies are likewise involved in the foreign exchange market either through banks or through their own foreign exchange departments. Traditionally, corporations (e.g., producers of consumer products) and service organizations (e.g., travel agencies) have seen foreign exchange as an unwanted necessity of doing business internationally. Today, however, a number of international corporations have become highly sophisticated in their foreign exchange operations, building their own trading departments that boast trading and information technology matching those of banks. Usually, however, corporations do not trade directly in the interbank market, but take part in the market through banks.

One of the foremost reasons for the involvement of corporations in the foreign exchange market is currency hedging (i.e., protecting business by offsetting the risk of unfavorable currency movements). Companies that operate internationally consider foreign exchange rates when deciding, for example, where to locate their production sites, where to buy supplies and hire workers, and how to determine the prices of their products. For example, a European importer of Japanese cars buys these cars with Japanese yen. If the yen appreciates, the price for a delivery of cars in six months might turn out considerably higher than it is now, at the time of ordering the cars. In order to hedge against this risk, the European importer could buy yen forward from his bank[xi] (i.e., agree with his bank on a fixed price at which he will receive the needed amount of yen six months from today for a fixed amount of euro).

[xi] For a definition of forward transactions, see the section "Instruments" in this chapter.

Even smaller companies that purchase materials, hire workforces, and sell products only domestically may have to develop hedging strategies in order to manage foreign exchange risk. Often, there are foreign competitors who are also involved in the domestic market.[7]

Corporations also may attempt to increase their business performance by speculating on currency fluctuations. For example, corporations may decide selectively as to which of their foreign exchange transactions they hedge, based on their expectations of currency movements. Corporations may decide to operate their trading department as an independent profit center, thereby supporting their revenues. Temporarily, some international corporations earn more money by their investments in the foreign exchange market than by their commercial businesses.

As the demarcation line between hedging and speculating of corporations is blurred, it is difficult to assess the extent to which corporations actively speculate in the foreign exchange market. Regardless of whether the reason for the foreign exchange trading of corporations is the protection against market risk or the ambition to profit from currency movements, these corporate trading activities are both significant and powerful influences of exchange-rate movements. Thus the hedging activities by corporations may have played a bigger role in the British pound's exit from the European Exchange Rate Mechanism than such speculators as the Quantum Fund cited above.[7]

Individuals

Individuals play only a limited role in the foreign exchange market. Their transactions, primarily related to international travel or the purchase of foreign goods, are generally too small to move the market. Speculation by individuals has historically been limited, as it was too costly to speculate at the retail level, and only extremely wealthy individuals could qualify to participate in the wholesale market. Recently, however, foreign exchange Internet trading platforms (such as Oanda.com), have begun to permit less wealthy individuals to speculate in currencies. These services often offer advice about day trading. "It's never been easier to play the foreign exchange market!" shouts one service seeking investors. "Can you trust the stock market? Learn about our strategy trading in the foreign currency exchange. See how $10,000 can leverage 1,250,000 Euro," advertises another. Thus, substantive leverage effects allow investors to gain (and of course lose) significant amounts from minor exchange-rate swings. Whether this development will significantly affect market dynamics is not clear yet.

Global financial news agencies

In addition to the traders, news services also play a fundamental daily role in the foreign exchange market. As one trading expert remarked in the interviews, "Everybody is a market participant, whether he trades or he provides information." Traders and financial news services are indeed symbiotically intertwined. Traders base their decisions on the information available to them. Financial news agencies provide information including exchange rates, political news alerts, economic statistics, and comments from significant policy-makers.

The main, global, online financial news providers come from the U.S. and the U.K. AP-Dow Jones, Bloomberg News, and Bridge News (formerly Knight-Ridder) are American, while the largest, Reuters, is British. For traders, these electronic, real-time, global news providers are a critical "window" to the foreign exchange market. The importance of these global financial news services has increased along with the size of the foreign exchange market itself. Indeed, the number of news terminals increases much more rapidly than trading itself. For example, Bloomberg has grown from zero screen-based terminals in 1983 to more than 70,000 in 1995. Reuters has grown from 50,000 terminals in 1985 to 300,000 in 1995.[8]

Recent developments have witnessed a dramatic change in the role of news providers, where the boundaries to the trading institutions are frequently crossed. Banks try to increase their influence on the suppliers of financial news or even provide their own news service. The electronic screens supplied by the news services allow banks to feed wide parts of the market with their own information. News services have developed systems that allow trading institutions not only to collect market information, but also to actually trade with one other.

Thus, without global financial news services, the foreign exchange market as we know it today would not exist. As one financial journalist astutely puts it, "Without news, there is *no* market. There would not be any exchange, any change, any trade without news."

ABBREVIATED REFERENCES

See the reference chapter at the end of the book for full details.

1 Bank for International Settlements (2002)
2 Clark, G. (1999)
3 Swiss Bank Corporation (1992)

4   Roth, P. (1996)
5   Newby, A. (2002)
6   Liebenberg, L. (2002)
7   Millman, G. J. (1995)
8   J. P. Morgan (1996)

Appendix
The European and
the North American Survey

A total of 321 foreign exchange traders in the U.K., Germany, Switzerland, and Austria participated in the European survey (return rate 54%). Of the participating traders, 92% were commercial or investment bank traders, 5% central bank traders, and 3% indicated that they worked for a different financial institution. Thirty-eight percent of the traders worked in Switzerland, 32% in the U.K., 18% in Austria, and 12% in Germany. The sample consisted to a large part of senior traders (75%) and smaller parts of junior traders (22%) and foreign exchange trainees (3%). In terms of traded foreign exchange instruments, 51% of the traders traded spot, 13% forward, 8% money market, 8% foreign exchange derivatives, and 19% of traders a combination of these instruments. Ninety-one percent of the traders were male and 9% female.

In addition to foreign exchange traders, the European survey also included answers from 59 financial journalists working for leading financial news providers (return rate 30%). These journalists were active for news wire services (64%), daily financial news (19%), financial television (14%), and financial periodicals (3%). They were reporters (56%), editors and subeditors (32%), and other financial news journalists (12%). Seventy-four percent of the financial journalists were male and 26% female.

Of the traders who participated in the North American survey, about half (53%) worked in New York, one-third (33%) in the U.S. outside New York, and one-seventh (14%) worked in Canada. Three-quarters of the traders (73%) mostly traded spot, one-third (33%) forward, one-fifth (23%) derivatives, and 6% money market. About 6 in 10 traders (59%) worked in the interbank market, 3 in 10 (32%) as customer traders or foreign exchange salespeople, and 2 in 10 (20%) as proprietary traders. A very small percentage of respondents (1%) indicated that they worked as currency strategists and analysts. Traders reported an average trading experience of 12 years. The survey sample consisted of a majority of senior traders (75%), followed by equally large groups of junior traders (12%) and treasurers or foreign exchange managers (12%), and a very small group of foreign exchange trainees (1%). Also the North American survey sample reflects the high prevalence of male foreign exchange traders. About 9 in 10 of surveyed traders (88%) were male, and about 1 in 10 traders (12%) female.

Trading floors of 21 out of the 26 leading banks in the North American foreign exchange market participated in the North American survey. Leading foreign exchange banks were defined as those institutions included in one of the following lists:

1. Banks represented in the New York Foreign Exchange Committee in 2001 and/or 2002.
2. Positioned among the top-10 institutions of the Global Top 50 Foreign Exchange Market Companies by Estimated Market Share annual ranking published by *Euromoney* magazine in May 2001.
3. Positioned among the top-10 institutions in the Annual Ranking of Banks' FX Revenues 2001 published by *FX Week* in December 2001.
4. Positioned among the top-10 institutions of the Best Provider of FX Services Overall annual ranking published by *Global Investor* Magazine in March 2001 and/or March 2002.
5. Positioned among the top-10 institutions of the annual Best Bank Overall for FX Dealing ranking published by *FX Week* in December 2001.

Three hundred and twenty-six foreign exchange traders from these leading foreign exchange institutions participated in the survey (return rate 60%). Additional data were included from 90 traders working for other foreign exchange institutions in North America,[1] raising the total number of surveyed traders to 416.[i]

In-depth research interviews were conducted with 54 foreign exchange trading experts (treasurers, senior members of trading management, heads of

---

[i] Both in the European and the North American surveys, return rates compared favorably with other surveys of foreign exchange professionals. For example, response rates of 8% and 6% were reported for mail surveys conducted with foreign exchange traders in the U.S. and in the U.K.[2,3] A response rate of 41% was reported for questionnaires distributed to German foreign exchange professionals,[4] and a questionnaire survey conducted among traders in London obtained a response rate of 60%.[5]

trading, and senior traders) and 16 foreign exchange news experts (editors, subeditors, and senior journalists) who were guaranteed that their identity would be protected.

ABBREVIATED REFERENCES

See the reference chapter at the end of the book for full details.

1   Nicolson, A., ed. (2002)
2   Cheung, Y.-W. and Chinn, M. D. (2001)
3   Cheung, Y.-W. et al. (1999)
4   Menkhoff, L. (1998)
5   Taylor, M. P. and Allen, H. (1992)

References

Abelson, R. P. (1976). Social psychology's rational man. In: S. I. Benn and G. W. Mortimore (eds), *Rationality in the Social Sciences* (pp. 58–87). London: Routledge & Kegan Paul.

Abrams, D. and Hogg, M. A. (1988). Comments on the motivational status of self-esteem in social identity and intergroup discrimination. *European Journal of Social Psychology*, **18**(4), 317–334.

Allais, M. (1953). Rational man's behavior in the presence of risk: Critique of the postulates and axioms of the American school. *Econometrica*, **21**, 503–546.

Allen, F., Morris, S., and Shin, H. S. (2002). Beauty contests, bubbles and iterated expectations in asset markets. Retrieved from the World Wide Web: http://www.econ.yale.edu/~sm326/beauty.pdf

Allen, H. and Taylor, M. P. (1990). Charts, noise and fundamentals in the London foreign exchange market. *Economic Journal*, **100**(400), 49–59.

Allport, G. W. and Postman, L. J. (1947). *The Psychology of Rumor*. New York: H. Holt & Co.

Altman, M. (1990). How not to do things with metaphors we live by. *College English*, **5**(52), 495–506.

Anderson, J. R. (1990). *Cognitive Psychology and Its Implications* (3rd edn). New York: W.H. Freeman.

Anderson, M. A. and Goldsmith, A. H. (1994a). Economic and psychological theories of forecast bias and learning: Evidence from U.S. business manager's forecasts. *Eastern Economic Journal*, **20**(4), 413–427.

Anderson, M. A. and Goldsmith, A. H. (1994b). Rationality in the mind's eye: An alternative test of rational expectations using subjective forecast and evaluation data. *Journal of Economics*, **15**, 379–403.

Andreassen, P. B. (1987). On the social psychology of the stock market: Aggregate attributional effects and the regressiveness of prediction. *Journal of Personality and Social Psychology*, **3**(53), 490–496.

Antonides, G. and van der Sar, N. L. (1990). Individual expectations, risk perception and preferences in relation to investment decision making. *Journal of Economic Psychology*, **11**(2), 227–245.

Arkes, H. R. and Blumer, C. (1985). The psychology of sunk cost. *Organizational Behavior and Human Decision Processes*, **35**(1), 124–140.

Aronson, E. (2004). *Social Psychology* (4th edn). New York: Pearson/Prentice Hall.

Asch, S. E. (1951). Effects of group pressure upon the modification and distortion of judgments. In: H. Guetzkow (ed.), *Groups, Leadership, and Men* (pp. 177–190). Pittsburgh: Carnegie Press.

Bagozzi, R. P. (1978). The construct validity of the affective, behavioral, and cognitive components of attitude by analysis of covariance structures. *Multivariate Behavioral Research*, **13**(1), 9–31.

Banerjee, A. V. (1992). A simple model of herd behavior. *Quarterly Journal of Economics*, **107**(3), 797–817.

Bank for International Settlements (2002). *Triennial Central Bank Survey: Foreign Exchange and Derivatives Market Activity in 2001*. Basle, Switzerland: Bank for International Settlements.

Banz, R. W. (1981). The relationship between return and market value of common stocks. *Journal of Financial Economics*, **9**(1), 3–18.

Barber, B. M. and Odean, T. (2000). Trading is hazardous to your wealth: The common stock investment performance of individual investors. *Journal of Finance*, **55**(2), 773–806.

Barber, B.M. and Odean, T. (2001). Boys will be boys: Gender, overconfidence, and common stock investment. *Quarterly Journal of Economics*, **116**(1), 261–292.

Barberis, N., Shleifer, A., and Vishny, R. (1998). A model of investor sentiment. *Journal of Financial Economics*, **49**(3), 307–343.

Barkow, J. H., Cosmides, L., and Tooby, J. (1992). *The Adapted Mind: Evolutionary Psychology and the Generation of Culture*. New York: Oxford University Press.

Baron, J. (2000). *Thinking and Deciding*. Cambridge, UK: Cambridge University Press.

Barrick, M. R. and Mount, M. K. (1991). The big five personality dimensions and job performance: A meta-analysis. *Personnel Psychology*, **44**(1), 1–26.

Barrick, M. R., Mount, M. K., and Judge, T. A. (2001). Personality and performance at the beginning of the new millennium: What do we know and where do we go next? *International Journal of Selection and Assessment*, **9**(1–2), 9–30.

Basu, S. (1983). The relationship between earnings' yield, market value and return for NYSE common stocks: Further evidence. *Journal of Financial Economics*, **12**(1), 129–156.

Bazerman, M. H. (2002). *Judgment in Managerial Decision Making* (5th edn). New York: John Wiley & Sons.

Beach, L. R. (1997). *The Psychology of Decision Making: People in Organizations*. Thousand Oaks, CA: Sage Publications.

Bechara, A., Damasio, H., Tranel, D., and Damasio, A. R. (1997). Deciding advantageously before knowing the advantageous strategy. *Science*, **275**(5304), 1293–1294.

Beck, A. T. (1967). *Depression: Clinical, Experimental*, and *Theoretical Aspects*. New York: Hoeber Medical Division, Harper & Row.

Bell, D. E. (1982). Regret in decision making under uncertainty. *Operations Research*, **30**(5), 961–981.

Belsky, G. and Gilovich, T. (1999). *Why Smart People Make Big Money Mistakes—and How to Correct Them: Lessons from the New Science of Behavioral Economics*. New York: Simon & Schuster.

Bennett, A. (1994). Who's news: An economist investigates the irrationality of people. *Wall Street Journal*, July 29, 1.

Berelson, B. and Steiner, G. A. (1964). *Human Behavior: An Inventory of Scientific Findings*. New York: Harcourt, Brace & World.

Berkowitz, L. (1986). Situational influences on reactions to observed violence. *Journal of Social Issues*, **42**(3), 93–106.

Bernoulli, D. (1738/1954). Exposition of a new theory on the measurement of risk. *Econometrica*, **22**(1), 23–36.

Bernstein, P. L. (1996). *Against the Gods: The Remarkable History of Risk*. New York: John Wiley & Sons.

Biais, B., Hilton, D., Mazurier, K., and Pouget, S. (2001). Psychological traits and trading strategies. Unpublished manuscript.

Biek, M., Wood, W., and Chaiken, S. (1996). Working knowledge, cognitive processing, and attitudes: On the determinants of bias. *Personality and Social Psychology Bulletin*, **22**(6), 547–556.

Bikhchandani, S., Hirshleifer, D., and Welch, I. (1992). A theory of fads, fashion, custom, and cultural change in informational cascades. *Journal of Political Economy*, **100**(5), 992–1026.

Black, F. (1986). Noise. *Journal of Finance*, **3**(41), 529–544.

Black, M. (1977). Mehr über die Metapher [More about the metaphor]. In: A. Haverkamp (ed.), *Theorie der Metapher* (pp. 379–413). Darmstadt, Germany: Wissenschaftliche Buchgesellschaft [in German].

Blanz, M., Mummendey, A., and Otten, S. (1995). Positive–negative asymmetry in social discrimination: The impact of stimulus valence and size and status differentials on intergroup evaluations. *British Journal of Psychology*, **34**(4), 409–419.

Bordia, P. and Rosnow, R. L. (1998). Rumor rest stops on the information highway: Transmission patterns in a computer-mediated rumor chain. *Human Communication Research*, **25**(2), 163–179.

Borges, B., Goldstein, D. G., Ortmann, A., and Gigerenzer, G. (1999). Can ignorance beat the stock market? In: G. Gigerenzer and P. M. Todd (eds), *Simple Heuristics that Make us Smart* (pp. 59–72). Oxford, UK: Oxford University Press.

Borman, W. C. and Motowidlo, S. J. (1997). Task performance and contextual performance: The meaning for personnel selection research. *Human Performance*, **10**(2), 99–109.

Bower, G. H. (1981). Mood and memory. *American Psychologist*, **36**(2), 129–148.

Bower, G. H. and Cohen, P. R. (1982). Emotional influences in memory and thinking: Data and theory. In: M. S. Clark and S. T. Fiske (eds), *Affect and Cognition* (pp. 291–331). Hillsdale, NJ: Erlbaum.

Bower, G. H. and Forgas, J. P. (2000). Affect, memory, and social cognition. In: E. Eich, J. F. Kihlstrom, G. H. Bower, J. P. Forgas, and P. M. Niedenthal (eds), *Cognition and Emotion* (pp. 87–168). Oxford, UK: Oxford University Press.

Bower, G. H., Gilligan, S. G., and Monteiro, K. P. (1981). Selectivity of learning caused by affective states. *Journal of Experimental Psychology: General*, **110**(4), 451–473.

Boyd, M. (2001). On ignorance, intuition, and investing: A bear market test of the recognition heuristic. *Journal of Psychology and Financial Markets*, **2**(3), 150–156.

Bradley, J. V. (1981). Overconfidence in ignorant experts. *Bulletin of the Psychonomic Society*, **17**(2), 82–84.

Brandstaetter, E., Kuehberger, A., and Schneider, F. (2002). A cognitive-emotional account of the shape of the probability weighting function. *Journal of Behavioral Decision Making*, **15**(2), 79–100.

Bray, R. M. and Noble, A. M. (1978). Authoritarianism and decisions of mock juries: Evidence of jury bias and group polarization. *Journal of Personality and Social Psychology*, **36**(12), 1424–1430.

Breckler, S. J. (1984). Empirical validation of affect, behavior, and cognition as distinct components of attitude. *Journal of Personality and Social Psychology*, **47**(6), 1191–1205.

Broemer, P. (1998). Ambivalent attitudes and information processing. *Swiss Journal of Psychology—Schweizerische Zeitschrift fuer Psychologie—Revue Suisse de Psychologie*, **57**(4), 225–234.

Brown, R. (1986). *Social Psychology* (2nd edn). New York: Free Press.

Brown, R. (2000). Social identity theory: Past achievements, current problems and future challenges. *European Journal of Social Psychology*, **30**(6), 745–778.

Bruner, J. S. and Goodman, C. C. (1947). Value and need as organizing factors in perception. *Journal of Abnormal and Social Psychology*, **42**, 33–44.

Buvinic, M. L. and Berkowitz, L. (1976). Delayed effects of practiced versus unpracticed responses after observation of movie violence. *Journal of Experimental Social Psychology*, **12**(3), 283–293.

Carew, E. and Slatyer, W. (1989). *Forex: The Techniques of Foreign Exchange*. Sydney: Allen & Unwin.

Cavaglia, S. M. F. G. and Wolff, C. C. P. (1996). A note on the determinants of unexpected exchange rate movements. *Journal of Banking and Finance*, **20**(1), 179–188.

Chan, L. K. C., Hamao, Y. and Lakonishok, J. (1991). Fundamentals and stock returns in Japan. *Journal of Finance*, **46**(5), 1739–1764.

Chang, P. H. K. and Osler, C. L. (1999). Methodical madness: Technical analysis and the irrationality of exchange-rate forecasts. *Economic Journal*, **109**(458), 636–661.

Chapman, L. J. and Chapman, J. P. (1967). Genesis of popular but erroneous psychodiagnostic observations. *Journal of Abnormal Psychology*, **72**(3), 193–204.

Cheung, Y.-W., and Chinn, M. D. (2001). Currency traders and exchange rate dynamics: A survey of the US market. *Journal of International Money and Finance*, **20**(4), 439–471.

Cheung, Y.-W., Chinn, M. D., and Marsh, I. W. (1999). How do UK-based foreign exchange dealers think their market operates? Traders, market microstructure and exchange rate dynamics. Unpublished manuscript.

Chu, J. and Osler, C. L. (2004). Identifying noise traders: The head-and-shoulders pattern in U.S. equities. Unpublished manuscript.

Clark, G. (1999). *Betting on Lives: The Culture of Life Insurance in England, 1695–1775*. New York: Manchester University Press.

Clasing, H. and Craig, R. (1990). Deciphering the market's moods and modes. *Futures*, **19**(10), 32–34.
Cohen, D. (2001). *Fear, Greed and Panic*. Chichester, UK: John Wiley & Sons.
Combs, B. and Slovic, P. (1979). Newspaper coverage of causes of death. *Journalism Quarterly*, **56**(4), 837–843.
Condon, T. (2000). Atriax arrives. *Bank Technology News*, December, pp. 12–18.
Cosmides, L. and Tooby, J. (1994). Better than rational: Evolutionary psychology and the invisible hand. *American Economic Review*, **84**(2), 327–332.
Costa, P. T. (1996). Work and personality: Use of the NEO-PI-R in industrial/organizational psychology. *Applied Psychology: An International Review*, **45**(3), 225–241.
Costa, P. T. and McCrae, R. R. (1985). *The NEO Personality Inventory Manual*. Odessa, FL: Psychological Assessment Resources.
Costa, P. T. and McCrae, R. R. (1992). *Revised NEO Personality Inventory (Neo-PI-R) and NEO Five-Factor Inventory (NEO-FFI): Professional Manual*. Odessa, FL: Psychological Assessment Resources.
Crocker, J., Thompson, L., McGraw, K. M., and Ingerman, C. (1987). Downwards comparison, prejudice, and evaluations of others: Effects of self-esteem and threat. *Journal of Personality and Social Psychology*, **52**(5), 907–916.
Czernik, A. and Steinmeyer, E. (1974). Experience of loneliness in normal and in neurotic subjects. *Archiv fuer Psychiatrie und Nervenkrankheiten*, **218**(2), 141–159.
Daniel, K., Hirshleifer, D., and Subrahmanyam, A. (1998). Investor psychology and security market under- and overreactions. *Journal of Finance*, **53**(6), 1839–1885.
Daniel, K. D., Hirshleifer, D., and Subrahmanyam, A. (2001). Overconfidence, arbitrage, and equilibrium asset pricing. *Journal of Finance*, **56**(3), 921–965.
Davis, F. D., Lohse, G. L., and Kottemann, J. E. (1994). Harmful effects of seemingly helpful information on forecasts of stock earnings. *Journal of Economic Psychology*, **15**(15), 253–267.
De Bondt, W. F. M., and Thaler, R. (1985). Does the stock market overreact? *Journal of Finance*, **40**(3), 793–805.
De Bondt, W. F. M. and Thaler, R. H. (1994). *Financial Decision-making in Markets and Firms: A Behavioral Perspective* (Working Paper 4777). Cambridge, MA: National Bureau of Economic Research.
De Long, J. B., Shleifer, A., Summers, L. H., and Waldmann, R. J. (1991). The survival of noise traders in financial markets. *Journal of Business and Psychology*, **64**(1), 1–19.
DiFonzo, N. and Bordia, P. (1997). Rumor and prediction: Making sense (but losing dollars) in the stock market. *Organizational Behavior and Human Decision Processes*, **71**(3), 329–353.
DiFonzo, N., Bordia, P., and Rosnow, R. L. (1994). Reining in rumors. *Organizational Dynamics*, **1**(23), 47–62.
Digman, J. M. (1990). Personality structure: Emergence of the five-factor model. *Annual Review of Psychology*, **41**, 417–440.
Dreman, D. (1995). Outpsyching the market—1995 money guide. *Forbes [FBR]*, June 19, 162–168.

Duchon, D., Ashmos, D., and Dunegan, K. J. (1991). Avoid decision making disaster by considering psychological bias. *Review of Business*, **1–2**(13), 13–18.

Eagly, A. H. (1998). Attitudes and the processing of attitude-relevant information. In: J. G. Adair and D. Belanger (eds.), *Advances in Psychological Science, Social, Personal, and Cultural Aspects* (Vol. 1, pp. 185–201). Hove, UK: Psychology Press/Erlbaum (UK)/Taylor & Francis.

Eagly, A. H. and Chaiken, S. (1998). Attitude structure and function. In: D. T. Gilbert, S. T. Fiske, and G. Lindzey (eds), *The Handbook of Social Psychology* (Vol. 2, pp. 269–322). New York: McGraw-Hill.

Earles, J. A., Driskill, W. E., and Dittmar, M. J. (1996). Methodology for identifying abilities for job classification: An application of job analysis. *Military Psychology*, **8**(3), 179–193.

Ederington, L. H. and Lee, J. H. (1993). How markets process information: News releases and volatility. *Journal of Finance*, **48**(4), 1161–1191.

Edwards, D. (1991). Categories are for talking: On the cognitive and discursive bases of categorization. *Theory and Psychology*, **4**(1), 515–542.

Edwards, D. (1997). *Discourse and Cognition*. London: Sage Publications.

Edwards, W. (1954). The theory of decision making. *Psychological Bulletin*, **51**, 380–417.

Ellis, A. and Harper, R. A. (1961). *A Guide to Rational Living*. Englewood Cliffs, NJ: Prentice Hall.

Ellsberg, D. (1961). Risk, ambiguity, and the savage axioms. *Quarterly Journal of Economics*, **75**, 643–699.

Etzioni, A. (1988). Normative-affective factors: Toward a new decision-making model. *Journal of Economic Psychology*, **2**(9), 125–150.

Evans, J. S. B. T. (1987). Beliefs and expectations as causes of judgmental bias. In: G. Wright and P. Ayton (eds), *Judgmental Forecasting* (pp. 31–47). New York: John Wiley & Sons.

Fama, E. F. (1970). Efficient capital markets: A review of theory and empirical work. *Journal of Finance*, **25**(2), 383–417.

Fama, E. F. (1998). Market efficiency, long-term returns, and behavioral finance. *Journal of Financial Economics*, **49**(3), 283–306.

Fama, E. F. and French, K. R. (1992). The cross-section of expected stock returns. *Journal of Finance*, **47**(2), 427–465.

Farr, R. M. and Moscovici, S. (1984). *Social Representations*. Cambridge, UK: Cambridge University Press.

Fazio, R. H. (1986). How do attitudes guide behavior? In: R. M. Sorrentino and E. T. Higgins (eds), *Handbook of Motivation and Cognition: Foundations of Social Behavior* (Vol. 1, pp. 204–243). New York: Guilford Press.

Fazio, R. H. and Towles-Schwen, T. (1999). The MODE model of attitude–behavior processes. In: S. Chaiken and Y. Trope (eds), *Dual-process Theories in Social Psychology* (pp. 97–116). New York: Guilford Press.

Feather, N. T. (1994). Values, national identification and favouritism towards the ingroup. *British Journal of Social Psychology*, **33**(4), 467–476.

Feather, N. T. (1996). Social comparisons across nations: Variables relating to the subjective evaluation of national achievement and to personal and collective self-esteem. *Australian Journal of Psychology*, **48**(2), 53–63.

Fenton O'Creevy, M., Nicholson, N., Soane, E., and Willman, P. (1998). Individual and contextual influences on the market behaviour of finance professionals. Unpublished manuscript.

Ferguson, R. (1989). On crashes. *Financial Analysts Journal*, **45**(2), 42–52.

Festinger, L. (1957). *A Theory of Cognitive Dissonance*. Stanford, CA: Stanford University Press.

Fischhoff, B. and Beyth, R. (1975). "I knew it would happen": Remembered probabilities of once-future things. *Organizational Behavior and Human Decision Processes*, **13**(1), 1–16.

Forgas, J. P. and Bower, G. H. (1988). Affect in social judgments. *Australian Journal of Psychology*, **40**(2), 125–145.

Frankel, J. A. and Froot, K. A. (1986). Understanding the US dollar in the eighties: The expectations of chartists and fundamentalists. *Economic Record Supplementary Issue*, **62**, 24–38.

Frankel, J. A. and Froot, K. A. (1987). Using survey data to test standard propositions regarding exchange rate expectations. *American Economic Review*, **77**(1), 133–153.

Frankel, J. A. and Froot, K. A. (1990a). Chartists, fundamentalists, and trading in the foreign exchange market. *American Economic Review*, **80**(2), 181–185.

Frankel, J. A. and Froot, K. A. (1990b). *Exchange Rate Forecasting Techniques, Survey Data, and Implications for the Foreign Exchange Market* (Working Paper WP/90/43). Washington, DC: International Monetary Fund.

Frenkel, J. A. (1981). Flexible exchange rates, prices, and the role of "news": Lessons from the 1970s. *Journal of Political Economy*, **41**(89), 665–705.

Freud, S. (1900). *The Interpretation of Dreams*. New York: Macmillan.

Freud, S. ([1933] 1965). *New Introductory Lectures on Psychoanalysis* (trans. James Strachey). New York: W.W. Norton & Company.

Frey, B. S. (1990). Entscheidungsanomalien: Die Sicht der Ockonomie. *Psychologische Rundschau*, **41**, 67–83.

Friedman, M. (1953). *Essays in Positive Economics*. Chicago: University of Chicago Press.

Froot, K. A. and Frankel, J. A. (1989). Forward discount bias: Is it an exchange risk premium? *Quarterly Journal of Economics*, **104**(1), 139–161.

Gardner, J. (1978). *On Moral Fiction*. New York: Basic Books.

Garland, H. (1990). Throwing good money after bad: The effect of sunk costs on the decision to escalate commitment to an ongoing project. *Journal of Applied Psychology*, **75**(6), 728–731.

Ghiselli, E. E. (1973). The validity of aptitude tests in personnel selection. *Personnel Psychology*, **26**(4), 461–477.

Gigerenzer, G. and Todd, P. M. (1999). *Simple Heuristics that Make Us Smart*. Oxford, UK: Oxford University Press.

Gilovich, T., Vallone, R., and Tversky, A. (1985). The hot hand in basketball: On the misperception of random sequences. *Cognitive Psychology*, **17**(3), 295–314.

Gimpl, M. L. and Dakin, S. R. (1984). Management and magic. *California Management Review*, **1**(27), 126–136.

Goldberg, J. and Nitzsch, R. v. (2001). *Behavioral Finance* (English edn). Chichester, UK: John Wiley & Sons.

Goldberg, L. R. (1992). The development of markers for the Big-Five factor structure. *Psychological Assessment*, **4**(1), 26–42.
Goldberg, L. R. (1993). The structure of phenotypic personality traits. *American Psychologist*, **48**(1), 26–34.
Goldstone, N. B. (1988). *Trading Up*. London: Sidgwick & Jackson.
Golec, J. and Tamarkin, M. (1995). Do bettors prefer long shots because they are risk-lovers, or are they just overconfident? *Journal of Risk and Uncertainty*, **11**(1), 51–64.
Goodhart, C. (1988). The foreign exchange market: A random walk with a dragging anchor. *Economica*, **55**(220), 437–460.
Goodhart, C. and Demos, A. A. (2000). Reuters' screen images of the foreign exchange markets: The yen/dollar and the sterling/dollar spot market. In: C. Goodhart and R. Payne (eds), *The Foreign Exchange Market: Empirical Studies with High-frequency Data* (pp. 75–133). New York: St Martin's Press.
Goodhart, C., Ito, T., and Payne, R. (1996). One day in June 1993: A study of the working of the Reuters 2000–2 electronic foreign exchange trading system. In: J. A. Frankel, G. Galli, and A. Giovannini (eds), *The Microstructure of Foreign Exchange Markets* (pp. 107–179). Chicago: University of Chicago Press.
Goodstein, L. D. and Lanyon, R. I. (1999). Applications of personality assessment to the workplace: A review. *Journal of Business and Psychology*, **13**(3), 291–322.
Gotthelf, P. (2003). *Currency Trading: How to Access and Trade the World's Biggest Market*. Hoboken, NJ: John Wiley & Sons.
Gray, J. (1997). Overquantification. *Financial Analysts Journal*, **6**(53), 5–12.
Groysberg, B. (2001). Can they take it with them? The portability of star knowledge workers' performance: Myth or reality. Unpublished manuscript.
Guion, R. M. and Gottier, R. F. (1965). Validity of personality measures in personnel selection. *Personnel Psychology*, **18**(2), 135–164.
Gump, B. B. and Kulik, J. A. (1997). Stress, affiliation, and emotional contagion. *Journal of Personality and Social Psychology*, **72**(2), 305–319.
Hackman, R. J. (2002). *Leading Teams: Setting the Stage for Great Performances*. Boston: Harvard Business School Press.
Hake, H. W. and Hyman, R. (1953). Perception of statistical structure of a random series of binary symbols. *Journal of Experimental Psychology*, **45**, 64–74.
Hakkio, C. S. and Pearce, D. K. (1985). *The Reaction of Exchange Rates to Economic News* (Research Paper No. 8501). Kansas City: Federal Reserve Bank.
Hall, C. S., Lindzey, G., and Campbell, J. B. (1998). *Theories of Personality*. New York: John Wiley & Sons.
Hardouvelis, G. A. (1988). Economic news, exchange rates and interest rates. *Journal of International Money and Finance*, **7**(1), 23–35.
Harris, E. S. and Zabka, N. M. (1995). The employment report and the dollar. *Current Issues in Economics and Finance*, **8**(1), 1–6.
Harvey, J. T. (1996). Long-term exchange rate movements: The role of the fundamentals in neoclassical models of exchange rates. *Journal of Economic Issues*, **2**(30), 509–516.
Hastie, R. and Dawes, R. M. (2001). *Rational Choice in an Uncertain World: The Psychology of Judgment and Decision Making*. Thousand Oaks, CA: Sage Publications.

Hatfield, E., Cacioppo, J. T., and Rapson, R. L. (1993). Emotional contagion. *Current Directions in Psychological Science*, **2**(3), 96–99.

Hatfield, E., Cacioppo, J. T., and Rapson, R. L. (1994). *Emotional Contagion*. New York: Cambridge University Press.

Hawawini, G. and Keim, D. B. (2000). The cross section of common stock returns: A review of the evidence and some new findings. In: D. B. Keim and W. T. Ziemba (eds), *Security Market Imperfections in Worldwide Equity Markets* (pp. 3–43). Cambridge, UK: Cambridge University Press.

Herkner, W. (1983). *Sozialpsychologie* (3rd edn). Bern: Hans Huber [in German].

Hirshleifer, D. (2001). Investor psychology and asset pricing. *Journal of Finance*, **56**(4), 1533–1597.

Ho, T. S. Y. and Michaely, R. (1988). Information quality and market efficiency. *Journal of Financial & Quantitative Analysis*, **23**(1), 53–70.

Hodgson, G. M. (1993). The economy as an organism—not a machine. *Futures*, **25**(4), 392–403.

Hoelzl, E., Kirchler, E., and Rodler, C. (2002). Hindsight bias in economic expectations: I knew all along what I want to hear. *Journal of Applied Psychology*, **87**(3), 437–443.

Hofstaetter, P. R. (1956). Color symbolism and ambivalence. *Psychologische Beitraege*, **2**, 526–540.

Hogan, R., Hogan, J., and Roberts, B. W. (1996). Personality measurement and employment decisions: Questions and answers. *American Psychologist*, **51**(5), 469–477.

Hogarth, R. (1981). Beyond discrete biases: Functional and dysfunctional aspects of judgmental heuristics. *Psychological Bulletin*, **2**(90), 197–217.

Hogarth, R. M. (2001). *Educating Intuition*. Chicago: University of Chicago Press.

Hogarth, R. and Makridakis, S. (1981). Forecasting and planning: An evaluation. *Management Science*, **2**(27), 115–138.

Hogarth, R. and Reder, M. W. E. (1987). *Rational Choice: The Contrast between Economics and Psychology*. Chicago: University of Chicago Press.

Hogg, M. A. and Abrams, D. (1988). *Social Identification: A Social Psychology of Intergroup Relations and Group Processes*. London: Routledge.

Hogg, M. A. and Sunderland, J. (1991). Self-esteem and intergroup discrimination in the minimal group paradigm. *British Journal of Social Psychology*, **30**(1), 51–62.

Hogg, M. A., Terry, D. J., and White, K. M. (1995). A tale of two theories: A critical comparison of identity theory with social identity theory. *Social Psychology Quarterly*, **58**(4), 255–269.

Huberman, G. and Regev, T. (2001). Contagious speculation and a cure for cancer: A nonevent that made stock prices soar. *Journal of Finance*, **56**(1), 387–396.

Hunter, J. A., Stringer, M., and Coleman, J. T. (1993). Social explanations and self-esteem in Northern Ireland. *Journal of Social Psychology*, **133**(5), 643–650.

Ichheiser, G. (1949). Misunderstandings in human relations: A study in false social perception. *American Journal of Sociology*, **55**(Supplement).

Inwald, R. E. and Brockwell, A. L. (1991). Predicting the performance of government security personnel with the IPI and MMPI. *Journal of Personality Assessment*, **56**(3), 522–535.

Isozaki, M. (1984). The effect of discussion on polarization of judgments. *Japanese Psychological Research*, **26**(4), 187–193.

Ito, T. (1990). Foreign exchange rate expectations: Micro survey data. *American Economic Review*, **3**(80), 434–449.

Jegadeesh, N. and Titman, S. (1993). Returns to buying winners and selling losers: Implications for stock market efficiency. *Journal of Finance*, **48**(1), 65–91.

Johnson, M. (1987). *The Body in the Mind: The Bodily Basis of Meaning, Imagination, and Reason*. Chicago: University of Chicago Press.

Jonas, E., Schulz-Hardt, S., Frey, D., and Thelen, N. (2001). Confirmation bias in sequential information search after preliminary decisions: An expansion of dissonance theoretical research on selective exposure to information. *Journal of Personality and Social Psychology*, **80**(4), 557–571.

JP Morgan (1996). *The Information Revolution in Financial Markets*. Prague: JP Morgan.

Jungermann, H. and Thüring, M. (1987). The use of mental models for generating scenarios. In: G. Wright and P. Ayton (eds), *Judgmental Forecasting* (pp. 245–266). New York: John Wiley & Sons.

Kahn, H. and Cooper, C. L. (1993). *Stress in the Dealing Room*. London: Routledge.

Kahn, H. and Cooper, C. L. (1996). How foreign exchange dealers in the City of London cope with occupational stress. *International Journal of Stress Management*, **3**(3), 137–145.

Kahneman, D. and Tversky, A. (1973). On the psychology of prediction. *Psychological Review*, **80**(4), 237–251.

Kahneman, D. and Tversky, A. (1979). Prospect theory: An analysis of decision under risk. *Econometrica*, **2**(47), 263–291.

Kahneman, D. and Tversky, A. (1982). The psychology of preference. *Scientific American*, **246**, 160–173.

Kahneman, D. and Tversky, A. (1984). Choices, values and frames. *American Psychologist*, **39**, 341–350.

Katona, G. (1972). Theory of expectations. In: B. Strumpel, J. N. Morgan and E. Zahn (eds), *Human Behavior in Economic Affairs* (pp. 549–582). Amsterdam: Elsevier Scientific.

Katona, G. (1975). *Psychological Economics*. New York: Elsevier Scientific.

Kelly, G. A. (1955). *The Psychology of Personal Constructs*. New York: W.W. Norton.

Keynes, J. M. (1936). *The General Theory of Employment, Interest, and Money*. London: Macmillan.

Kichuk, S. L. and Wiesner, W. H. (1998). Work teams: Selecting members for optimal performance. *Canadian Psychology*, **39**(1–2), 23–32.

Kirman, A. (1991). Epidemics of opinion and speculative bubbles in financial markets. In: M. P. Taylor (ed.), *Money and Financial Markets* (pp. 354–368). Cambridge, UK: Blackwell.

Kirman, A. (1995). The behaviour of the foreign exchange market. *Bank of England— Quarterly Bulletin*, **3**(35), 286–293.

Klein, G. A. (1993). A recognition-primed decision (RPD) model of rapid decision making. In: G. A. Klein, J. Orasanu, R. Calderwood, and C. E. Zsambok (eds), *Decision Making in Action: Models and Methods* (pp. 138–147). Norwood, NJ: Ablex.

Klein, G. A. (1998). *Sources of Power*. Cambridge, MA: MIT Press.

References

Knox, R. E. and Inkster, J. A. (1968). Postdecision dissonance at post time. *Journal of Personality and Social Psychology*, **8**(4), 319–323.

Krieger, A. J. and Claflin, E. (1992). *The Money Bazaar: Inside the Trillion-dollar World of Currency Trading* (1st edn). New York: Times Books.

Kristof, A. L. (1996). Person–organization fit: An integrative review of its conceptualizations, measurement, and implications. *Personnel Psychology*, **49**(1), 1–49.

Kritzman, M. (1998). Risk and utility: Basics. In: P. L. Bernstein and A. Damodaran (eds), *Investment Management* (pp. 27–57). New York: John Wiley & Sons.

Kubon-Gilke, G. (1996). Institutional economics and the evolutionary metaphor. *Journal of Institutional and Theoretical Economics*, **152**(4), 723–738.

Kyle, A. S. and Wang, F. A. (1997). Speculation duopoly with agreement to disagree: Can overconfidence survive the market test? *Journal of Finance*, **52**(5), 2073–2090.

Lakoff, G. (1987). *Women, Fire, and Dangerous Things: What Categories Reveal about the Mind*. Chicago: University of Chicago Press.

Lakoff, G. and Johnson, M. (1980). *Metaphors We Live By*. Chicago: University of Chicago Press.

Lakoff, G. and Johnson, M. (1999). *Philosophy in the Flesh: The Embodied Mind and Its Challenge to Western Thought*. New York: Basic Books.

Lamont, O. A. and Thaler, R. H. (2003). Can the market add and subtract? Mispricing in tech stock carve-outs. *Journal of Political Economy*, **111**(2), 227–268.

Land, D. (1996). Partial views. In: R. Hutterer, G. Pawlowsky, P. F. Schmid and R. Stipsits (eds), *Client-centered and Experiential Psychotherapy: A Paradigm in Motion* (pp. 67–74). Frankfurt, Germany: Peter Lang.

Langer, E., Blank, A., and Chanowitz, B. (1978). The mindlessness of ostensibly thoughtful action. *Journal of Personality and Social Psychology*, **36**(6), 635–642.

Lazarus, A. A. (1971). *Behavior Therapy and Beyond*. New York: McGraw-Hill.

Lee, S. B. and Kim, K. J. (1994). Does the October 1987 crash strengthen the co-movements among national stock markets? *Review of Financial Economics*, **3**(1–2), 89–102.

Leeson, N. W. (1996). *Rogue Trader: How I Brought Down Barings Bank and Shook the Financial World*. Boston: Little & Brown.

Levin, J. H. (1997). Chartists, fundamentalists and exchange rate dynamics. *International Journal of Finance and Economics*, **2**(4), 281–290.

Liberman, A., de la Hoz, V., and Chaiken, A. (1988). Prior attitudes as heuristic information. Unpublished manuscript.

Liebenberg, L. (2002). *The Electronic Financial Markets of the Future*. New York: Palgrave Macmillan.

Long, K. M., Spears, R., and Manstead, A. S. R. (1994). The influence of personal and collective self-esteem on strategies of social differentiation. *British Journal of Social Psychology*, **33**(3), 313–330.

Loomes, F. and Sugden, R. (1982). Regret theory: An alternative theory of rational choice under uncertainty. *Economic Journal*, **92**(368), 805–824.

Lopes, L. L. (1995). On modeling risky choice: Why reasons matter. In: J. P. Caverni, H. M. Bar-Hillel, H. Barron, and H. Jungermann (eds), *Contributions to Decision Making* (Vol. 1, pp. 29–50). Amsterdam: North-Holland.

Lovell, M. C. (1986). Tests of the rational expectations hypothesis. *American Economic Review*, **76**(1), 110–124.

Luca, C. (2000). *Trading in the Global Currency Markets*. New York: New York Institute of Finance.

Lucas, R. E. (1978). Asset prices in an exchange economy. *Econometrica*, **46**(6), 1429–1445.

Lui, Y.-H. and Mole, D. (1998). The use of fundamental and technical analyses by foreign exchange dealers: Hong Kong evidence. *Journal of International Money and Finance*, **17**(3), 535–545.

Lux, T. (1995). Herd behavior, bubbles and crashes. *Economic Journal*, **105**(431), 881–896.

Lyons, R. K. (1998). Profits and position control: A week of FX dealing. *Journal of International Money and Finance*, **17**(1), 97–115.

Maas, P. and Weibler, J. (1990). *Boerse und Psychologie; Plaedoyer für eine neue Perspektive*. Koeln: Deutscher Instituts-Verlag GmbH [in German].

MacDonald, R. and Marsh, I. W. (1996). Currency forecasters are heterogeneous: Confirmation and consequences. *Journal of International Money and Finance*, **15**(5), 665–685.

MacDonald, R. and Taylor, M. P. (1992). Exchange rate economics: A survey. *International Monetary Fund Staff Papers*, **39**(1), 1–57.

Maital, S. (1982). *Minds, Markets, and Money: Psychological Foundations of Economic Behavior*. New York: Basic Books.

Malinowski, B. (1925). *Magic, Science, and Religion, and Other Essays*. New York: Doubleday.

Malkiel, B. (1990). *A Random Walk down Wall Street*. New York: W.W. Norton.

March, J. G. and Simon, H. A. (1958). *Organizations*. New York: John Wiley & Sons.

Markowitz, H. (1952). Portfolio selection. *Journal of Finance*, **7**(1), 77–91.

Maslow, A. H. (1962). *Toward a Psychology of Being*. Princeton, NJ: Van Nostrand.

McCloskey, D. N. (1990). *If You're So Smart: The Narrative of Economic Expertise*. Chicago: University of Chicago Press.

McCloskey, D. N. (1995). Metaphors economists live by. *Social Research*, **2**(62), 215–237.

McCloskey, J. C. and McCain, B. (1988). Variables related to nurse performance. *Journal of Nursing Scholarship*, **20**(4), 203–207.

McGoun, E. G. (1996). Fashion and finance. *International Review of Financial Analysis*, **1**(5), 65–78.

McNeil, B. J., Pauker, S. G., Sox, H. C., Jr, and Tversky, A. (1982). On the elicitation of preferences for alternative therapies. *New England Journal of Medicine*, **306**(21), 1259–1262.

Meese, R. A. and Rogoff, K. (1983). Empirical exchange rate models of the seventies: Do they fit out of sample? *Journal of International Economics*, **14**(1–2), 3–24.

Meier-Pesti, K. and Kirchler, E. (2003). Attitudes towards the euro by national identity and relative national status. *Journal of Economic Psychology*, **24**(3), 293–299.

Menkhoff, L. (1997). Examining the use of technical currency analysis. *International Journal of Finance and Economics*, **2**(4), 307–318.

Menkhoff, L. (1998). The noise trading approach—questionnaire evidence from foreign exchange. *Journal of International Money and Finance*, **17**(3), 547–564.

References

Mero, L. (1998). *Moral Calculations: Game Theory, Logic, and Human Frailty*. New York: Springer-Verlag.

Merton, R. (1948). The self-fulfilling prophecy. *Antioch Review*, **8**, 193–210.

Miller, P. H. (2001). *Theories of Developmental Psychology* (4th edn). New York: Worth.

Millman, G. J. (1995). *The Vandal's Crown: How the World's Currency Traders Overthrew the World's Central Banks*. New York: Free Press.

Mitchell, M. L. and Harold, M. J. (1994). The impact of public information on the stock market. *Journal of Finance*, 3(49), 923–949.

Morris, S. and Shin, H. S. (1998). Unique equilibrium in a model of self-fulfilling currency attacks. *American Economic Review*, **88**(3), 587–589.

Moscovici, S. and Zavalloni, M. (1969). The group as a polarizer of attitudes. *Journal of Personality & Social Psychology*, **12**(2), 125–135.

Mullen, B. and Riordan, C. A. (1988). Self-serving attributions for performance in naturalistic settings: A meta-analytic review. *Journal of Applied Social Psychology*, **18**(1), 3–22.

Muth, J. F. (1961). Rational expectations and the theory of price movements. *Econometrica*, **29**, 315–335.

Myers, D. G. (2002a). *Intuition: Its powers and perils*. New Haven, CT: Yale University Press.

Myers, D. G. (2002b). *Social Psychology* (7th edn). Boston: McGraw-Hill.

Neely, C. J. (1997). Technical analysis in the foreign exchange market: A layman's guide. *Federal Reserve Bank of St. Louis Review*, September/October, 23–38.

Neuman, G. A., Wagner, S. H., and Christiansen, N. D. (1999). The relationship between work-team personality composition and the job performance of teams. *Group and Organization Management*, **24**(1), 28–45.

Newby, A. (2002). 2002 Euromoney foreign exchange poll. *Euromoney*, May, p. 58.

Newcomb, T. M. (1972). Expectations as a social-psychological concept. In: B. Strumpel, J. N. Morgan, and E. Zahn (eds), *Human Behavior in Economic Affairs* (pp. 109–117). Amsterdam: Elsevier Scientific.

Nicolson, A. (ed.) (2002). *SG Dealers Directory 2002* (45th edn). London: Société Générale.

Niederhoffer, V. (1997). *The Education of a Speculator*. New York: John Wiley & Sons.

Nisbett, R. E. and Ross, L. (1980). *Human Inference: Strategies and Shortcomings of Social Judgment*. Englewood Cliffs, NJ: Prentice Hall.

Northcraft, G. B. and Neale, M. A. (1987). Experts, amateurs, and real estate: An anchoring-and-adjustment perspective on property pricing decisions. *Organizational Behavior and Human Decision Processes*, **39**(1), 84–97.

Norton, L. P. (1996). The outliers. *Barron's*, May 20, 43–44.

Oakes, D. W., Ferris, G. R., Martocchio, J. J., Buckley, M. R., and Broach, D. (2001). Cognitive ability and personality predictors of training program skill acquisition and job performance. *Journal of Business and Psychology*, **15**(4), 523–548.

Oberlechner, T. (2001a). Evaluation of currencies in the foreign exchange market: Attitudes and expectations of foreign exchange traders. *Zeitschrift fuer Sozialpsychologie*, **32**(3), 180–188.

Oberlechner, T. (2001b). Importance of technical and fundamental analysis in the European foreign exchange market. *International Journal of Finance and Economics*, **6**(1), 81–93.

Oberlechner, T. (2003). *Psychology of Trading in the Foreign Exchange Market: Insights from North American Market Participants*. Cambridge, MA: Harvard University.

Oberlechner, T. (2004a). The alchemists of finance: Personality and trading performance of foreign exchange traders. Unpublished manuscript.

Oberlechner, T. (2004b). Perceptions of successful traders by foreign exchange professionals. *Journal of Behavioral Finance*, **5**(1), 23–31.

Oberlechner, T. and Hocking, S. (1997). *Market Psychology and the Dynamics of Information: An Interdisciplinary View of the Foreign Exchange Market*. Vienna: Webster University.

Oberlechner, T. and Hocking, S. (2004). Information sources, news, and rumors in financial markets: Insights into the foreign exchange market. *Journal of Economic Psychology*, **25**(3), 407–424.

Oberlechner, T. and Osler, C. L. (2004). Overconfidence in currency markets. Unpublished manuscript.

Oberlechner, T., Slunecko, T., and Kronberger, N. (2004). Surfing the money tides: Understanding the foreign exchange market through metaphors. *British Journal of Social Psychology*, **43**(1), 133–156.

Olsen, R. A. (1997). Desirability bias among professional investment managers: Some evidence from experts. *Journal of Behavioral Decision Making*, **10**(1), 65–72.

Osgood, C. E. (1952). The measurement of meaning. *Psychological Bulletin*, **49**, 197–237.

Osgood, C. E., Suci, G. J., and Tannenbaum, P. H. (1957). *The Measurement of Meaning*. Urbana, IL: University of Illinois Press.

Oskamp, S. (1965). Overconfidence in case-study judgments. *Journal of Consulting Psychology*, **29**(3), 261–265.

Osterberg, W. P. and Wetmore Humes, R. (1993). The inaccuracy of newspaper reports of U.S. foreign exchange intervention. *Economic Review (Federal Reserve Bank of Cleveland)*, **4**(29), 25–33.

Ostrom, T. M. (1969). The relationship between the affective, behavioral, and cognitive components of attitude. *Journal of Experimental Social Psychology*, **5**(1), 12–30.

Pennington, N. and Hastie, R. (1992). Explaining the evidence: Tests of the story model for juror decision making. *Journal of Personality and Social Psychology*, **62**(2), 189–206.

Perraudin, W. and Vitale, P. (1994). *Information Flows in the Foreign Exchange Market* (Working Paper 9412). Cambridge, MA: University of Cambridge Department of Applied Economics.

Pieters, R. G. M. and Van Raaij, W. F. (1988). Functions and management of affect: Applications to economic behavior. *Journal of Economic Psychology*, **9**(2), 251–282.

Plous, S. (1993). *The Psychology of Judgment and Decision Making*. New York: McGraw-Hill.

Polanyi, M. (1962). *Personal Knowledge: Towards a Post-Critical Philosophy*. Chicago: University of Chicago Press.

Polanyi, M. (1964). *Science, Faith and Society*. Chicago: University of Chicago Press.

Pring, M. J. (1991). *Technical Analysis Explained: The Successful Investor's Guide to Spotting Investment Trends and Turning Points* (3rd edn). New York: McGraw-Hill.

Pruitt, S. W., Reilly, R. J., and Hoffer, G. E. (1988). The effect of media presentation on the formation of economic expectations: Some initial evidence. *Journal of Economic Psychology*, **9**(3), 315–325.

Pulford, B. D. and Colman, A. M. (1997). Overconfidence: Feedback and item difficulty effects. *Personality and Individual Differences*, **23**(1), 125–133.

Rabin, M. (1998). Psychology and economics. *Journal of Economic Literature*, **36**(1), 11–46.

Rashes, M. S. (2001). Massively confused investors making conspicuously ignorant choices (MCI-MCIC). *Journal of Finance*, **56**(5), 1911–1927.

Reynolds, R. I. (1982). Search heuristics of chess players of different calibers. *American Journal of Psychology*, **95**(3), 383–392.

Reynolds, R. I. (1991). The application of a search heuristic by skilled problem solvers. *Bulletin of the Psychonomic Society*, **29**(1), 55–56.

Ricoeur, P. (1975). *The Rule of Metaphor*. Toronto: Toronto University Press.

Riggio, R. E. and Taylor, S. J. (2000). Personality and communication skills as predictors of hospice nurse performance. *Journal of Business and Psychology*, **15**(2), 351–359.

Robertson, I. T. and Kinder, A. (1993). Personality and job competences: The criterion-related validity of some personality variables. *Journal of Occupational and Organizational Psychology*, **66**(3), 225–244.

Rogers, C. (1951). *Client-centered Therapy: Its Current Practice, Implications, and Theory*. Boston: Houghton-Mifflin.

Rogers, C. (1961). *On Becoming a Person*. Boston: Houghton-Mifflin.

Rosenberg, B., Reid, K. and Lanstein, R. (1985). Persuasive evidence of market inefficiency. *Journal of Portfolio Management*, **11**(3), 9–16.

Rosenberg, D. (2003). Early modern information overload. *Journal of the History of Ideas*, **64**(1), 1.

Rosnow, R. L. (1991). Inside rumor: A personal journey. *American Psychologist*, **5**(46), 484–496.

Rosse, J. G., Miller, J. L., and Stecher, M. D. (1994). A field study of job applicants' reactions to personality and cognitive ability testing. *Journal of Applied Psychology*, **79**(6), 987–992.

Roth, P. (1996). *Mastering Foreign Exchange*. London: Pearson Education.

Rubinstein, A. (2003). "Economics and psychology"? The case of hyperbolic discounting. *International Economic Review*, **44**(4), 1207–1216.

Russo, E. J. and Schoemaker, P. J. H. (1989). *Decision Traps—The Ten Barriers to Brilliant Decision-making and How to Overcome Them*. New York: Simon & Schuster.

Russo, E. J. and Schoemaker, P. J. H. (2002). *Winning Decisions: Getting It Right the First Time*. New York: Doubleday.

Salgado, J. F. (1997). The five factor model of personality and job performance in the European community. *Journal of Applied Psychology*, **82**(1), 30–43.

Samuelson, W. and Zeckhauser, R. (1988). Status quo bias in decision making. *Journal of Risk and Uncertainty*, **1**(1), 7–59.

Scharfstein, D. S. and Stein, J. C. (1990). Herd behavior and investment. *American Economic Review*, **80**(3), 465–479.

Schmidt, F. L. and Hunter, J. E. (1998). The validity and utility of selection methods in personnel psychology: Practical and theoretical implications of 85 years of research findings. *Psychological Bulletin*, **124**(2), 262–274.

Schmitt, R. (1995). *Metaphern des Helfens [Metaphors of Helping]*. Weinheim: Beltz, Psychologie Verlags Union [in German].

Schwager, J. D. (1989). *Market Wizards: Interviews with Top Traders*. New York: New York Institute of Finance.

Schwager, J. D. (1992). *The New Market Wizards: Conversations with America's Top Traders*. New York: HarperCollins.

Shapira, Z. (1986). On the implications of behavioral decision making theory to economics. In: A. J. MacFadyen and H. W. MacFadyen (eds), *Economic Psychology: Intersections in Theory and Application* (pp. 621–644). Amsterdam: North-Holland.

Shefrin, H. (2000). *Beyond Greed and Fear: Understanding Behavioral Finance and the Psychology of Investing*. Boston: Harvard Business School Press.

Shefrin, H. and Statman, M. (1985). The disposition to sell winners too early and ride losers too long. *Journal of Finance*, **40**(3), 777–790.

Sherif, M. (1936). *The Psychology of Social Norms*. New York: Harper.

Shiller, R. J. (1984). Stock prices and social dynamics. *Brookings Papers on Economic Activity*, **2**.

Shiller, R. J. (1989). *Market Volatility*. Cambridge, MA: MIT Press.

Shiller, R. J. (2000). *Irrational Exuberance*. Princeton, NJ: Princeton University Press.

Shiller, R. J. and Pound, J. (1989). Survey evidence of diffusion of interest and information among investors. *Journal of Economic Behavior and Organization*, **12**, 47–66.

Shleifer, A. (2000). *Inefficient Markets: An Introduction to Behavioral Finance*. New York: Oxford University Press.

Shleifer, A. and Summers, L. H. (1990). The noise trader approach to finance. *Journal of Economic Perspectives*, **2**(4), 19–33.

Simon, H. A. (1957). *Models of Man: Social and Rational*. New York: John Wiley & Son.

Simon, H. A. (1959). Theories of decision-making in economics and behavioral science. *American Economic Review*, **3**(49), 254–283.

Simon, H. A. (1987). Making management decisions: The role of intuition and emotion. *Academy of Management Executive*, February, 57–64.

Skinner, B. F. (1974). *About Behaviorism*. New York: Knopf.

Slovic, P. (1986). Psychological study of human judgment: Implications for investment decision making. In: H. R. Arkes and K. R. Hammond (eds), *Judgment and Decision Making: An Interdisciplinary Reader* (pp. 173–193). New York: Cambridge University Press.

Slovic, P. (1990). Choice. In: D. N. Osherson and E. E. Smith (eds), *An Invitation to Cognitive Science—Thinking* (pp. 89–116). Cambridge, MA: MIT Press.

Slovic, P., Fischhoff, B., and Lichtenstein, S. (1976). Cognitive processes and societal risk taking. In: J. S. Carroll and J. W. Payne (eds), *Cognition and Social Behavior* (pp. 165–184). Oxford, UK: Lawrence Erlbaum.

Snyder, W. (1978). Decision-making with risk and uncertainty: The case of horse-racing. *American Journal of Psychology*, **91**, 201–209.

Soros, G. (1987). *The Alchemy of Finance: Reading the Mind of the Market*. New York: John Wiley & Sons.

References

Soros, G. (1994). *The Theory of Reflexivity*. New York: Soros Fund Management.
Stael von Holstein, C. A. (1972). Probabilistic forecasting: An experiment related to the stock market. *Organizational Behavior and Human Decision Processes*, **8**(1), 139–158.
Starmer, C. (1993). The psychology of uncertainty in economic theory: A critical appraisal and a fresh approach. *Review of Political Economy*, **5**(2), 181–196.
Staw, B. M. and Ross, J. (1989). Understanding behavior in escalation situations. *Science*, **246**(4927), 216–220.
Steiner, I. D. (1972). *Group Process and Productivity*. New York: Academic Press.
Steiner, I. D. (1980). Attribution of choice. In: M. Fishbein (ed.), *Progress in Social Psychology*. Hillsdale, NJ: Erlbaum.
Sternberg, R. J. (2002). *Cognitive Psychology* (3rd edn). Belmont, CA: Wadsworth Publishing.
Stoner, J. A. (1961). *A Comparison of Individual and Group Decisions Involving Risk*. Cambridge, MA: MIT.
Svenson, O. (1981). Are we all less risky and more skillful than our fellow drivers? *Acta Psychologica*, **47**(2), 143–148.
Swiss Bank Corporation (1992). *Foreign Exchange and Money Market Operations*.
Tajfel, H. (1974). Social identity and intergroup behaviour. *Social Science Information*, **13**(2), 65–93.
Tajfel, H. and Turner, J. C. (1979). An integrative theory of intergroup relations. In: W. G. Austin and S. Worchel (eds), *The Social Psychology of Intergroup Conflict* (pp. 33–47). Monterey, CA: Brooks-Cole.
Tajfel, H. and Turner, J. C. (1986). The social identity theory of intergroup behavior. In: W. G. Austin and S. Worchel (eds), *Psychology of Group Influence*. Hillsdale, NJ: Erlbaum.
Taleb, N. N. (2001). *Fooled by Randomness*. New York: Texere.
Taylor, M. P. and Allen, H. (1992). The use of technical analysis in the foreign exchange market. *Journal of International Money and Finance*, **11**(3), 304–314.
Tett, R. P., Jackson, D. N., and Rothstein, M. (1991). Personality measures as predictors of job performance: A meta-analytic review. *Personnel Psychology*, **44**(4), 703–742.
Thaler, R. (1985). Mental accounting and consumer choice. *Marketing Science*, **4**(3), 199–214.
Thaler, R. H. (1991). *Quasi-rational Economics*. New York: Russell Sage Foundation.
Thaler, R. H. (1992). *The Winner's Curse: Paradoxes and Anomalies of Economic Life*. Princeton, NJ: Princeton University Press.
Thaler, R. H. and Johnson, E. J. (1990). Gambling with the house money and trying to break even: The effects of prior outcome on risky choice. *Management Science*, **36**(6), 643–660.
Tokar, D. M., Fischer, A. R., and Subich, L. M. (1998). Personality and vocational behavior: A selective review of the literature, 1993–1997. *Journal of Vocational Behavior*, **53**(2), 115–153.
Tupes, E. C. and Christal, R. E. (1961). *Recurrent Personality Factors Based on Trait Ratings* (Technical Report 61–97, p. 40). Lackland AFB, TX: USAF Aeronautical Systems Division.

Turner, J. C. (1982). Towards a cognitive redefinition of the social group. In: H. Tajfel (ed.), *Social Identity and Intergroup Relations* (pp. 15–40). Cambridge, MA: Cambridge University Press.

Turner, J. C. (1985). Social categorization and the self-concept: A social cognitive theory of group behavior. In: E. J. Lawaler (ed.), *Advances in Group Processes: Theory and Research* (Vol. 2, pp. 77–122). Greenwich, CT: JAI.

Turner, R. L. and Killian, L. M. (1957). *Collective Behavior*. Englewood Cliffs, NJ: Prentice Hall.

Tversky, A. and Kahneman, D. (1971). Belief in the law of small numbers. *Psychological Bulletin*, **76**(2), 105–110.

Tversky, A. and Kahneman, D. (1973). Availability: A heuristic for judging frequency and probability. *Cognitive Psychology*, **5**(2), 207–232.

Tversky, A. and Kahneman, D. (1974). Judgment under uncertainty: Heuristics and biases. *Science*, **185**, 1124–1131.

Tversky, A. and Kahneman, D. (1981). The framing of decisions and the psychology of choice. *Science*, **211**(1), 453–458.

Tversky, A. and Kahneman, D. (1982). Judgments of and by representativeness. In: D. Kahneman, P. Slovic, and A. Tversky (eds), *Judgment under Uncertainty: Heuristics and Biases*. Cambridge, UK: Cambridge University Press.

Tversky, A. and Kahneman, D. (1988). Rational choice and the framing of decisions. In: D. E. Bell, H. Raiffa, and A. Tversky (eds), *Decision Making—Descriptive, Normative, and Prescriptive Interactions* (pp. 167–192). Cambridge, UK: Cambridge University Press.

Vanden Abeele, P. (1988). Economic agents' expectations in a psychological perspective. In: W. F. Van Raaij, G. M. van Veldhoven, and K. E. Wärneryd (eds), *Handbook of Economic Psychology* (pp. 497–515). Dordrecht, The Netherlands: Kluwer Academic.

Van Raaij, W. F. (1986). Economic phenomena from a psychological perspective: Economic psychology. In: A. J. MacFadyen and H. W. MacFadyen (eds), *Economic Psychology: Intersections in Theory and Application* (pp. 9–23). Amsterdam: North-Holland.

Van Raaij, W. F. (1989). Economic news, expectations and macro-economic behavior. *Journal of Economic Psychology*, **10**(4), 473–493.

Vigfusson, R. (1997). Switching between chartists and fundamentalists: A Markov regime-switching approach. *International Journal of Finance and Economics*, **2**(4), 291–305.

von Neumann, J. and Morgenstern, O. (1947). *Theory of Games and Economic Behavior*. Princeton, NJ: Princeton University Press.

Wagenaar, W. A. (1971). Appreciation of conditional probabilities in binary sequences. *Acta Psychologica*, **34**(2–3), 348–356.

Wagner, U. and Zick, A. (1990). The psychology of intergroup relationships: The social identity approach. *Gruppendynamik*, **21**(3), 319–330.

Watzlawick, P. (1967). *Pragmatics of Human Communication: A Study of Interactional Patterns, Pathologies, and Paradoxes*. New York: W.W. Norton.

Watzlawick, P. (1976). *How Real Is Real? Communication, Disinformation, Confusion*. New York: Random House.

Watzlawick, P. (1984). *The Invented Reality: How Do We Know What We Believe We Know?: Contributions to Constructivism* (1st edn). New York: W.W. Norton.

Weatherall, A. and Walton, M. (1999). The metaphorical construction of sexual experience in a speech community of New Zealand university students. *British Journal of Social Psychology*, **4**(38), 479–498.

Wertlieb, D. L. (1996). Affective development. In: R. J. Corsini (ed.), *Encyclopedia of Psychology* (2nd edn, Vol. 1). New York: John Wiley & Sons.

Wiggins, J. S. and Trapnell, P. D. (1997). Personality structure: The return of the big five. In: R. Hogan, J. A. Johnson, and S. R. Briggs (eds), *Handbook of Personality Psychology* (pp. 737–765). San Diego: Academic Press.

Williams, A. C. (1966). Attitudes towards speculative risks as an indicator of attitudes towards pure risks. *Journal of Risk and Insurance*, **33**, 577–586.

Yates, F. J. (1990). *Judgment and Decision Making*. Englewood Cliffs, NJ: Prentice Hall.

Yates, F. J., McDaniel, L. S., and Brown, E. S. (1991). Probabilistic forecasts of stock prices and earnings: The hazards of nascent expertise. *Organizational Behavior and Human Decision Process*, **49**(1), 60–79.

Zeckhauser, R., Patel, J., and Hendricks, D. (1991). Nonrational actors and financial market behavior. *Theory and Decision*, **31**(2–3), 257–287.

Zeelenberg, M., Beattie, J., van der Pligt, J., and de Vries, N. (1996). Consequences of regret aversion: Effects of expected feedback on risky decision making. *Organizational Behavior and Human Decision Processes*, **2**(65), 148–158.

Index

3Com Corporation, 2
Affects, 41–4, 57
  and crashes, 39
  and decisional escalation, 44–5
  definition, 41
  emotions (*see* Emotions)
  feelings (*see* Feelings)
  importance, 41–2
  and information processing, 43
  and market constructions, 43
  and market overshooting, 42
  moods (*see* Moods)
  and risk-taking (*see also* Risk-taking, willingness), 43
  and status quo tendency, 44
  in trading decisions, 42
Alchemists, 125
Ambivalence, 22
Anchoring-and-adjustment heuristic, 64–6
  in expectations, 65
  and experts, 65–6
  in predictions, 65
  process, 64
Arbitrage, 9, 12
  arbitrageurs, 9–10, 16
    and noise traders, 97
  dangers, 10, 12
  limitations, 10, 12
Attitudes, 16, 46, 96, 130
  ABC tripartite model, 110
  biased self-attributions, 7
  characteristics, 108–11
  towards coins, 108
  and confirmation bias, 130–1
  towards currencies, 111–17
    evaluation, potency, and activity, 115–16
  definition, 25
  and exchange-rate expectations, 116–17
  and expectations, 16, 108–17
  external and internal, 7, 25
  and information processing, 109
  and news media, 122–3
  risk-taking, 79
  self-enhancing bias, 25
Autonomous organization, 159
Availability heuristic, 39, 63–4
  and financial news, 63–4
  recency, 64
  in rumors, 146
  triggers, 64
  vividness, 63–64

Back office, 215
Balance of payments, 95
Bank Negara, 217
Banks
  central banks, 217–18
    and herding 37
    intervention, 37, 136, 143–4, 217–8
  commercial and investment banks, 216–17
  dealing rooms, 213–15
  influence on financial news, 141
  trading, 212–13

Barings Bank, 83
Base-rate fallacy, 59–60
Battle of Waterloo, 156
Bazaar metaphor, 170, 171–2
Beast metaphor, 170, 174
Beauty contest, 119–21
Behavioral finance, 3–7, 15, 16, 47, 150
 and cognitive psychology, 15
 and human decision making, 6
Behaviorism, 4
Belief bias (*see also* Confirmation bias), 130–1
Bernoulli, D., 27, 74
Black box, 4, 32, 33, 109
Bounded rationality, 2, 29
Brandywine mutual fund, 10
Bretton Woods, 163, 217
Brokers, 218–19
 auditory and visual 219
 automatic broking systems, 134
 electronic brokerage, 134, 218–19
 voice broker, 134, 218–19
Bubbles, 66, 126

Call option, 212
Cancer treatment, 31, 79
Cells
 healthy and sick, 196–7
Chartism (*see* Technical/chartist analysis, chartism)
Chartist analysis (*see* Technical/chartist analysis, chartism)
Chief dealer, 215
Choice, 21, 27
 dilemma, 28
 risky and riskless, 28
Cognitions
 interplay with affects, 55–6
Cognitive dissonance, 45, 46–7
 post-decisional dissonance, 46
Cognitive linguistics, 168
Cognitive psychology, 15
Cognitive-behavioral approaches, 4
Competitive advantage, 203–4
 and market size, 204
Concorde, 47

Confirmation bias, 33, 130–1, 196
Conformity (*see also* Herding), 15, 35–6
 social conformity, 36
Conjunction fallacy, 60–2
Conservatism, 7
Corporations, 21, 22, 203, 220–1
Crashes, 38–9, 40, 59, 99
 affects, 39
 news, 99
 self-fulfilling dynamics, 99
Credit line, 210, 211
Cross rates, 208

Daily press, 125
 rumors 143–4
Daylight position limit, 84
Dealing rooms, 213–15
Decision-making
 behavioral, 29
 biases, 5, 7, 9, 15, 25, 44, 56–7, 62, 66–7, 90, 115, 116
 decisional escalation 44–5, 47
 history, 27–30
 narrative approaches 30
 normative and descriptive approaches, 30–4
 prescriptive approaches, 30
 scenarios 30, 50
Decisions
 best and worst, 23–5
 and communication, 23
 types, 21
Diminishing marginal utility, 27
Discipline, 77, 87, 154–6
Disjunction fallacy, 62
Dreams, 188

Economic fundamentals (*see* Fundamentals)
Efficient frontier, 3
Efficient markets, 2, 4, 5–6, 9, 150
 anomalies, 6, 7
 defense, 7–10
 "as if" defense, 7
 departures, 2, 6–7
 effects of competition, 33

Index

hypothesis, 5, 6, 7, 126
expertise and learning, 9–10
informational efficiency, 4
Electronic trading systems, 141, 216–17
Emotions (*see also* Affects), 14, 41–2, 44–5
   and availability, 63–4
   emotional contagion, 39
   emotional stability, 157–9
   in living being metaphor, 173–4
   and loss aversion, 76
   perception of market and own decisions, 102–3
Employment rates (*see* Unemployment rates)
Endowment effect, 81
EntreMed, 6
European Exchange Rate Mechanism, 220, 221
European survey, xvi–xvii, 50–1, 54–5, 61–2, 73, 82, 100–1, 102, 103, 104, 112–16, 128, 131, 136–7, 139, 141, 153, 168, 201, 225–7
Exotics, 208
Expectations, 203–4
   and anticipatory market reality, 93, 129
   and attitudes, 108–17
   cognitive, affective, and behavioral, 110
   descriptive approach, 91
   desirability bias, 90
   discounting into market prices, 93–4, 120–1, 129
   division of work, 118
   economists, 118
   importance, 90, 92
   influencing and manipulating, 91, 118–19
   as intervening variables, 109
   learning, 108
   meta-expectations, ix–x, 119, 121
   and news, 93–4
   and news media, 121–3
   normative approach, 90
   other market participants, 91
   psychological understanding, 91
   second-order, 120
   self-reinforcing nature, 111
   social dynamics, 117–19
   as time machine, 92
   uncertain, 89
   unconscious, 111
   wishful thinking, 90
Expected utility (*see also* Utility), 193
   theory, 28
   contradictions 29, 56–7
   and prospect theory, 72
Explicit metaphors, 185–8

Feedback loops (*see also* Information processing, circular), 15, 99
Feelings (*see also* Affects) 23, 27
FFM, 152
Financial news agencies (*see* News media)
Financial news providers (*see* News media)
Financial news reporting
   speed, 139–40 (*see also* News characteristics, speed)
   trends, 139–43
Financial news services (*see* News media)
Financial television, 125
Five Factor Model, 152
Forecasts, computer-assisted, 96
Foreign exchange market
   as bowl in motion, 32
   connection to other financial markets, xv
   as construct, 192, 193, 198–9, 202, 204
      changing construct, 199, 200–4
      rules change over time, 200–1
   demystification, xvi
   effects of new information technologies, 203
   formal exchanges, 211, 212
   function, 207, 208
   geographic rule variations, 201
   influence, xv
   interpretations, xv–xvi
   location, 209–10
   perspectives, xvii
   rules
      adapting to, 202
      and consensus, 202
      genesis, 202–3
      geographic variations, 201
      influencing, 204
      and metaphors, 171, 183–5, 199, 200

Foreign exchange market (*cont.*)
  as social institution, 168
  theories
    explanatory fictions, 197
    illusion of control, 197
    subjective, 196–8
    unpredictability effects, 195–7
  traded currencies, 208
  traded objects, 210
  trading centers, 209
  unpredictability, 200
  volume, 207
Forward market, 211
  forward trader, 213
  forward transaction, 211, 213, 220
Framing, 5, 8, 29, 31–2, 73, 77–82
  example, 78–9
  metaphors, 167
  and risk-taking, 8
Freud, S. 4, 188
Front-running, 214
Fundamental analysis 95–6
Fundamentals, 16, 25, 39, 52, 94, 97, 98, 100, 101, 105, 144, 159, 199, 202
Futures, 211

Gambler's fallacy, 62
Gambling metaphor, 170, 175
Groups
  and compensatory judgment tasks, 15–16
  conflict, 115
  conformity, 35
  consensus, 35
  dynamics, 15–16
  and identity, 113
  norms, 34–5
  polarization, 26
  process loss, 16
  pressure, 35
  risky shift, 26
  and self-enhancement, 115
  size and performance, 16
  teamwork, 25
  in trading decisions, 23, 25

Head-and-shoulders, 9, 96

Hedge funds, 214, 220
Hedging, 21, 22–3, 220–1
Herding,
  and affects, 39
  augmenting irrationality, 15
  building and integration stage, 37–8
  and chartism, 41
  conformity, 35
  crashes, 38–9
  dissolution stage, 38
  emotional contagion, 39
  and feedback loops, 15
  and information processing, 37
  market dynamics, 36–41
  and new technologies, 40
  and news, 40–1
  reasons, 34–6
  and regret (*see also* Regret theory), 36
  as search for rules, 35–6
  and trading systems, 40
  triggers, 36–7
  and volatility, 40
Heuristics, 5, 17, 29, 57–8
  chess masters, 58
  definition, 57–8
  simplifying information, 57
  in trading decisions, 57–8
  usefulness, 57–8
Hiding, 169
Highlighting, 169
Hindsight bias, 66–7
  in financial markets, 67
  illusory logic, 67
Hiring traders, 163
Home bias, 115, 116
Home currency, 112–13, 115
Homo economicus, 57
Hot hand, 197
House money effect, 81–2
Humanistic theory, 4
Hypnosis, 110
  post-hypnotic suggestion, 110

Illusion of control, 153, 156, 197–8
  definition of illusions, 199
  weather forecasts, 197–8

Imitation
  in herding 34–5
  inefficiency intensification, 8–9, 100
Implicit metaphors, 185–8
Impulsiveness, 153, 157
Individuals
  as market players, 221
Inflation, 95, 126
Information (*see also* News)
  cascades, 39
  circular information processing, 99, 137–8, 146
  collective information processing, 137–8
  loops (*see also* Information, circular information processing), 137–8, 146
  overload, 49, 58, 126, 127, 147
  private and public, 201–2
  quantitative and qualitative, 201
  selection, 126, 127–8, 130
  sources, 131
    analysts, 134
    brokers (*see also* Brokers), 134
    daily newspapers, 133–4
    financial magazines, 133–4
    financial television, 135
    of journalists, 135–7
    personal contacts, 133, 135–6
    print media, 133–4
    of traders, 131–5
    wire news media, 131–3, 137
Information handling, 160
Insurance
  history, 212
Interaction-oriented metaphors, 181–2
  predictability, 184–5
Interbank trader, 213–14, 215
Interest rates, 59, 60–1, 90, 94, 109, 110, 129, 199, 213, 217
Intuition, x, 25, 27, 44, 51–5, 157
  and analytical thinking, 52
  applying, 53
  best and worst trading decisions, 54–5
  chess players, 52–3, 54
  and experience, 53–4, 55, 157
  importance, 52
  in living being metaphor, 173–4
  learning, 53

neurological research, 52
  pattern recognition, 52–4
  and rationality/irrationality, 53–4
Invariance, 28, 29, 33
Investment companies, 219
Irrationality (*see also* Rationality), 4, 8, 9, 10, 11, 12, 13, 14, 15, 16, 17, 38, 41, 45, 121
  blurred line to rationality, 14, 193
  examples, 13–14
  irrational exuberance, 9
  in living being metaphor, 174
  in machine metaphor, 172
  and non-rationality, 17, 53

Junior trader, 215

Learning, 29, 53, 67, 190, 196
  and arbitrageurs, 9–10
  and personality, 152, 163
  resistance to learning from mistakes, 5, 10
Leeson N., 2, 83, 87, 156
Line-matching task, 35
Living being metaphor, 170, 173–5
Loss aversion, 76
  and experience, 77
  and status quo tendency, 45
Loss limit (*see* Stop-loss limit)
Lover metaphor, 170, 174–5
Luck
  in gambling metaphor, 175
  and personality, 160
  and survivorship bias, 151
Lung cancer treatment, 31, 79

Machine metaphor, 170, 172–3
Magical rites, 198
Market approaches
  outcomes vs. actual dynamics, 1, 14–15, 21–2, 198–9
  static vs. dynamic, 34
Market maker, 22, 212, 213, 218
Market meaning-making, 157
Market psychology (*see also* Psychology), x, 14–18, 25
  beyond cognitive aspects, 15–16

Market psychology (*cont.*)
  connecting subjective experience to objective market processes, 16
  contributions, 3
  importance, 2
  individual differences, 16
  need for, 14–18
  realistic understanding of market dynamics, 6
  and social psychology, 15
Market rules (*see* Foreign exchange market, rules)
Market theories (*see* Foreign exchange market, theories)
Market-to-book-value, 5, 7
Maslow, A., 4
Mean-variance optimization, 3
Memory
  availability heuristic, 55–6, 63
  hindsight bias, 66–7
  and intuition, 52–3, 54
  and moods, 43
  as psychological reconstruction, 66
Mental accounting, 79–82
  and risk, 79–80
Metaphors, x, 164, 204
  analysis, 168, 169
    cognitive approach, 169
    discourse theory, 169
  central bank trader, 188–9, 191
  commercial bank trader, 190–1
  definition, 168
  entailment, 180, 182, 191, 192
  explicit and implicit, 185–8
  and framing, 167
  gendered nature, 192
  highlighting and hiding, 169
  interaction-oriented metaphors, 181–2
  interplay, 191
  main market metaphors, 169–71, 181
    bazaar, 170, 171–2
    beast, 170, 174
    gambling, 170, 175
    living being, 170, 173–5
    lover, 170, 174–5
    machine, 170, 172–3
    ocean, 171, 178–9
    sports, 170–1, 176–7
    war, 171, 177–8
  and market developments, 192
  and market predictability, 183–5
  ontological, 182, organic, 187
  and psychological other, 180–3
  and rationality, 192
  secondary metaphors, 188–9
  and traditional finance, 187
  unconscious use 185–6
Middle office, 215
Momentum effects, 5–6, 7
Money supply, 95, 126, 199, 200
Moods, 41, 42–3
  definition, 42
  and expectations, 43
  and learning, 43
  linking market participants, 43
  and living being metaphor, 185
  media, 43
  and memory, 43
Multinational companies, 220–1
Mutual funds, 151

Narcissus, 21–2
Naturalistic decision theories, 30
NEO personality inventory, 152
Neural networks, 96
News (*see also* Information)
  characteristics, 126
    accuracy, 129–30
    confirmation, 130
    contradicting expectations, 129
    impact on others, 129
    market influence, 130
    source reliability, 129–30
    speed, 126, 128–9, 132
    surprise, 130
    timing, 130
    unanticipated, 129
  events and background analysis, 140
  influence of irrelevant news, 6
  misreporting, 140
  new technologies, 140, 141
News media, 222
  attributions, 122–3
  dependence, 135–7

as financial brokers, 141
financing, 141
influencing and manipulating, 142–3
interdependence with trading participants, 139, 142
print, 142
public, 125
relationship with trading institutions, 140–3, 222
reporting trends, 139–43
types, 125–6
wire, 125, 126, 131–3, 137, 142
News providers (*see* News media)
Nixon, 66
Noise traders, 16, 97
Norse mythology, 17
North American survey, xvi–xvii, 23, 49, 50, 85, 112, 116–17, 132, 161, 168, 201, 225–7

Ocean metaphor, 171, 178–9
Ontological metaphors, 182
  predictability, 184–5
Options, 71, 76, 212
Over-the-counter, 211, 212
Overconfidence, 7, 47–51, 55–6, 153, 164
  available information, 48–9
  and availability heuristic, 55–6
  and disciplined cooperation, 156
  danger 48
  and emotional stability, 158–9
  excess trading, 49
  foreign exchange market, 49
  positive consequences, 50
  risk, 49
  self-esteem, 55
  volatility, 49
Overnight position limit, 84

Pavlov, 98, 190
Pension funds, 219
Personality
  characteristics, ix, 16, 149
  Five Factor Model, 152
    Agreeableness, 152
    Conscientiousness, 152
    Emotional Stability, 152
    Extraversion, 152
    Neuroticism, 152
    Openness to Experience, 152
  link to work performance, 152
  and trading, 163
  and trading performance, 162
  and trading styles, 163–4
  and trading institution, 162
  and trading roles, 162
  in traditional economics, 150
Person–environment fit, 160–1
Pip 213
Pleasure principle, 4
Polarity profiles, 112
Pony Express, 139
Portfolio allocation, 3
Portfolio insurance, 40
Position limit, 84, 215
Predictions
  regressive and extrapolative, 123
Profit maximization (*see also* Utility, maximization), 4, 33, 45, 80
Proprietary trader, 21, 215
Prospect theory, 29, 72–6, 78, 80
  loss aversion, 45, 76
  probability weighing function, 74
  reflection effect, 74
  subjective reference point, 73, 77, 78, 79–80
    dependent on previous trades, 80
    independence from previous trades, 80, 86
    influencing, 77, 80
  value function, 74–5, 76
Psychoanalysis, 4
Psychology (*see also* Market Psychology)
  key to future, 294
  organizational psychology, 151–2
  personnel psychology, 151–2
  psychological theories, 4
  role in market theories, 195–8
  subjective theories, 196–8
Purchasing power theory, 199
Put option, 212

Quasi-rational economics, 58

Random walk, 5
Randomness
  pattern perception, 197
Rationality (*see also* Irrationality), 1–2, 3, 4, 5, 6, 7, 8, 31, 150
  arbitrageurs, 9–10
  and asset pricing, 3
  axioms, 28
  and behavioral finance, 6–7
  bounded, 2, 29
  departures, 4, 5, 8, 31, 45, 57, 90, 198
  in expectations, 3, 90
  and feelings, 102–3
  and framing, 8, 31, 80, 86
  and heuristics, 57, 58
  limitations, 2
  limiting consequences, 16–17
  imperfect rationality, 2, 5, 8, 9
  and informationally efficient markets, 4
  and market psychology, 14–18
  and metaphors, 192, 193
    in bazaar metaphor, 172
    in gambling metaphor, 175
    in machine metaphor, 173
    market rationalities, 17, 192
  in normative–economic approach, 30–4
  and personality, 150
  and psychological theories, 4, 17–18
  and time horizon, 12–13
  subjective explanatory concept, 11
  traders and journalists, 102–3
  traders' views, 10–14
  and utility maximization, 28
Real-time news, 40, 126, 127, 131–3, 139, 141, 203
Recognition heuristic, 58
Recognition primed decision model, 30
Reference point (*see* Prospect theory, subjective reference point)
Reflexivity, 100
Regret, 36, 45
Regret theory, 45–6
Representativeness heuristic, 7, 58–63, 197
  functional and dysfunctional aspects, 59
  local representativeness, 62
  vivid information, 60
Reversal effects, 5–6, 7

Risk (*see also* Risk-taking)
  alpha, 4
  asset-specific, 3
  aversion, 28, 72, 74, 75, 79, 80
  definition, 71
  diversification, 3
  feedback systems, 86
  and future, 72
  hedging (*see* Hedging)
  institutional regulations, 84–6
  and insurance, 212
  management 82–7
  market risk, 3–4, 5
  and options, 212
  personal regulations, 86–7
  precommitment techniques, 86
  seeking, 72, 73, 74, 75, 76, 79, 80
  and volatility, 3
Risk-taking (*see also* Risk)
  asymmetric, ix, 45, 72–7, 158
    and mathematical trading models, 75
    and trading experience, 75–6
  bias, 156
  choice dilemma, 26
  and discipline, 77
  in real-life conditions, 22, 27
  risky shift, 26
  and trading position size, 56
  willingness 50
    regarding gains and losses, 74–5
    after group discussion, 26
    and framing, 78
    and house money effect, 81–2
  in personality, 157
Rogers, C., 4
Rothschild, 156
Rumors, x, 143–8
  and availability, 146
  content adaptation, 144
  definition, 143
  development, 145–5
  dissemination stage, 147
  evaluation stage, 145–6
  functions, 145
  and future, 146–7
  generation stage, 145
  and herding, 40

Index

importance in trading, 144
and information loops, 138, 146
and new information technologies, 147–8
press reports, 143
reality shaping, 147
technological adaptation, 144
triggering conditions, 144–5
Rusnak, J., 83, 87, 156

Sales trader, 213–14, 215
Salesperson (*see Sales* trader)
Satisficing, 29
Selecting traders, 163
Self-esteem, 55, 115
Self-fulfilling prophecy, 99–100
chartism, 100
definition, 99
Semantic differential, 111–12, 115
Senior trader, 215
Settlement date, 211
Sherlock Holmes, 169
Skinner, B.F., 4
Social dynamics, 23, 26–7, 34, 41, 92
in bazaar metaphor, 172
and expectations, 117–23
in groups (*see also* Groups), 16
self-fulfilling, 37
Social identity theory, 113–15
Social representations, 168
Speculation, 208–9, 221
derived, 209
Sports metaphor, 170–1, 176–7
Spot market, 211
trader, 133–4, 213
trading, 213
transaction, 211
Spread, 213, 214
Status quo bias (*see* Status quo tendency)
Status quo tendency, 44–7
and affects, 44
and emotional commitment, 45
and loss aversion, 45
and psychological commitment, 47
in trading style, 44
Stock market, 2, 5, 9, 10, 14–15, 39, 40, 49, 66, 99, 133, 202, 210, 221

Stop-loss limit, 84–5, 156
Sunk cost effect, 47
Superstitions, 196, 198
Survivorship, 16, 151
Swaps, 211

Technical/chartist analysis (*see also* Fundamental analysis), 9, 16, 94–108
attitudes of market participants, 96
chartism, 96
definition, 96
motives, 98–9
as self-fulfilling prophecy, 99–100
definition, 96
exchange-rate patterns, 96
imaginary pattern perception, 8–9
and forecasting horizon, 97, 100–1, 107
head-and-shoulders, 9, 96
and herding, 41
heterogeneous expectations, 97, 108
importance over time, 103–4
mix with fundamental analysis, 104–5
positive feedback trading, 9
as quasi-psychology, 98
as repetitive expectation formation mechanism, 111
technical break, 26
among traders and journalists, 100–3
and trading location, 107
usage styles, 105–6
Terminator, 41, 44, 109
Time machine, 92–3, 94
Trade balance, 91, 97, 129, 199, 200
Trade deficit (*see* Trade balance)
Trade numbers (*see* Trade balance)
Trading instruments, 211–212
Trading interval, 132
Trading performance, 151
chance, 151
organizational contributions, 161–2
person–environment fit, 160–1
successful traders, 152
autonomous organization, 159
disciplined cooperation, 154–6, 158
emotional stability, 157–9
information handling, 160

Trading performance (*cont.*)
   information-processing, 159
   interested integrity, 159
   market meaning-making, 157
   tackling decisions, 156–7
  survivorship bias, 151
  trading potential, 161–2
  trading profit, 161–2
Trading profits, 54, 149, 161, 163
  and herding, 37
  and overconfidence, 50
Trading style
  and gender, 164
  and personality, 163–4
  and status quo tendency, 44
Traditional economic theory (*see* Traditional economics)
Traditional economics, 1, 3, 5, 6, 8, 11, 12, 14, 15, 18, 31, 32, 33, 57, 58, 90, 91, 109, 126, 150, 163, 192, 199
Traditional finance, 3–7, 8, 9, 32 (*see also* Traditional economics)
  and metaphors, 187
Traits, 16, 150, 151, 153, 161, 162, 163, 182
  definition, 149
  and job performance, 152
  and learning, 152
Transitivity, 28, 33
Treasurer, 215
Trobriand Archipelago, 198
Truthfulness requirement, 8
Tulip mania, 126

Unconscious, 4, 111
  Metaphors 186, 188
Unemployment rates, 62, 109, 121, 122, 129, 136, 176, 199, 200, 217, 198
Utility, 27 (*see also* Expected utility)
  diminishing marginal utility, 27
  function, 27–8, 74
  maximization (*see also* Profit maximization) 28–30, 45

War metaphor, 171, 177–8
Wheel-of-fortune, 65
Wire news services (*see* News media, wire)
Wire news terminals, 214